Successful Business Models For Filmmakers

John Sweeney

Bloomington, IN Milton Keynes, UK

authorHOUSE®

AuthorHouse™
1663 Liberty Drive,
Suite 200
Bloomington, IN 47403
www.authorhouse.com
Phone: 1-800-839-8640

AuthorHouse™ UK Ltd.
500 Avebury Boulevard
Central Milton Keynes, MK9 2BE
www.authorhouse.co.uk
Phone: 08001974150

First published by AuthorHouse 4/12/2007

ISBN: 978-1-4259-7628-6 (sc)

Printed in the United States of America
Bloomington, Indiana

This book is printed on acid-free paper.

Original idea for cover by Pauline Cain.

Cover Graphics by David Wood

Internal Graphics by Alisha Miller

This book is dedicated to:

Mrs Flump – my beautiful granddaughter Keira.

and

Raisa

Editorial Acknowledgements

Jane Howard

Every book needs a good editor and I was incredibly fortunate to have Jane Howard who, as well as being a colleague and friend, acted as a brilliant editor of the book right from the first. That she believed in the book was also an inspiration and inducement to enact the many corrections and suggestions she proffered.

Always her ideas and suggestions were thoughtful and constructive and she managed, over many months and rewrites, to turn a gawky clumsy first draft into something far more cogent and presentable.

Gerry O'Sullivan

I would also like to thank Gerry O'Sullivan who, as a good friend and keen reader, took on the arduous task of proof reading the final manuscript and spotting errors the rest of us missed.

Any remaining errors are of course my own.

Acknowledgements

The aim of this book is to take the many business disciplines, such as human resource management, marketing, financial planning and management and apply them to the filmmaking process. Therefore, the management constructs, the marketing principles, the financial formats and structures used in this book can be found in many classical business texts. However, their detailed application to the film industry is purely the author's own.

As with other art forms, filmmaking has a body of knowledge which all practitioners use and refer to. In writing this book, I have been influenced by the books and reports I have read, the conferences I have attended, the people I have worked with when making my films, the film industry professionals I have spoken to, the students I have taught. I have attempted, as with the business books, wherever possible and appropriate, to give all full acknowledgement within the text of the book.

Unfortunately, I cannot give full acknowledgement to all the sources, since to do so would require copious footnotes on each page, which would detract from the simple structure of the book and possibly deter the reader. Therefore, to all those whose books, articles, experiences or findings have been used, please accept this as my appreciation and acknowledgement of your work.

For a comprehensive, but doubtless not totally complete, list of books and reports that have informed and influenced the writing of this book, see the further reading section.

Contents

PART ONE
The filmmaking company, its products, services, and the industrial environment it operates in.

PART TWO
The management of resources both human and technical.

PART THREE
The Marketing, promotion and distribution of films.

PART FOUR
Financial planning to acquire funding for film projects and to generate income and profits.

Preface

"...... we need to reinvent our industry, and make it fit to face the future"

Building a Sustainable UK Film Industry – Keynote speech by Sir Alan Parker as Chairman of the Film Council.

This book is for those who believe that good and great films can be made outside the Hollywood studio system; and that independent film production companies can be built and sustained if they have the right business model. And, that by developing and applying a business model, it doesn't mean diminishing or losing creativity, but rather it facilitates the full expression of creativity by maximising the use of all the filmmaker's resources.

The Film Business Model

All successful enterprises, either commercial or non-profit making, work to a business model, which is why it is so important for all aspiring filmmakers to have one. There is no consensus as to what a business model should be or what it should contain, and all business models vary according to the product or services they are offering. However, they all have four basic elements and these are: the product or service; the management of resources both human and technical; the promotion and distribution of the product or service; a financial plan to generate income and profits. Therefore, the film business model developed here has these four parts.

- *The filmmaking company, its products, services, and the industrial environment it operates in.*

- *The management of resources both human and technical.*

- **The marketing, promotion and distribution of films.**

- **Financial planning to acquire funding for film projects and to generate income and profits.**

A business model for a filmmaker needs to comprise a complete overview of the whole process of running a successful filmmaking enterprise – what kind of films you intend to make, how you develop or find ideas or scripts for each film, how you compose the budgets for each film, how you will make the most of the resources available and how you intend to distribute the films. By integrating all these core elements within a model, you are able to plan and evaluate each key stage of the filmmaking process. This also means that you are in control of the process and can respond to changes, be they loss of finance, locations, changes to lead actors, or sudden opportunities such as the kind of films you want to make becoming very popular. With a business model you are able to respond in an informed and strategic manner.

Viability Threshold Theory

The most radical aspect of the model I propose is the Viability Threshold Theory. (See chapter six for a full explanation). I have developed the theory to help ascertain the commercial viability of a film while it is still in script form. The theory is premised on the notion that if a script contains key elements that will enable the finished film to be easily marketed, then it is likely to be a commercial success. This does not mean that creativity is sacrificed, but rather creativity expressing itself within a structure, just as in all other arts forms. This aspect of the model is based on research into all the successful UK films made since 1991 and which cost less than £5m to produce.

The business model for a Hollywood studio is to produce, on average, 12 films each year on the basis that 8 will fail, 2 will break-even and 2 will make money. This business model relies on the fact that the two films that make money will generate enough income to cover the costs of making all the other films. Given that each studio can spend $600m plus each year on making and marketing their movies, then independents can in no way compete by using the same business model.

My research showed that the average cost of each successful UK film was £2.6m and average earnings were £10.6m. It is therefore not just a question of big finances, as with the Hollywood model, but rather choosing the right script, that can be made for the right price and which contains enough key marketing determinants to make it successful at the box-office. This book addresses all these key constructs and shows how they can be integrated into a viable and sustainable business model.

Since there is no limit for the number of good films that can be consumed by an increasingly eager film market, we all benefit from good stories being well told through film.

Integrated Approach

All too often in the UK, and in the European film industry, business modelling and planning do not take place and everything tends to happen on an ad-hoc basis. Writers write scripts and send them out on spec to hundreds of agents, producers or directors; directors, if they are fortunate enough to raise the cash, make films and then look for a distributor; distributors roam festivals and editing rooms hoping to find a gem they can market that others have overlooked, and so buy it cheap. All these aspects of the filmmaking process should not be separate but should be planned for from the beginning within a film business model. It follows that if UK and European filmmakers and producers are to build a sustainable film industry, creating and applying business models is crucial.

Introduction

"I don't think anyone out of the business realises (nor should they) just how fragile movies are, how even the greatest successes run, at least for a while, neck and neck with failure." **Goldman – Which Lie Did I Tell?**

All filmmaking outside the Hollywood studio system needs to address four crucial requirements – an understanding of how the film industry works, a good original script that meets the expectations of a defined market, a comprehensive marketing strategy, and the effective management of the financial and human resources available. This book fully addresses these key filmmaking issues. Their crucial importance was reinforced by the findings of the most recent investigation into the UK film industry, the Relph Report – March 2002 and Alan Parker's keynote speech as Chair of The BFI – November 2002. Alan Parker declared that UK films must be distribution led, and the Relph report said they must be made at a cost that can be recouped from potential box office earnings.

It could be argued that the reason the UK and European film industries are in such a poor state is because the above two key recommendations have yet to be implemented. Good and innovative film, like other art forms, is vital for the health of any civilised society and at its best good film is life-enhancing. Yet, all too often good films never see the light of day because they are failed by either the wrong production costs or a poor marketing strategy. This is an immeasurable loss to our culture. This book seeks to help redress that situation and to provide future generations of filmmakers with the tools to create sustainable careers in the film industry.

The UK and Europe have the biggest cinema audiences outside the US, yet they seem incapable of creating and sustaining a viable film industry that can compete with America. This situation is not new. As far back as the beginning of the making of films for public viewing, the UK film industry was complaining about the dominance of US films in the UK market which by 1918 had captured 80% of films shown in Britain. At this time, UK filmmakers also began asking for regulations to protect the home industry "against marauding Americans." (**British Cinema – The Lights That Failed** James Park B.T. Batsford Ltd, London 1990)

The problem, then as now, is that the US makes films that people want to see, and in a market driven industry audience tastes and needs will determine success.

Often, US film companies develop and produce internationally successful films such as the **James Bond** series and **Harry Potter** that are made in the UK, written by British writers and performed by British acting talent. So why is it that UK companies didn't make these films? The only US contribution to this scenario was the development, production, marketing and the distribution process, or, in other words, the business side of the film industry. I say, the only contribution, but it seems to have been the key one and the one that, according to many observers and analysts, is most lacking in the UK and European film industries.

Filmmaking As A Business

That business skills need to be brought to the UK and European filmmaking process seems to have been amply demonstrated in recent times by Simon Franks who founded Redbus, one of the success stories of the UK film industry. He said *"I had been to business school, had worked in the City, and knew that I could bring a business professionalism and discipline to the company that would make Redbus stand out from its competitors."* Redbus has been responsible for major successes such as **Bend It Like Beckham**.

This understanding of the need to apply business and marketing skills to the filmmaking process, along with creativity and choosing the right talent, is what has driven other success stories in the UK film industry such as Goldcrest, Polygram and Working Title. That only one of these companies still exists, Working Title, in no way diminishes the films produced by Polygram and Goldcrest, nor the way these companies were run.

Goldcrest was indeed possibly our most successful film company ever, having developed and produced more Oscar winners, such as **Chariots of Fire** and **Gandhi**, than any other UK company. However, by their own admission, Goldcrest's demise can be traced to their having strayed from the path of sound business management. **My Indecision Is Final-The rise and fall of Goldcrest Films** by Jake Eberts and Terry Ilott, Faber and Faber 1990, shows that their demise can be traced to this factor.

There have been many reasons cited for this lack of business skills by UK and European filmmakers. The main one alleged is that there are too many government subsidies in Europe and the UK, encouraging filmmakers to reflect national cultures in films, which play only to small culturally based audiences and do not need to make a profit. This scenario is in contrast to the US, where there are no subsidies, and films are made to appeal to a wide range of audiences. Such films seek to entertain and are more likely to be commercially viable. In other words, writers and filmmakers in the US create with the audience in mind, whereas in the UK and Europe, screenplays are often written and films made as dramas that are personal visions without universal appeal. To sum up, the writers, filmmakers and studios in the US treat the process of making films as a business. This doesn't mean that US or Hollywood films are not art forms, but they show that films can be both culturally and commercially successful. At the moment there are a growing number of American financiers bankrolling films outside the studio system that are thoughtful with a political edge. These films are clearly aimed at making a political or social statement but also aim to reach a wide audience by being entertaining. In fact, since they have a message their primary aim is to reach a wide audience; otherwise, they are a voice in the wilderness. As an article in the Observer newspaper said, when reporting on the new more socially aware and politically charged movies being made in America, "But if the film is too preachy ... no one will listen, so the films must also be commercially viable. So far, they have been a spectacular success." *(Observer Features 08-01-06).* The following sections will unpack some of these key points.

Art Versus Commerce

It is a fallacy, often repeated by non-professional wannabe filmmakers, that to build a film around a business plan will stop the film from being art. To be aware that a film needs to succeed commercially does not mean having to compromise on originality and creativity. In 2005 the film that achieved the second highest box-office rating of the year was **Syriana**, a highly political film "about an ideology". The film's success goes against the notion that films have to be "feel good" to be successful.

In fact, it can be a form of arrogance to assume that a film because it seeks, by appealing to a market, to retrieve the investment made in it, can never be great art. It's fair to say that most great works of art were commissioned within a marketing environment; in other words, what the existing commercial environment demanded and what those with money were willing to commission. The Medicis during the Italian Renaissance are a prime example. One of England's greatest writers, Charles Dickens, wrote for the public and often serialised his work in newspapers in order to reach a wider audience.

Creating viable business models for film production does not mean compromising on originality or creativity. Appropriate planning, no matter what the budget, allows time to formulate strategies that are only limited by the individual filmmaker's abilities and imagination. All works of art are created and exist in time and place. Film is, I believe, set to become the central art form of the 21st century. It is the only art form that can fuse all the other art forms together: Music, Painting as visual composition, Drama, and others. But if the UK and Europe are to build and sustain film production they need to develop the business skills to do so. The aim of this book is to help get more films made because they are artistically good and commercially viable. There is too much hit and miss in the UK and European film industry, with many potentially great films left unmade. By hit and miss I mean films that are made which are then hawked around the festivals in the hope of finding a distributor and becoming a hit. Needless to say, this method leads to many more misses than hits.

People who want to simply make films that please themselves should perhaps seek another form of artistic expression such as song-writing or painting, where minimal resources are needed and they can indulge themselves. That is not to say that a producer or director should not have a strong and focused vision of what kind of film they want to create, but their idea does need to have the potential to attract an audience. There is no dichotomy between creative work that is seen and admired by a wide audience, and true art. However, many failed filmmakers blame the audiences for not going to see what is considered to be a good film. Films may be good and work on all sorts of levels, but in the end the film must be able to sustain the infrastructure that supports it, namely the cost of distribution and exhibition.

Importance Of A Market-led Approach

The book unashamedly sets out to nurture producers into creating viable film projects that are market led. This of course means that the film's budget is determined by its potential earnings, which in turn means "writing to budget". A third of all UK films made in the past ten years, never made it to the big screen and those that did make it, often produced poor box office takings.

It is generally considered that part of the reason that the UK film industry is not successful is that, unlike in the US, British filmmakers are reluctant to accept that filmmaking is a business. Sure, it is a business based on creativity, but like any other commercial activity it produces a product. The clear aim of the book is to develop, in independent non-studio filmmakers, those skills that make the US film industry so powerful.

In creating a film you are basically setting up and running a small, or sometimes not so small, business with a turnover of £2m to £5m per year. And as with all businesses, the first questions are, what shall the business produce, and what is the market potential for the product.

Make no mistake, a completed film is a product, just as a designed object is and any of the other things produced by the creative industries. In America this is clearly understood, which is why their films dominate the world and the UK film market.

As with all businesses, after the questions of what shall we produce, what is the market potential for the product, come the further questions: what are the revenue streams and how will the business sell the film to the consumers? This book aims to answer these questions by applying the classic business tools of marketing, management and finance. There are those in Hollywood who say that marketing is the most important of all these business tools and underpins everything else. I have therefore dealt in depth with this aspect of the business model and developed a unique tool for calculating the market potential for a film project by establishing a Marketing Potential Score for the film while it is still in the development stage. (See chapter 6)

Comments from established members of the film industry suggest that a lack of a clear marketing vision by new filmmakers plays a crucial role in their being unable to obtain funding. Distributors complain that UK films often have not clearly identified a potential audience. Distributing films under any circumstances is risky with no guaranteed result, but with no clearly defined audience to aim at then it is almost suicidal. All too often UK and European filmmakers create films they hope will be crossover films, that is films made for a low budget that become big box office hits. Examples of these are **Four Weddings and a Funeral** and **The Full Monty**. What should happen is that from the very beginning when the idea for the film is being developed, and possibly even before the script is written, the questions of what market it will be aimed at and what the budget should be need to be asked.

Why Business Plans Are Vital

Business plans and business models are crucial to the filmmaker because they allow the producer and potential investors to evaluate the context within which the film is being made. It shows that the filmmaker or producer is being professional. It is also the case that public funding bodies, such as the UK Film Council, require some form of business and marketing plan in order to judge the potential of the proposed film. While it is generally considered true, as the script writer William Goldman said, that "nobody knows anything" in the film industry, and so nobody can say for sure if a film is going to be a success, a good business plan shows the potential viability of the film. The plan is what ultimately financiers base their judgement on. The plan also acts as a strategic device for developing and co-ordinating the various stages of creating the film.

Finance, as Jean-Luc Godard observed, is the key to getting films made, and the key to getting finance is having a structured proposition that appeals to those who have the money and/or resources needed to make the film. Therefore, those seeking to be professional filmmakers and film producers and who wish to build successful careers, need to adopt sound business practices. It is only by doing so that they will earn the trust of financiers and major film production and distribution companies and be continually offered resources for filmmaking. Everyone is aware that investing in films is risky, but they are also aware that it can provide returns on capital invested many times greater than in other industries. What the professional film producer or filmmaker must do is reduce the risk for investors by developing and working with a sound business model that suits their talents and goals.

The aim of this book is to provide a comprehensive framework for creating a business model that will attract finance for filmmaking. It sets out an integrated approach that covers all the aspects of the business of films. This helps, since as a filmmaker and or producer you will need to convince a lot of different people – from film directors to distributors – that you fully understand the film industry and that any artistic or financial backing they give you is in safe hands.

Speaking The Right Language.

Often, filmmakers and producers seem not to realise that when seeking finance for a film, they are asking investors to stake millions of pounds in an enterprise which has no clear outcomes. Nobody can guarantee that the investors will not lose all their money. Film, unlike most other products, is not a tangible entity that can be easily measured.

There are a lot of financiers in the City of London and throughout the world who would like to invest in films for lots of reasons, including tax breaks. Where else, as Louise Levison points out in her excellent book **Filmmakers & Financing – Business Plans for Independents** Focal Press 2001, could investors get such mind boggling returns for their money. However, what holds most investors back from investing in films is that financiers find that producers don't understand or appreciate their needs and concerns. At the same time film producers feel the money-men don't appreciate their art. It is the deaf talking to the blind. What is needed is a bridge that will allow both sides to communicate effectively, which means learning to speak each other's language and to see and properly evaluate the opportunities and the risks. It is important that film producers learn to formulate proposals in such a way as to attract the money that is there and ready to be invested in filmmaking. The aim should be, and this is the central aim of this book, for film-producers and filmmakers to possess skills to financially manage projects that have clear marketing potential. They also need to demonstrate that they have the management skills to make the best use of the technical and artistic resources that are available to them.

There is no doubt that much more money would be released to make films if the legitimate concerns of the investors were addressed. This doesn't mean making purely commercial films, but it does mean showing the possession of skills to financially manage projects that have clear marketing potential. Whether filmmakers like it or not, potential earnings from a film are what drive interest in the project. This is how both distributors and exhibitors judge a film.

Business Plans Help Planning

It is the quality of the planning and preparation that determines if a film gets the finance for it to be made, and, when shooting begins, the quality of the finished film. Yes, the initial pitch, a short summary of the proposed film, is important in engendering initial interest, but it is considered that the best pitch comes across in the form of someone speaking and enthusing about a film they have just seen. To achieve this, the film should already exist in some form, and a business plan, built around a good script or treatment, is a way of achieving this. It will also enable you to answer authoritatively, all the questions that will be thrown at you. It is an adage in the film industry that nobody got fired for playing safe and saying no. What producers need to do is to instil enough confidence to elicit a yes.

Time, and not having the right understanding of the methods and structures needed to make the planning process a success, have been the downfall of many talented producers. The major Hollywood studios understand this need, which is why they have a whole corporation whose sole aim is to identify concepts, in script or other form, that have the potential to be good films, and then plan their development and creation.

The co-chairman of Working Title says that: ***"No film ever suffered for taking too long in development".***

A crucial element in having a business plan is that it allows you to plan ahead and, where necessary, change and adapt to changing conditions and opportunities. When I discussed this with Eric Felner at Working Title he said it was crucial to have at least three projects on the go at any one time, because things change constantly. It might be that your director or star dies or becomes unavailable, or that funding might suddenly appear for a comedy or other genre film following the surprise success of a similar film. Therefore, a balance is needed between flexibility and rigidity – the business plan and business model provides this.

Making Films That Are Seen

It is a sad fact that the majority of films made by UK producers never see the light of day. They are made in the hope of finding a distributor, but end up on the shelves collecting dust. UK, and European producers and filmmakers, must learn to think first about who will want to see the film, rather than just making a film because they think it is a good idea. Yes, there are plenty of ideas that need to be expressed that reflect the current human condition, but whether film is the right medium has to be thought about. It seems very strange that people will ask for millions of pounds or dollars or euros, just on the strength of an idea for a film that they want to make. Yes, it might prove to be the break-out film of the year, but if you have no previous history of managing 40 to 100 people, all with a wide range of complex jobs to do, then nobody is going to take you seriously.

We have stressed that a film is a product like any other consumable. You are asking people to cross town and pay £5 to £10 to watch your film. You need to ask would they? Why should they? Especially given that in London, like other major cities around the world, on average five major films open each week. So the competition is fierce. Understanding why and how people make choices as to which films they will pay money to see, will greatly enhance your ability to get your film funded. The ideas you want to express in the form of a film need to be those that others would find interesting. If not, you are simply making the film for yourself.

Hollywood Versus The World

The US studio system, and to a lesser extent the one or two successful UK and European film production companies, work on a formula of high concept films with big stars and wide distribution and marketing. These films can cost from £3m to £200m. This makes it very difficult for non US independent producers or filmmakers to compete. It is highly doubtful, at least in the foreseeable future, that Europe can compete with the US in terms of making films with large budgets. It has been estimated that to set up a studio similar to one of the Hollywood majors would cost in the region of £300m. Add to that, that to make it a going concern it would need the in-depth support systems in terms of scriptwriters, directors, actors, agents and studio executives. At present, this kind of support is only found in the US. This is because, in the real meaning of the term, they have a film industry.

Europe, and especially the UK, has a collection of people and organisations who make films, but not an industry. Whether or not one can be created, or even if it is desirable, is a moot point. However, like other industries, the film industry is becoming globalised and there appears an opportunity for individuals and organisations to set up virtual studios. The skills to do this are the same as those needed within the studio system: good scripts that translate into good films, the artistic and technical input to ensure high cinematic values within the film, and a highly effective marketing and distribution strategy. These are the main elements addressed in this book, with the aim of focusing on the skills UK and European filmmakers and producers need to develop if they are to sustain and develop a viable filmmaking industry outside the Hollywood system.

Most film companies, including those in the US, started small and built their business over a number of years. Unfortunately, very few UK and European filmmakers have this longer perspective in mind when they set out on their careers. It is a sad fact that the vast majority of directors and producers only make one film. All too often budding producers and filmmakers are advised to work within the system, and so lose their independence.

The Future

In spite of the difficulties outlined above, I believe the signs for the future of the UK and European film industries are good.

In the past ten years there has been a growth in scriptwriting courses, some as MAs, which are raising the level and quality of scripts produced. The film-schools and various courses, along with in-house training, continue to feed into a body of filmmaking talent in the UK and Europe that is as good as anywhere in the world. However, there is a need to address the issue of the business of film: overseeing the development of a script that has a clear market potential, and the development of a business plan for the script that ensures the cost of making the film reflects and is in relationship with its potential earnings in various markets. Furthermore, to bring the management skills, evident in many other areas of UK and European commerce, both in artistic and non-artistic areas, to bear on the filmmaking process, so that the best film is made from the resources available.

Can we change things? I believe we can, but we must stop being amateur in our approach to the commercial side of filmmaking and realise it is a business, albeit a creative one.

If UK and European independent producers and filmmakers are to compete with Hollywood then they must adopt a more business-like approach to film projects. They must learn to adopt modern business strategies as used successfully in other creative enterprises. It is often said that problems arise for the UK film industry when it tries to compete with Hollywood; that we do not have the resource to do it well, since we would need to be able to make 12 big budget films a year. Given that the average cost of a UK film last year was £2.2m and the average Hollywood studio spend is £15m, we clearly do not have the resources to compete. Those who have tried to compete, such as Rank, have failed. What the future holds is anybody's guess, but there is now a clear message coming from bodies like the UK Film Council, that if we are to build a film industry in Europe we need to address the issue of business skills for filmmakers and producers.

So, the challenge to UK and European filmmakers is: given that we have the talent and the creativity, can we develop the business and management side to match it? I think we can, and hopefully this book helps, in some small way, that development.

PART ONE

The filmmaking company, its products, services, and the industrial environment it operates in.

Chapter 1

The Film Industry

"It's a crazy business full of crazy people" **Goldman – Which Lie Did I Tell?**

In this chapter we will:

Provide a tool for you to check you are fully conversant with the industry.

Show you how to demonstrate to investors and partners that you fully understand the business you are in.

Show how you, as an independent producer, fit into the industry.

Introduction

In order for you to achieve your aims and get your film project off the ground, you will need to demonstrate to your financial backers and potential distributors, that you understand the industry you are in. This means understanding not just how a film is storyboarded and shot, but also how the pre-production, post production editing and marketing and distribution all fit

1

together. In analysing and explaining the way the film industry works, you reassure investors and other important backers, such as distributors or agents, that you know what you are doing. It also allows you to focus on the important issues relating to your specific film project, and how these would relate to a critical time line, from pre-production through to editing and distribution.

It may be that you are guiding an investor who is not familiar with the film industry, or you are demonstrating to a studio, distributor or production company that you know what you are talking about. Either way, explaining the process puts everything into context. Also, it helps investors or distributors to say the magic word – Yes. It is often quoted in Hollywood, that no film executive got fired for saying no. In Hollywood it is the film executives who identify and nurture film projects, and so they are judged not only on how many successful projects they have created, but also how many loss making films they have avoided. In Hollywood the life of the film executive is as precarious as that of a football manager in Europe's top clubs.

There are many different aspects of the film industry, from the crafts side of making sets and story boards to cashflow and budgets. However, for the business plan itself, you should stick to focussing on the process of production and distribution in relation to theatrical and ancillary markets. This is because these are the key factors that determine whether or not a film is attractive to investors and distributors. Yes, they want to make films they think are worth making, but they will only invest in, and support, such films if they think they will achieve their objectives in the various markets. These objectives should always be expressed in terms of volume of sales – that is, the box office take and ancillary sales, such as pay TV or sales of DVDs, in various territories. These are the income streams that drive the industry and define each sector, be it defining the size of markets for various genres, or defining viable film budgets or distribution strategies. You should give an overview of the industry as a whole, and then deal with that area of the film industry that relates specifically to your project/s. So, rather than talking about the technical side of the various distribution opportunities, such as details of how the DVD's will be made, you should talk about them in terms of markets and potential sales, how big the markets are, how they are currently performing and the opportunities that arise for the investor from this analysis. (See chapter nine)

What Attracts The Investor

Investors, be they studios, distributors or private individuals or companies, are aware of the potentially vast return on investments made in film projects. Only gambling scenarios offer better odds. There are many financial companies and financiers who would like to invest in films for reasons other than the opportunity for massive returns on investments. These include tax breaks, and, in some cases, the wish to invest in a more art-based enterprise and so experience the glamour and kudos of being part of the artistic fraternity. However, many investors are put off investing in films because they have difficulty in assessing the potential gains, as well as risks. This is where the business plan really helps.

The lack of investment by mainstream investors has led the UK government, like those in many other European states, to create tax breaks to try to lure private capital to invest in the making of films for theatrical distribution. At this moment, the UK and other European governments, are looking at new ways of helping film producers raise funds for new, European based, films. However, as senior figures in the film industry that dominates the world, Hollywood, point out, they are not subsidised. They feel that if there is a market for the films then there is no need for government subsidies. Indeed a leading film critic and writer on the UK film industry, Alexander Walker, makes the same point. In his posthumously published book, **Icons In The Fire: The Decline and Fall of Almost Everybody in the British Film Industry. 1984-2000.** Published by **Orion 2004**, he said that when Hollywood wanted to make a film they went to the banks, whereas in the UK, we go to the government and the appointed bureaucrats. This he felt is why the US has a film industry and we do not.

Indeed, it has been said that the Canadian film industry only really took off when government subsidies were withdrawn. In actual fact, Europe, and especially London as Europe's main financial centre, is well able to provide private finance for filmmakers, but its reluctance to do so is often premised on the fact that potential investors are unable to assess the risks. Again, this shows the importance of having a well structured business plan that details the investment opportunities in a professional manner.

Public Funding Versus Private

In the UK, and other European countries, government finance for films is available and should be seen as one of the potential elements within the finance part of the business plan. However, the aim of the producer or filmmaker, if they wish to build a filmmaking career, should be to create commercial viability movies. In this context, so called Art House movies, those films often with a more literary and intellectual content, can also be described as commercially viable. This can happen with Art House movies that reach their target audience and recoup their costs, often over a long period as they play to small but discerning audiences world-wide. It could be very dangerous to have your film totally subsidised by public funds, without any commercial considerations, since, in the end, the film must have the potential to reach a target audience, or it will just be shelved and never see the light of day. After all, no matter where you got the original investment from, if your film is shelved because it has no perceivable audience, then it will be very hard to convince people in the future to invest in your next film.

Those who provide public funds in the UK, make it clear that they require private funding to be a part of any project they invest in. This applies to the UK's Film Council who, in their latest guide to applying for finance, will require at least 50% of the final budget to be raised from private finance. This, the Film Council hopes, will ensure that commercial viability has been taken into consideration; otherwise private investors would not invest. You will not be taken seriously by the UK Film Council unless you do develop a business plan and can demonstrate you will husband and spend public money effectively. However, the UK Film Council, like all film financiers, know that there is no such thing as a definite box office hit.

Suffice to say, that film projects, based on sound business plans, stand more chance of success at the box office and so are much more likely to attract both private and public investment. Also, they give the filmmaker the opportunity of building on success by developing a slate of films. That is how careers are made in the film industry. Governments are also beginning to realise that just giving grants, without any planning for production and distribution, is not a recipe for building a thriving and successful film industry. One of the aims of government funding is to receive a return on the capital they invest in films so that a pool of finance is built for investment in future projects. If it were not so, then the government would have to be willing to set aside money each year for investment in films no matter what their commercial viability.

The UK Franchise Experiment

In 1997 the UK government decided to use £92m from National Lottery money to help fund the British Film industry. This would be done via the Arts Council of England and would involve three film companies who it was deemed had the potential to grow into major players within the UK and, hopefully, internationally. When the plan was unveiled at the Cannes film festival in 1997, a major film distributor said, **"the government might as well have taken £100 million into the street and set alight to the whole fucking lot, for all the good it's going to do."**

It is now seven years since the franchises were given out and most people feel that they have not achieved what they set out to do. The franchises are no longer in place and it will be interesting to see if the money invested did actually allow these companies to build a platform from which they can now become serious players on the world film stage.

Film As One Of The Nation's Art Forms

Some argue that films should be subsidised and paid for by the state, because they reflect the stresses, strains and aspirations of an individual society. That grants should be given for films to be made that are deemed to be art, and therefore cathartic, and express the current concerns of the nation. Such films, it is argued, would also be a way of protecting the nation's culture at home, and promoting it abroad.

Some would say that this is what France has attempted to do. However, such an approach can also generate xenophobia and be used to stop what many see as the rampant spread of US culture via films. Many would argue that films have been the main way in which the world has been culturally colonised by the US and that since non-Hollywood film industries cannot compete on a economically level playing field, state intervention to save cultural diversity is advisable and necessary.

It is often argued that we need a UK or European studio that could rival the Hollywood majors. Against this argument is the consideration that the UK doesn't have sufficient scriptwriters, directors and producers to form a basis for a major studio to thrive here. The assertion is that Europe doesn't have the business mentality that creates a large pool of highly motivated, competitive and talented film people with a professional outlook to filmmaking. In short, that it is not just that we do not have the money, but rather we do not have the human resource to make the twelve big budget films a year needed to be viable. Others argue that we need to think European, and create a true European based studio that can develop and fund films no matter where they are from and who is producing them, as long as they are made with European resources and reflect European culture.

Replicating The Hollywood Model

One possible way forward for UK and other European countries, is to build virtual studios: that is, to create corporate infrastructures that reflect the way the major Hollywood studios work, but without the actual studio. This will entail encouraging and supporting people with judgement and vision and, at the same time, being willing to make difficult decisions when people do not produce the desired results. This seems to be the methodology adopted by the European football industry and nobody seems to complain, even those managers who lose their jobs because of poor results. It is also worth noting that the European football industry is the most vibrant and successful in the world, with many players from outside Europe eager to come and play for European teams.

Many would say that by adopting the Hollywood model and creating a virtual studio, filmmakers do not sacrifice quality, but rather create the potential to make a broad spectrum of films that suit many tastes. After all, Hollywood, as well as giving us what are often considered mind-numbing blockbusters, also produced **Blade Runner, Lost In Translation, Casablanca, Citizen Kane, Blue Velvet, Apocalypse Now, Videodrome, LA Confidential** and many more films that are popular as well as being considered works of art.

However, the big issue is, and always will be, distribution. As Michael Khun amply demonstrated in his book, **One Hundred Films and a Funeral**, without the power to effectively distribute world wide, non-Hollywood studio filmmakers will always be at a disadvantage.

John Sweeney

Reaching The Parts Others Don't Reach

It could be argued, that unless a film is popular and therefore commercially viable, it is not achieving the aim of promoting national cultures since it needs to reach a wide audience and engage with it on many levels. This reflects the arguments about grants given to fringe theatre groups in the UK in the sixties and seventies. Many of these theatre companies had a clear polemical stance, usually left of centre, which they sought to promote via the stage. However, it is generally accepted that they failed since audience numbers were low and the plays were preaching to the converted. The plays therefore failed to promote the values they were proselytising, since they were not seen by their target audiences – those who needed to be converted. This is often the accusation levelled at art films.

Many see the Holy Grail as producing works of art that engage a wide audience, as is the case with great works of literature. However, the problem remains as to who can judge what films have the potential to be real works of art and should therefore be produced. Publishing houses have often, though not always, managed to identify and produce great works of literature, but they were able to judge the final work. Publishers and fine art gallery owners are in the same position as the film distributor who is able to look at the finished work and decide whether or not to buy it for exhibition and distribution. The public bureaucrat or private investor or Hollywood executive, are all faced with the same dilemma. They must judge from a script or treatment, outline of a story, whether the film has real potential. They are also aware that a great script can be ruined by a director, no matter how good the director's films have been in the past. By the same token, a director can take what is perceived as a mediocre script and turn it into a smash hit. This is what is considered to have happened to **Casablanca. Casablanca** was bought by Hollywood as a published, but unperformed, play. It was completely rewritten by a team of writers, brilliantly directed, an excellent music score was created and there was, of course, inspired casting and acting.

8

(Imagine, wooden-top B movie actor **Ronald Reagan** nearly got the part of Rick which, in the film, was played by Humphrey Bogart). **Casablanca** was just one of fifty two studio movies made that year. The rest, as they say, is history.

Command Economy Versus Free Market

Some commentators believe that when the state becomes a player in the market place it creates a situation similar to when the soviet model was the alternative to the free market capitalist model. In the soviet model a group of state employees decided what would be produced. The criteria they used varied from what factory capacity was available, to what the government thought was good for the people. This could be said to be the ultimate in films that are "product-led". Product-led is when a film or any other product is created without any consideration as to who the target market might be.

It has been observed, that at the initial decision making stage concerning whether or not to make a film, the so called private sector or free market is not so different from the government or command structure. Proposals for a film will be put forward and ultimately rejected or accepted by a small group of people, or even one person. Possibly, the real difference between the two models is that in the free market model the decision maker/s need to ensure that overall they make a profit. This means they are basically driven by public taste. The state model assumes that each year funds will be allocated, as for other state institutions such as museums, and so profit is not an issue in the sense that even if the film does not make a profit there will be more money next year. In the private sector, if you continue to make losses then you will eventually go bankrupt.

The Filmmaker

The issue for filmmakers is to define their basic aims. Do they want to reach a wide audience with whom they engage emotionally and psychologically and so possibly change the way people view the world? Or, have they got just one way of seeing the world and wish to share this vision with like-minded people, no matter what the size of this group is? This is clearly a judgement that only the filmmaker can make. It is possible to have a defined focus on the world, as Ken Loach does, in making films that highlight the travails of the working classes. He still finds funds to go on making the same kind of films and has mostly been backed by Channel 4 which has a remit to produce socially relevant broadcast content. The same could be said of Woody Allen, in terms of making films for a target audience. However, many of Woody Allen's films are not released and so do not make any money at all in box office terms, but often go on to make money via TV and video and DVD sales.

However, these two filmmakers have built their reputations over a number of years and have used the system. Ken Loach saw a small, but clearly defined, market that was left of centre and oriented himself within an organisation, Channel 4, that had the resources and the remit from the state, to encourage non-mainstream films. Woody Allen achieved some critically and financially successful films and also showed he could make films for very small amounts of money. It is also the case that he is much more successful in France than in the US.

Opportunity And Entry Costs

Songwriters or comedians or painters or writers, have the opportunity to express themselves in their chosen medium and deliver a finished product without external funding. This is because the cost of creating one of these art forms is usually within the reach of most people. However, the cost of producing a film that can be theatrically released is out of the reach of most individuals.

Whether or not the state should play a role in producing films, and it what form, is a debate that shows no signs of being resolved in the near future.

The Markets For Film

In presenting a case for funding it is helpful to have an overview not just of how films are made, but of how and why they are shown. This will of course vary from one country to another, and you will need to focus on those countries in which the film will be made and distributed. If you are thinking of doing a co-production involving two or more countries, you will need to separately analyse and explain each country. The key elements for analysis are:

- *Number of theatrical tickets sold – box-office.*
- *Film territories – size of markets and activity.*
- *Type and volume of ancillary sales (DVD etc.)*
- *Trends – in terms of admissions and genre.*

The Studio System And The Independents

The big differences between European and US films are the manner in which they are financed and distributed. The major Hollywood studios develop, finance, create and distribute their own films. In Europe, it is often the case that once a film has been completed, the producer must then go looking for a distributor. Hollywood therefore has a huge advantage in that film projects can be developed over time, and marketing, production and distribution strategies integrated. Also, since most majors are currently owned by conglomerates, they have access to vast sums of money to invest in the pictures. This gives them enormous advantages when marketing the films, which can often cost more than the shooting of the film. However, even within the studio system, marketing and business plans are developed for each film. By the time an initial version of the script is in place, the marketing departments are already putting together a marketing strategy and campaign. This may even happen when the film is just an idea. They may only have the poster and the producer's pitch – from this they can decide to create a script and make a film. A pitch, in movie terms, is the initial, brief verbal outline of the idea for a film. Pitching a movie is considered an art form and many words and books have been written on the subject. Pitching ideas for films to major studios is a substantial part of an independent producer's job. We will discuss this in more detail later in the chapter.

Pitching is the manner in which **The Usual Suspects** got made. The independent producer, Robert Jones, had a poster and an idea for the film. The pitch may be only three or four sentences long, but if you already have a business and marketing plan, the pitch can be a distillation of that. There are highly successful producers in Hollywood who first create the key art, poster images and the tag-lines or one liners that go on the poster, such as in **Jaws 2**, *"Just when you thought it was safe to go back in the water"*, and then take this to the studio executives and use it to pitch the film.

Sometimes, the overseas distribution arms of the majors will be asked to make comments about the script, potential stars, director and genre to ascertain the film's likely success in the various territories. The studio executives are attempting to forecast the film's potential earnings in those areas based on the track records of the genre, stars, director and production values. They are seeking to analyse and quantify the market potential for each of these elements in relation to the various territories. They will then assess each territory's maximum potential earnings based on past records. It could be said that the exercise is market-led not product-led. However, the end product is still a film which people will either choose to go and see or not. It is also recognised that despite all the marketing analysis and planning, the majority of films fail at the box office. And this is not because they are bad films. It may be that a film reaps critical acclaim, but fails to make any money – that is, it fails to make more money than it cost to produce and distribute. It is estimated that eight out of ten

Hollywood films will create a loss, in that the revenue streams will not equal the cost of production, marketing and distribution. The business plan cannot guarantee success, but it can stop you making obvious mistakes and it gives you an overview of what the cost of the film should be in relation to its potential earnings.

The crucial thing to be aware of is that the markets, and therefore the opportunities for returns on investments and therefore success, are always in a state of flux and change. A few years ago a trend was observed that showed the US film industry was dividing into two distinct markets – one that produced Christmas or Summer $70m plus blockbusters and their sequels, and the other that turned out films below the $10m mark. The trend is now for the majors not to get involved with the production of really low budget movies, but to provide finance or distribution deals once the film is made. It is assumed that the centre ground left for the $25 – $45m picture will get ever smaller.

If this trend continues, it will create lots of opportunities for the independent, non-studio, filmmaker. With cinema attendance growing and the majors spending ever more resources making bigger and bigger blockbusters and sequels, the opportunities for independent filmmakers will expand. The independent filmmaker is able to be more cost effective when developing film projects and can spend more time looking for new and emerging talent. This is because the new and emerging talent is often first seen at minor film festivals, which the major studio executives do not have the time, or inclination, to attend. Also, on low budget films, the producer can take more risks and give the writer or director more creative scope to experiment, with the hope that they will come up with something unique that has mass market appeal. This will give the film a buzz factor and create a "must see" feeling within the target audience, often by word of mouth. This happened with **Leaving Las Vegas**.

If a low budget film turns out to be marketable, then a distributor is much more likely to acquire it and promote it, since the potential for creating a profit is much greater. If a film can be made for

£1m and has potential sales of £3m and has low marketing and distribution costs, it is much more attractive than a film costing £45m that needs another £15 to £20m P&A (cost of film Prints and Advertising) spent on it. Also the £45m film would need clear mass-market appeal that would enable it to recoup its costs. Often, it is only the blockbusters costing $100m plus that are the safe bets for reaching a mass market. Studio blockbusters, and their sequels, may be predictable and boring, but they usually have all the ingredients that their audiences are looking for. However, well made low budget films aimed at a clearly defined market also do well, as recent figures show a clear trend within Europe for well made locally produced films.

As far as the majors are concerned, as long as the main losses occur with the lower-budget films, and the main successes are with the higher costing films, they remain in business. Remember, it is a business, show business, and no business will last very long unless it makes profits.

The Studio System

It is generally held that there are eight Hollywood Majors. These are currently, Columbia Pictures, Walt Disney, MGM, Paramount, 20th Century Fox, Universal, Fox, Warner Bros.

It is worth having an idea of how the studio system works since you may find the perfect combination for collaboration with a major studio or production company. It may be that you are sent a hot new script and find a first time, but talented director, and the project has the interest of, and is just right for, a major actor with box-office appeal. You may not see as much money back if the studio does all the work, but your film will get distributed in a professional manner. This is because the studios have the resources and the clout to ensure that the film gets the maximum exposure.

Clearly there are pluses and minuses for going with a studio or a large European production company. On the plus side, the studio is able to bankroll the film if the money runs out or it goes over budget. Because of technical difficulties, amongst other things, **Jaws** went over budget, but the work that was in the can looked good and so more money was provided. It is very difficult going back to individual investors for extra money, since they will feel that they appraised the initial request for investment capital and now the budget has increased with no discernible extra value to the film. Also, if there is more than one investor, why should one of them give money unless they all do? The problem will be persuading all of them to contribute towards the extra money that is needed. If you have kept back some of the equity for yourself, you may be able to trade this for the extra cash you need. This is where pre-production strategic and financial planning is crucial. You must build in contingencies because "sod's law" manifests itself on a regular basis in the film industry.

Needing extra funds could be crucial if the ending of the film doesn't work, as with **The Crying Game**. Or you have carried out a test screening and the results show you have to re-shoot expensive scenes to make the film commercially viable, as was the case with **My Best Friend's Wedding**. Also, if the theme and values of the film warrant it, the studio has the clout to open in 3,000 plus cinemas. A film print costs approximate £1,000, so a wide distribution strategy will be expensive for an independent producer and distributor.

On the minus side, the studio controls everything including the final cut. It is very rare for a director to have the final cut, and those that do hold onto this right. If you are a new producer with a new director then it is very unlikely you will be allowed to have the final say as to what the film eventually looks like. The studio will be keen to control the whole process to ensure that the shooting schedules are met and the artistic form of the film is right for the market it is aimed at. This also means they can hire and fire anyone, including the director or producer, and control who gets the final credits.

They may also radically change the script, and not give the original writer the screenplay credit.

With **The Last Action Hero**, the original writers ended up with the credit of the original story, but the studio appointed writers got the credit for the screenplay. If an Oscar is awarded for best screenplay, this could be galling to the original writers!

Hollywood

The main source of film finance and funding lies with the Hollywood majors. They each spend on average between $450m and $600 every year on making films. The logic is that if you can make sufficient films, then one or two of them will make enough profit to cover the costs of all of them. In his book **Independent Feature Film Production**, **Gregory Goodell** quotes from a survey by **Paul Kagan** and associates, which shows that for movies costing over $4m a random slate of five films did not make a profit. Nor was a random slate of ten films able to produce a profit. However, when twentyfive films were selected randomly, one of them produced enough profit to cover the cost of all the others. This could be seen as critical mass. These movies included those that were made for reasons other than commercial considerations, so the studios aim for half this output but with a commercial focus and this seems to work. This, I believe, is the basis of the model that needs to be developed by the UK or European film industry.

As quoted before, one of the real masters of screenwriting, William Goldman, in his book **Adventures in the Screen Trade,** says that the truth is that as regards picking films that are likely to be hits, "nobody knows anything". He goes on to say that the problem is that because films take a long time to make, usually three years from conception to release, we are trying to guess what public taste will be in three years time. He says that this means it is a lottery, because "no one knows what will work". However, thinking through a project and building a business model can stop you making obvious mistakes, such as making a high budget film in a genre, eg a $200m slasher/horror movie, that will never recoup its production costs.

Films do get made from a simple pitch or somebody seeing a good script, but it is generally accepted that to improve the chances of acceptance, an independent producer will need to have a substantially developed package before they approach a studio. By "package" is meant a script, director, stars and budget. A clear indication that the independent producer is well aware of how, and why, the movie will perform well in its target market would also be helpful. The studio executive who first hears the proposal, must, if he or she likes it, then go on and sell it to others within the studio, especially the person who can green-light the project. So the studio executive needs all the reason possible to say yes to your proposal because he will use these same reasons to get others to say yes.

Developing Movies Within The Studio System

The Deal Memo

If a studio is interested in working with an independent producer on a specific project, both parties will enter into a development agreement in the form of a Deal Memo. A deal memo will outline the crucial elements of the agreement between the producer and the studio. It is very important that producers spend time making sure they understand exactly what they are entering into. This applies equally to the UK and European producers and production companies, as to Hollywood. The kind of issues the deal memo will cover are: the salaries of the various participants; the time schedule; who gets the credits on screen and in any advertising materials; how the profits will be distributed and what are called "turnaround rights" should the film not be made by that particular studio or production company.

Turnaround agreements define who controls the property, how the money spent on development by the studio will be repaid if the project is successfully set up elsewhere, interest on any monies the studio has paid out to help develop the project, and what percentage of the profit should come back to the studio should the film be successfully developed and produced elsewhere. These details are usually hammered out during active development of the project. But the producer needs to be very careful about the details of a deal memo, especially as regards the terms of the turnaround aspect of the deal. The producer may have problems getting back ownership of the property if the studio decides not to proceed with the project. Studios would often rather bury the project than see it go elsewhere, since if they turn it around and then it is taken to another studio who make it into a major success, there is deep embarrassment and people lose their jobs. This happened to **Forrest Gump**, **Home Alone**, and even to **Gone With The Wind**. So the producer needs to make sure that the deal memo is clear about who owns the rights to the film if the studio decides not to proceed with it.

Step Deal

Basically a deal memo outlines a series of steps that will be taken during the development of the film project. The first step is often a first draft of the script. The writer and the producer are likely to receive a fee for this work. If the studio wishes to go to the next step, a rewrite and the producer possibly contacting acting and directing talent, then another fee will be paid. Clearly it is an incremental scale that allows payments to be made to the parties as the development process proceeds. It is often only the writers who get any significant amounts of money, since it is they who do most of the work during the initial stages of development. If they complete the script, then they will expect to be, and are, paid in full. The producer may receive only ten percent of his fee even if the development stage has been fully completed. The producer receives his full fee when the film is completed and ready for distribution.

The studio or production company will have the right to stop the development process at any time, but they will also be liable for the payment of fees they have agreed to pay, such as writer's fees for rewrites of the script.

When approaching a studio or production company for a development deal, it is vitally important that the producer knows how the studio or the production company like to do business. Some like just a minimum outline for a project and they then use their own system for budgeting and attaching acting and directing talent that suits their resources. In the UK, Working Title likes to use certain stars, directors and writers when they are developing and producing romantic comedies. As discussed previously, other studios and companies like you to come to them with a full package that includes the finished script, completed budget and what acting or directing talent has either agreed to be involved or should be approached with offers. However, you should find out beforehand which actors or directors would be available and those who have agreements or relationships with various studios or production companies. What is also important is that you should fully understand how a studio or production company develops its films before you approach them. This can be done by reading the trade magazines and seeing what the company has produced in the past and what they currently have in various stages of development and production.

Production And Distribution

It needs to be realised that for most producers, and certainly those beginning their careers, the deal they will have with the major studio or production company will be a production and distribution one. The production company or studio will want all the worldwide distribution rights for the film from the start. As said before, distribution is where the big money is made and the producer's film may be the only one that year that makes money for the studio, so they have to make sure they own all the crucial rights and thus receive the profits. The producer might have an agreement as regards a share in net profits, but net profits are considered as "monkey points" in Hollywood in that they never materialise.

The best thing for the producer is to secure a large producer's fee. Of course, as the producer builds his or her career with a series of successful films, the studios will beat a path to their door with deals that involve gross points. (See Glossary for full definition of Gross Points) However, these can be misleading and the small print must be read. As Goodall explains in his book **Independent Feature Film Production,** because the concept of net profits has been discredited in Hollywood, some studios now use euphemisms such as "participation points" – "contingency payments" – "net proceeds" and even "formula break even points". It is generally considered by accountants and lawyers that when you enter into financial agreements for film projects, the terms used in these agreements take on meanings not found in the normal world of finance and commerce. What is important is that the producer or filmmaker fully understands the terms of any agreement entered into and then they will not feel that they have been exploited or robbed or double-crossed.

Getting The Green Light

When the producer or filmmaker goes to the studio or production company, be it in Hollywood or Europe or elsewhere, they will usually be interviewed by a studio executive or development executive. These people are very busy and often would rather be somewhere other than listening to a producer or filmmaker. This is because they know that 99% of all proposals will be of no interest to them. This may be for a variety of reasons, such as it is not the kind of film they made, the cost of making the film clearly outweighs any revenue potential or, as it's most often the case, the proposal, or pitch, is for a film that has no potential for being successful in terms of quality. However, the executive is also well aware that you just might have the next **Four Weddings** or **Star Wars** in active development.

If the executive likes the proposal, he or she will contract with the producer or filmmaker and begin the development process. The thing to remember is that just because a film is in development with a major studio or production company, it doesn't mean it will get make into a movie and distributed. In his book, **Which Lie Did I Tell**, William Goldman says that there is only one person in each studio or organisation who can give the final go-ahead, or green-light, for a film to be produced and distributed.

A studio executive may receive a pitch, or have a book or script sent to them by an agent, that arouses his or her interest. However, there is a long way to go before production starts, and just because a script or treatment has been optioned doesn't mean it will be made into a film. Hundreds of films are in pre-production in any of the major Hollywood studios at any one time, but very few of them will reach the stage of going into production. It can be changes that happen completely outside the studio's control, such as 9/11 when disaster films were shelved.

When making a pitch, it is considered good practice to pitch only one film proposal at any one meeting. If the executive asks, then you can state what other ideas for film you have in the pipe-line. The pitch, the main idea of what the film is about, it is generally considered, should be just one or two sentences long. It should be delivered verbally and not read from notes. You should, however have a one or two page outline of the story of the film with you, which you can leave with the executive if he or she likes your original idea. There are many books and articles on pitching, but the basic ideas for a good pitch seem to be to keep it simple, one or two sentences, not to waste the executive's time, so the executive will therefore be more inclined to give you future meetings, and to do your homework on what kind of films the company makes. You should also know what films are currently in production around the world and how your film relates to these trends.

In his book, **Which Lie Did I Tell,** William Golding also explains that even if a studio executive loves your film and it is one week away from production, and he gets fired, the film will not be made. Golding explains that this is because the incoming executive throws out everything that has been developed by his predecessor. The new executive does this because if the film developed by his predecessor gets made and is a hit, everybody will know it wasn't the new executive's film, and will therefore see the new executive as a poor substitute for the sacked executive.

Co-Productions With Majors

The Hollywood majors, and the big European companies, are always on the look-out for co-productions with independent producers. This is because they are always seeking the next **Full Monty** or **Four Weddings** or **Amelie.** This means that projects initiated in the independent sector can be supported and developed by the majors. Since nobody knows what the next big hit will be, or where it will come from, the studio executives are desperate to be aware of any newly emerging talent. Therefore the key for new producers and filmmakers, is to seek out and work with up and coming talent, especially writers and directors. Often, it is the unique vision of the director, and the manner in which he or she interprets the script, that makes the difference between the film being a hit or a flop. Independent producers should be scouring the festivals looking for the next A list talent. It may be that you have a brilliant script and you find a director who wants to make the film and also align themselves with an actor, to the benefit of both their careers, such as Scorsese with De Niro.

One proven strategy for European production companies in forging links with major studios, is the creation of distribution deals. UK production company Working Title has a distribution agreement with the US studio, Paramount, and this seems to work well for both companies. As well as handling the distribution of the film, the US major may be willing to invest in the production of the film as well. The degree to which they invest will determine how much artistic control remains with the independent producer.

The Independent Producer

For our purposes, we will define Independent Producer as: *a person, or group of persons, who funds the film outside of the studio system and has full creative control*.

In the UK, funding for the negative, that is the actual shooting of the film and editing it to a form whereby it is ready to be distributed, can come from a mixture of private and public investors.

If you are an independent film producer, the crucial elements are production and distribution. In the early eighties a group of independent films made a lot of money. These included **Dirty Dancing**, which was made for under $5m (£2.84) and earned more than $100m (£56.8m) world-wide. **Four Weddings and a Funeral,** which was made for around £2.2m ($3.87m), has to date made over £113m ($200m) world-wide. There was also, **Look Who's Talking** which was made for less than $10m (£5.68) and took over $200m (£113m).

Since these films were made for what the major studios would call micro budgets, and yet recouped several times their initial investment, the studios became very interested in independent filmmaking. After all, the real money is made in distribution and so the studios thought that instead of buying low cost movies and promoting them, they could initiate them and even produce them. Miramax had bought **The Blair Witch Project** for $1m (£0.56m) at the Sundance Film Festival, and then spent another $20m (£11.36) getting it ready for distribution. It is estimated that it has taken over $100m (£56.8m) world-wide. The above figures, as with all figures for income relating to films, need to be approached with caution. Within the film industry it is accepted that the true figures for film receipts are never fully revealed for a variety of reasons.

However, it appears that the major studios either didn't have the experience or the patience to develop and make really low budget films. Low budget independent filmmaking requires something other than a corporate culture. It needs flexibility, patience and teamwork. That is not to say that these attributes cannot be found in large corporations, but film studios are not known for them. In most major studios projects are developed by studio executives operating within a traditional hierarchical management model, wherein it is much safer to say no, than to say yes. They want to keep their jobs and are desperate not to make mistakes; which means not taking any chances. However, when you, as an independent producer, go to them with a fully developed business and marketing plan, you are reducing the risk of their making a mistake if they choose to accept your project, and so they are much more likely to say yes.

For a variety of reasons therefore, but mainly because they cannot do it as well as the independent producers, the big studios have pulled out of very low budget filmmaking. However, they are still open to well thought-out film projects from independent producers who have a workable business plan and a marketing strategy. If these are present, then the majors may be willing to enter into deals whereby they will fund the making of the film in exchange for the distribution rights. This really is the model that independent filmmakers and producers should be aiming at, with the added strategy of keeping an ever increasing amount of the film's equity so that a production company can be built. The aim of the independent film producer should be to have ongoing income streams from films they have produced. This is usually in the form of equity or a share of the film's takings from the various distribution channels. This usually takes the form of gross points; that is if the producer has ten gross points then they receive 10% of the gross takings of the film. The independent producer needs to be aware that, unlike gross profits, net profits from a film are an extreme rarity.

Independent Slate

The term slate is used in the film industry to describe a collection of films that are being prepared for production. When the films have been completed and are owned by a company, they are referred to as a library. As we have seen, the big US studios have hundreds of films ready to go. Most small production companies have between five and ten projects they are working on. One model that successful UK independent producers use is the 3X3 model. This has three films ready to go into production; three films in active development; three films being seriously considered for development.

This model allows the production company to offset the losses from one film against the profits from others – a mini version of what the big studios do. However, each film must be geared towards a market and must be potentially viable in its own right, which is why separate planning is necessary for each one. Also, you must tell the investors and the studios if this is part of your business model. After all, if a film like **Four Weddings And A Funeral** makes phenomenal profits, then its investors will expect phenomenal returns. But these may be substantially reduced if cross-collateralisation is being exploited and there are loss-making films to be supported. This can mean that the investor in the successful film receives very little in way of a return on his investment, and at the same time has to watch while his film conquers the world.

Another reason why independent producers should have a slate of films is that if they focus on raising money for just one film the talent might suddenly disappear or die, or get a better offer.

Financing And Profit Distribution.

It is important for you and your investors to understand how the money flows through the system – from the time the audience hand over their money at the box office to when you can expect to see a return. It is vital that you explain all the details, so that investors do not feel they have been hoodwinked. After all, you want to build a relationship with them so that you can turn to them in the future for other projects. It is also worth pointing out that, in case some investors are surprised or sceptical, the studios did not make up this system and that it is standard business practice. Also be aware, and make sure that your investors know also, that even if a studio has been instrumental in producing and creating your film, the distribution of the film is treated as a separate entity, even though it may be being carried out by the same studio who made the film.

One crucial issue that is often overlooked by film producers is that investors want to know that they are being treated equitably, and that other investors or participants are not being given preferential treatment. So, be as open and transparent as possible, so that you are viewed as someone who can be trusted. Even if, by informing investors of all the organisations that need to be paid before they get their share, it means you lose them, they will still respect you and be willing to listen to you concerning future projects that might be structured more favourably towards them.

The business plan will include a finance plan, which we will deal with in a later chapter, that explains how you will raise the finance and from whom. What follows is an outline of the industry standard pattern.

Co-production Income Streams

Even though you may have private or state investors, if you are doing a co-production with a major studio, the flow is likely to be the following:

Cost of ticket at the box-office	**£6**	**($9)**

Exhibitor's share:		($4.50)
(50% in the US and most territories)		

* Note that in the UK the exhibitors often take anything up to 70% of the box office ticket. UK distributors say they feel vulnerable to the high cost of rents and other costs, and so are less likely to take a chance on films they are not sure will generate a profit. For this example I have applied 60% as the UK exhibitor's share.

Income:	**£2.40**	**($4.50)**
Studio Distribution Fee (30% of £2.40 ($4.50))	£0.72	($1.35)
Studio's fixed costs (12% of £2.40 ($4.50))	£0.28	($0.54)

(Fixed overheads not directly attributed to the film: staff salaries, rent, accountants etc.)

Amount left to apply to cost of film negative	**£1.4**	**($2.61)**

This amount goes towards paying off the cost of producing the film, up to creating the negative for the prints that are used by the distributor. The studio treats this as a loan to your company to create the film. Because they see it as a loan, they charge you interest at one or two points above base rate; so not only do you have to pay back the capital you were given to make the film with, but also interest on top.

Gross Points

Stars and the director may be entitled to "gross points", in which case they will be paid from the studio's gross dollar of $4.50 or pound sterling of £3.60. When this happens it is not unusual for a high grossing film to show a net loss on the bottom line.

Estimating Breakeven Points

Studios use a rough estimate to arrive at a breakeven point for film projects. What they do is multiply by 2.5 the production cost of a film to find the breakeven point. So a $10m (£5.7m) film needs to take $25m (£14.25) at the box-office. This is usually spread over a maximum of three months from the date of the release of the film. However, these days, in an attempt to beat the video pirates a film might have a limited time frame, but a wide distribution. So, it might be shown in all the UK's major cities over a two-week period.

In the US, it is generally considered that a low budget film is $15m (£8.25) or below, with another $15m (£8.25m) being spent on advertising and prints, so the film needs to take $75m (£42.6m) to break-even.

In the UK in 2003 the average cost of a film was £2.2m ($3.87m). So, to recover the costs of production, marketing and distribution it would need to take £5.3m ($9.6m) at the box office. Of course it may be a sleeper, like **Leaving Las Vegas**, which is said to have opened in one cinema in the US, and then, through word of mouth, gradually spread across the US. This film continues to make money through ancillary sales such as TV and video and DVD sales. Another film that bombed when it came out was **Blade Runner**, but then, ten years later when the director's cut was released, it became a hit as a cult movie. Being a "cult hit" means that the movie will generate income streams from ancillary sales such as TV and DVD. Often, these income streams have a long life, as new generations of film fans discover the film.

Independent Filmmaking And Distribution

There is no one-way to finance and distribute a film. A good, or great distribution deal will depend on many things, such as the type of film, the cast and/or director and the reputation of the producer or filmmaker. As to the distribution deal, this can be agreed before, during or after the making of the film. It is often thought to be a very good idea if a distribution deal can be arrived at before the film starts production. If a deal is in place before filming starts, and if the deal is an important one, such as selling the North American distribution rights, this can attract other investors and increase the budget of the film.

There are a lot of slang words and jargon used in the film industry and the producer or filmmaker will need to be familiar at least with the more commonly used ones. As far as distribution deals are concerned, the main terms used are:

Straight Distribution. The distributor acquires the rights to distribute the film in various territories. This may be just one territory, such as Japan, or all of Europe. The most valuable territory is the US and this is usually estimated to bring in 40% of the film's eventual revenues. Often this deal will be for a specific amount of time. It can also involve other factors. (See Chapter 7 on distribution deals)

Minimum Guarantee. This is when the distributor, often to make sure that he gets the rights to specific territory, will give an undertaking to pay a minimum amount of money to the producer once the film is made.

Outright Sales. This is possibly the most straightforward deal in that the distributor agrees to pay a set amount of money in exchange for the right to distribute the film in one or more territory. This will usually be for a set time, after which the distribution rights of that territory or territories revert back to the producer or filmmaker.

Negative Pick-up Deal. (See glossary)

Common Distribution Deals

How individual deals are put together and how the money is allocated once it starts to flow in, will depend on many things. How good the producer's negotiating skills are, will in part determine what the terms of the deal will be.

Gross Deal: This is a very straightforward deal with the income from the distribution of the film being divided between the producer and the distributor on an agreed percentage split. So the distributor may get 60% and the producer 40% of all incoming income from the film. With this kind of deal it is usual for the distributor to meet the costs of the Prints and Advertising (P&A) and the minimum guarantee (MG) commitments from his share.

Cost-Off-The-Top Deal: With this deal, as soon as the money starts to come in it is used to meet the cost of creating the prints and advertising (P&A budget). When these costs have been met, any further monies go towards the cost of any Minimum Guarantee commitments on the part of the distributor. When both these costs have been met, whatever comes in is divided on an agreed percentage basis between the distributor and the producer.

Net Deal: This deal is sometimes seen as a better deal for the new producer while at the same time protecting the interests of the distributor. What happens is that the all the costs and fees of the distributor are met and then all the rest of the money goes to the producer. So, first the distributor's fee is met, usually 35% of gross revenue, then the cost of the prints and advertising the film are met, then the cost of any minimum guarantee agreement. Once these items are met then all the monies go to the producer.

Of course it could be that the film never makes any money, or if it does it barely covers the cost of the distributor's fees and expenses. Or, as often happens, both the distributor and the producer lose money. That is why distributors need to be fully convinced about a film's commercial potential before they take it on.

Investor And Producer

The rest of the money is divided between the investor and the producer. However, all deals are different, and if the producer feels in a strong position with a hot script and with A list talent, then he/she is in a strong position to negotiate a deal that is favourable to them.

Build For The Future

Eric Felner, co-chairman of Working Title, widely regarded as Britain's most successful film company, believes that one of the main problems preventing UK film producers from building successful companies is that they work for a producer's fee, rather than retaining equity in the finished film. This can be easier said than done, especially if you are a new producer or filmmaker. However, building a film company by keeping equity in films the company has made, is a worthwhile strategy for those seeking to build a career as an independent film producer.

The producer should aim to protect as much of the revenues as possible, so that these can be used to build a base for the future development of the company. All too often UK and European filmmakers and producers do not look beyond the current film project. However, when starting out, it is often the case that he who pays the piper calls the tune, so that producers get paid only a producer's fee and have no share in the equity. But if the film is a success, or at least the process was managed professionally, then better deals can be struck for future projects.

What To Tell Investors

There is a great deal of information that can be provided under this heading, but basically investors are looking for reassurance that you understand the industry. They also want to know how it works in terms of the studio system and the independents.

Also, you want to explain that it is a healthy industry with growing markets in all sectors. At the moment, both in the US and Europe, there is a lot of good news out there, so use it. Most investors are savvy people, and they are aware that a healthy industry with expanding and growing markets is far more likely to give a return on their investment than one that is contracting. Make the most of the positive aspects of the film industry, but also make sure that you can back your assertions with facts.

Summing-up

It is best to assume that your investors have no knowledge of the film industry and how it works. This is especially true of new investors, and you will need to take them gently by the hand and lead them through the landscape. Remember, even if the investors are familiar with the film-industry landscape it demonstrates that you know what you are talking about and so gives the investors confidence in you. This is vital; after all you are wanting them to part with their hard earned millions to invest in your film.

Business Plan Data File

What are the crucial issues concerning the film industry in the country where the film will be produced?

How does the distribution system operate in the territories the film is most likely to do well in?

What are the key trends taking place in the film industry and how does your film relate to these?

Where do you intend to position your film, or film company, within the industry?

Are you spreading the risk over a slate of films?

How will you track the revenue streams?

By what method will you keep all investors, and other key interested parties, up to date?

Can you explain production, distribution and exhibition strategies, including time frames, as they relate to your projects?

Can you explain crucial financial elements, such as an ESCROW account? (See glossary)

Chapter 2

Creating A Film Company

"A business exists to create a customer." Peter Drucker, US
writer, educator, management consultant.

In this chapter we will:

**Look at why and how limited companies are formed to make
individual films**

**Emphasise the importance of building the right team to make
your films**

**Explain the need to have a clear focus on the kinds of films
you want to make**

**Show the importance of matching your team's skills and the
company's resources with the kind of films you propose to
make**

**Look at how and why you must identify your company's
strengths and weaknesses and how they relate to the film
projects you want to develop**

Introduction

*Running a company, even for one project, takes a wide spectrum
of skills and, in reality, no one person has all of them. And
if they did, they wouldn't have the time to attend to all the
things that need to be done. This is especially true for the film*

industry. *This means that you must choose carefully those team members with whom you will be closely working. It is a fact that there are more downs than ups in the film industry, and more negatives than positives on the road to getting the film financed, produced and distributed; you need people around you who can accept the disappointments and still stay focused on getting the film made.*

Forming A Company

It is common practice in the UK and other European countries for each film project to be developed and brought to fruition under the aegis of a limited company. Then, once the film is completed and is ready for distribution, the company formed to make the film is dissolved. It is also good practice to have a holding, or parent company, as a continuous trading entity. The parent company forms the individual companies to develop each film project and holds rights to the film. Just how many rights and what kind of rights, such as the distribution rights in various territories, depends on what has been sold prior to the finishing of the film. Creating a company solely to make the film allows protection for the producers should things go wrong. If things do go wrong, and they do, then only the company making the film, not the holding company, can be acted against. This protects the other films the holding company may be making and also the investors in the other films.

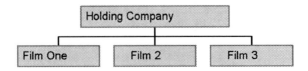

The form each company will take depends on which country the business is operating in, but the basic principles will remain the same. So will the reason for forming a parent company and companies for each film project, namely to protect those developing the film project and to place the business activity on a sound business footing.

Even if you are forming the company to make just one film, if that one film costs £3.2m ($5.6m), you are running a small business with a turnover way above the average for a small European company in any industrial sector. If you also take into account the pre-production and the post-production stages of making your film, you are looking at 18 months to two years during which you will be running the company. This is longer than most newly formed companies trade for.

Shared Vision

Because of the vicissitudes and many problems all film companies encounter, it is vital that all the key personnel agree on the goals and vision the company has, the strategy it has for achieving them, and the kind of films that will be made. It is often said that the film industry is all about being told no; the prevailing wisdom being that no studio or film production executive got fired for saying no, but that they do get sacked for saying yes to a film project that loses millions of pounds or dollars. Therefore there will be many disappointments and unfulfilled promises. Persistence is vital. It is essential that as well as sharing the corporate aims, all those involved in the enterprise should share a passion for the kind of films that are to be made, and believe they should be made. If the company is to run successfully, the company mission statement, and the methods it will use to achieve these goals, needs to be agreed and supported by all concerned. This is fundamental since it will underpin the implementation of the management strategy as discussed in chapter seven. In Jake Ebert's book: *My indecision is final: The rise and fall of Gold Crest Films*, he mentions several times that the company had no business plan. Would they have succeeded if they had one? Who knows? But from the book it appears clear that there were too many business styles.

Your aim should be to become expert at identifying good scripts and good ideas to be developed into films; identifying good writers, and so being able to give them ideas to work on that will make good scripts (David Puttnam asking Colin Welland to write Chariots of Fire); spotting brilliant directors before they become famous and working with them; spotting great actors before they become famous and working with them. You, personally, do not need to have all the expertise in identifying and working with these people, but you must have people on your team who can. You are aiming to build a reputation for being able to spot good scripts, attract top acting talent who want to work with you, and being able to run a shoot effectively both creatively and financially.

The mission statement should define what the company hopes to achieve. This not only helps to clarify and co-ordinate the thinking of the key personnel, but also helps others share your vision.

Protecting Your Business Idea

A **Patent** protects how your product **works**.

Design Registration protects how your product **looks.**

A **trademark** protects what your product is **called**.

A **copyright** protects your work on **record, paper or film.**

When establishing and running your parent company you must apply basic business skills and adhere to commercial considerations. This applies equally to each business plan you produce for each individual film. It is a matter of common sense, that unless you do adhere to and follow the basic rules of running a business, you wont be in business for long.

VAT Registered

If your company is in Europe you will need to consider if by law you should be registered for Value Added Tax (VAT). At the time of going to press the amount of turnover needed before you have to register for VAT in the UK is over £50,000. However, you can be voluntarily registered for VAT, even if your turnover is well below this figure. It is highly recommended that you do become VAT registered. This does mean you have to keep clear, and properly set out, accounts; but this discipline will be of immense value to you in ensuring that your company is run on a sound financial footing. Also, your VAT number, along with the address of your registered office if you are a limited company, will appear on your headed note paper and business cards, and this inspires confidence in those you are dealing with. Of course, being VAT registered means that not only do you charge your customers VAT, but you can claim all the VAT back on purchases made by the company.

The Producer

The producer is the manager of each of the film projects. You may wish to confine your role to being the executive producer, the one who puts the deal together, especially the financial aspects. You may then wish to appoint someone else as the production producer who will oversee the development of the script, the shoot and the editing. If you are appointing a production producer you must ensure that he or she is familiar with the genre of the film as well as the various processes that need to be skilfully managed in order to complete the film successfully. The investors and/or studio will want to see that the person in charge knows what he or she is doing. That doesn't mean that the producer has to do all the key jobs, but being able to identify what are the crucial activities, and being able to appoint the right people to fill these posts, is a vital skill and will impress investors.

Matching Skills To Budgets and Genre

The planned budget, genre and market should all relate to the skills of the key people managing the company and the projects.

If you do not have the relevant skills on board, then bring them in. This is where your SWOT analysis (see later in this chapter) helps you identify the key people you need and what skills they should possess. Most new companies are start-up companies and so do not have a track record. If you plan to make a £25m ($44m) film and the management team have never made a film before, you are highly unlikely to find investors or a studio ready to hand over large sums of money. Even if the new company has made low budget movies and even made a profit, it doesn't mean they can handle a large production budget.

Therefore, try to assemble a management team that reflects the projects being created. Aim to bring in a line producer who has line-produced a similar film in terms of genre and budget. A line producer is the person who organises the production of the film and coordinates all the activities of the various departments who are engaged in making the film. He or she will ensure that all the locations are available and booked and the right resources are in the right place at the right time such as actors, camera and sound equipment, costumes and make-up, and any other elements need to ensure the successful making of the film. One way of finding an appropriate line producer is this: once you have decided what the genre is, or the sub-section within that genre, rent and view those kinds of films and look at the credits to see who the line producer is. Contact them; if they like the script, they are likely to help.

Most of the successful independent companies, those outside the studio system, concentrate on specific genres and learn to do them well. They are then able to build a team who know how to produce specific kinds of film. Working Title have built their reputation on romantic comedies. Red Bus have concentrated on teen horror and comedy.

Planning

The main reason film companies fail is lack of financial management and planning. A key sin amongst new filmmakers is not planning the post-production route, and so running out of money and not being able to edit and so complete the film. When this happens they often have to give away all the remaining equity in the film to get a small amount of money to complete. This again compounds one of the main problems with UK film producers; they often give away all the equity in their films and take only a producer's fee, or they do not plan the post-production route and so give away any remaining equity; thus they have no ongoing income streams on which to build future projects. This is often cited as one of the reasons the UK seems unable to build film production companies that are able to develop into serious players, such as Working Title and Red Bus.

A viable strategy for a company would be to start out with a three to five year plan. During that timeframe they should plan to make three films. At the same time they should aim to organise the funding and distribution so that their company owns the equity and can therefore lease and rent the completed films to various markets and distributors. This will ensure future income streams that will enable more films to be made.

The Budget

We will deal with the budget in greater detail in chapter eight. However, it is worth pointing out that there are plenty of computer programmes that will enable you to put together a budget that meets the standards and conforms to the norms of the film industry. **Movie Magic** is one that is widely used, so I will not go into the structure here. Many producers develop their own budget templates, based on Excel. Whatever method you choose, what is important is that the producer is aware of all the items in the budget and how they have been costed. The executive and production producers cannot spend too much time ensuring that they are on top of all the individual budget heads and how they have been arrived at. Many major companies have their own methods for developing and creating budgets, but as a filmmaker or producer working in the independent sector you need to have a clear understanding of how much the film is likely to cost and how this relates to sales.

There is also the issue of how much money should be spent on making a film in order to ensure it reaches its full potential. Some major studios and distributors observe that producers or filmmakers often ask for too little money. That is, the proposed film, in order to be commercially viable and realise its full potential, needs a much bigger budget than the one asked for. Similarly, developing a script for a film that needs a large budget but which is unlikely to attract a wide audience is also not feasible.

Zero Accounting

One way of approaching budgeting is using a method based on zero accounting. This strategy means that you do not start off with a budget, but rather the notional sum of zero. This means that each area of the budget is built up on an essential cost basis. Money is only spent if it has to be, and before any item is put in the budget a case has to be made why it is essential. This means that each budget item is a building block that eventually goes to make up the whole of the budget.

What this does is focus clearly on each aspect of the film from the bottom up. You do not start off with "how much can I get", but rather "how much do I need to create the essential elements of the film". These are the elements that are vital in order to make a viable film in terms of the ratio of costs to sales. The costs to sales ratio is premised on how much the film costs to make in relation to how much money it is expected to recoup at the box office. If a producer is asking for £20m to make a film that is only likely to recoup £5m at the box office then they are not likely to meet with much success when seeking to raise the finance to make the film. The more that each pound or dollar, or euro is maximised in order to get the most from each budget head, the better the film will be. Within the constraints of the final budget, the producer must balance all the elements to ensure that he or she makes the best film from the resources available, and so maximise its commercial potential. The aim is to create a matrix within which all the values and production costs reflect the film's potential sales revenues from specific territories. We will look at this in much more detail later in chapter nine when we look at finance strategies.

Controlling Costs

It is generally thought that UK, and to a lesser extent European, filmmakers do not control their costs effectively and so do not get the most for their money. *(The Relph Report)* This is a very serious matter since it means that UK films, already on low budgets, have lower production values than they need to. UK filmmakers are not getting enough bangs for their bucks, as the US filmmakers would say. The objective should be to make films for £700k or £2.2m that look like £5m or £10 films. I believe it can be done, but it needs careful planning, sound financing management and good human resource management. These elements will be dealt with in greater detail later in the book, and also in examples of business models where they have been successfully applied.

SWOT Analysis

In order to make the most of the financial and other resources available to you as the filmmaker or producer, it is crucial that you are operating in an area of the film industry where your strengths matter and your weaknesses don't count. In order to ascertain if this is the case, you will need to carry out a full analysis of the company's strengths and weaknesses in relation to the kind of film, or films, the company is intending to make. This kind of analysis is standard practice in all kinds of companies large and small and the device used is a **SWOT Analysis.** This kind of preliminary analysis is a crucial stage in the planning process and will ensure that you make the right film for you and your company, and at the same time, greatly improve the possibility of the film being successful.

The aim is to be honest when assessing what your abilities and weaknesses are, and the resources you have available to you. Too often filmmakers embark upon the making of a film without all the necessary resources being available to make and complete the film ready for distribution. This can mean having to make compromises not only during the making of the film in terms of filmic values, but also during the post-production process. The result can be a finished film that is unable to find a distributor, or, more often than not, the producer runs out of resources after the film is shot and so is unable to edit the footage and the project just disappears.

Even if the film is finished, because of a lack of proper resources during the filming and editing stages, it may fail to realise the script's full potential. Of course the effective management of both the financial and human resources plays a crucial role in ensuring the film's success, and we will be dealing with this aspect of the filmmaking process in a later chapter.

The SWOT

A SWOT analysis, as its name implies, is made up of the following aspects:

Strengths

Weaknesses

Opportunities

Threats

Strengths And Weaknesses

This part of the SWOT is an internal analysis that relates to your, and your company's, ability to make the film you are developing. It is also worth repeating that your aim must be to be making a film where your strengths matter and your weaknesses don't count. But you can only do this when you know what your weaknesses and strengths are in relation to the needs of each of the film projects.

The first step should be to make a list of the aims and strategies for making the film, both artistically and commercially. Then make a list of all the jobs that need to be done to achieve these aims and accomplish these strategies. These might be:

- Fully realised and developed script.

- Skilled photographer who understands the genre.

- Appropriate director.

- Appropriate designer.

- Finance plan.

- Budget friendly script.

- Box office talent.

- Distribution deal.

- Defined genre and market.

Make a list of who is already committed, or whom you will be targeting for the job. Make sure you have a clear idea of whom you want for each of the key jobs such as Producer, Director, Director of Photography (DOP), Production Designer, Editor. You need to have a good idea of the strengths of each of these key personnel, since this could be the key in gaining the confidence of crucial supporters such as investors or distributors.

What is crucial is that you are honest and so are able to turn your weaknesses into strengths or eliminate their impact on the final project. This analysis is related directly to your film. One of your strengths might be that you are a strong swimmer, but if you are not making a film that requires you to swim, then it is not relevant.

When looking at your and the company's internal strengths, these might be:

Strengths:

- Clear understanding of your genre.

- Strong script.

- A list talent.

- Locations found.

- Screenplay rights

- Strong management team

Note: Screenplay rights. Set out clearly who has the rights to the screenplay or book, for how long, and if it is an option. These details can be put briefly here, and then expanded, if necessary, in the Project Section. No hard and fast rules.

Weaknesses:

- Not having the right actor for the lead role.

- Key locations are unavailable.

- You do not have a distribution agreement.

- Not all the money has been pledged or in the bank.

- No commitment from talent.

- No sales agent or distributor interested.

The aim is to identify weaknesses and if possible turn them into strengths. For example, you may decide to rewrite the script so that you can make use of the locations that are available. If you cannot turn these weaknesses into strengths, such as getting the right actor for the role, or securing the important locations at the right time, then attempt to negate them by finding alternatives. If that fails, then you must seriously question your ability to create the film you want to make.

Opportunities And Threats

These are the external forces that you cannot influence, but you need to be aware of their impact on your ability to make your films.

Opportunities

- Are more people going to see films?

- Is your target market expanding?

- Is there a trend to see the type of film you want to make?

- Has a film like yours recently been very successful?

- Has there been an increase in movie attendance, in recent years, in the key territories where your film is likely to be released?

Threats

- In your key territories, has there been an expansion of the number of films released without there being an increase in cinemas screens? Has this increased the competition your film will face?

- Is there a current boom, which looks like it is going to give way to a recession?

- Are other producers developing similar films?

- Are traditional finance sources ceasing to exist?

- Are US majors expanding their base and going into independent filmmaking territory?

What is vital is that you relate your SWOT to what you want to achieve and so it must relate directly to your company's goals and objectives. And again, it is worth repeating that you must be honest; if you're not, then you are only fooling yourself and putting the whole project in jeopardy. There is nothing wrong in acknowledging your, or the company's, weaknesses; in fact it will prove invaluable in helping you identify potential problem areas.

If your aim is to make, for example, slasher/horror films for the Japanese market, a weakness might be that you know nothing about how distribution works in Japan, or you know nothing about prosthetics and so how to cost and achieve the gory images you need to make the films a success. If success in the Japanese market is dependent on the fight scenes and the amount of gore produced, rather than on the quality of acting or a strong story line, then you need to be able to deliver this if you are to be successful.

Do not lie. Often in the film world we hear stories about how people blagged their way through: Orson Welles doing over 100 takes so that the meter on the camera clicked back and when the studio bosses came they thought he was still in the low digits. But most executives and investors are canny people and they will always find out what is really going on. This may be after the film has been made, and so when you look for support to make your next film it may be hard to find because you have a reputation of not telling the truth. The film industry is small, especially in the UK with only 50,000 employed in it, so your reputation will go before you. This might also be the reason Orson Welles found it almost impossible to get finance for his later films. Many felt he could not be trusted to stick to a budget.

Creating A Business Plan For a Film Production Company

The following is an example of how to create a notional business plan. It follows the usual format used to create a business plan; however, you may feel you wish to change the way you compose yours, but be careful, this format has been around for a long time and therefore changing it might suggest you are unfamiliar with the form.

Parent or holding company

It is usual and prudent to have one limited company as a base or holding company and then to form a limited company for each film you make. All commercial ventures are a risk and filmmaking is amongst the most risky, as well as potentially the most rewarding. The limited company is a person in law – this means the company makes the deals and signs the contracts. It also means that as well as being a director of the company you will also be an employee

49

of the company. As a director you have to file company accounts and act in a responsible way to the shareholders and those who invest in your company and its films.

The notion of a company being a person in law is sometimes difficult to conceive, but basically it means that if things go wrong, and you are sued, then it is the company that is sued, not you personally. If the action against you is successful, then all that you can lose is what the company owns, not what you own personally. This can be important if you are up against the big studios or international investors, for whatever reason, and you own a house or car or other assets. Your family would not be pleased to have their house taken away from them by a large studio or investors or those to whom the company owes money.

Although forming a limited company is the accepted norm in the film industry you may choose another type of company formation, such as:

Sole proprietor: This is when you register the company in your name and, as the name indicates, you are solely responsible for the company and all its activities. It also means that if the company should incur debts then those to whom the money is owed can proceed against you and your personal property in all its forms.

Partnership: This is the same as being a sole proprietor, but with the added danger that each partner is responsible for the company's debts. This means that if one partner, unbeknownst to the other partners, creates debts in the company's name then all the other partners are held responsible for the payment of those debts. And, as with a sole trader, those seeking redress can seize the personal property of the individual partners.

Co-operative: This is when all the members have an equal say in how the company is run. Critics of this form of association say that it is a recipe for disaster since it takes too long to make decisions because everybody must have their say, and when decisions are made they are often too woolly to be effective because they are based on consensus.

Company Mission Statement

Example:

The Pompous Film Company plans to make three feature films over the next five years. Scripts for all three films express themes of a philosophical and ethical nature that address fundamental moral issues currently facing humanity. Whilst each film will reflect a serious theme, they will also be entertaining and so reach a wide audience.

The films will range from £700k to £6m. The scripts for all three films have been completed and the company owns all the rights.

Once the mission statement is agreed and finalised, you will then need to determine how it translates into the company's goals and objectives.

Company Goals And Objectives:

By setting out clear goals and objectives you can then measure how well you are doing in achieving them. Also, by setting them within a time frame you can monitor your progress and make changes if necessary. Based on company mission statement above, these might be:

- *To develop and produce quality UK based films that can compete in national and international markets.*

- *To develop and produce films that can cross successfully from the specialist to mainstream sector.*

- *To make three feature films, of an inspirational nature that reflect deep human issues, over the next five years – one to be made approximately every eighteen months.*

- *To create a distribution strategy aimed at Europe.*

- *To create a financially viable film production company within the next five years that has income streams and the potential to grow.*

- *To create a skilled management team that can take the company forward.*

- *To explore co-production deals.*

Company Positioning Within The Film Industry

It is important that you show you have thought about how you will position your company within the film industry. This might be:

- *Our position within the market is to be an independent producer that has strong ties and working relationships with international distributors.*

- *We believe that there is a market for films that can both challenge the way we perceive society's moral framework, and at the same time be entertaining and engaging. Over the past few years the market for controversial films that deal in a thoughtful way with difficult themes has expanded.*

- *Although primarily aimed at the biggest market segment, 16 to 24 year olds, the films are likely to appeal to film watchers of all ages. Our films will have playability in terms of being able to create box office revenues through* selected theatrical release and other forms of viewing such as video, TV etc.

- **Our intention is to create a company with a stable and growing presence in the film industry and to establish a library of films that will generate a continuing income stream.**

Company's Short, Medium And Long Term Aims

Again, like goals and objectives, aims allow the company to plan what they want to achieve, within what time frame and monitor progress. Given the foregoing objectives and company positioning, these aims might be:

Short Term Aims:

- **To make, and successfully market, the film "Fen Fever".**

- **To begin to build a reputation for the sound management of financial and human resources in the filmmaking industry.**

- **To find and develop scripts, treatments or ideas for films that meet our goals.**

- **To receive income from producer fees.**

Medium Term Aims:

- **To have a portfolio of nine scripts in development, three of which are ready to be made into films.**

- **To have an emerging reputation within the film industry for professional management and good judgement in choosing scripts to be developed and packaged for presentation to distributors and production companies and investors in film.**

- **To begin to build stakes in the equity of films we have developed or produced.**

Long Term Aims:

- **To have an established a reputation within the film industry for professional management and good judgement in choosing scripts to be developed and packaged for presentation to distributors and production companies and investors in film.**

- **To have the resources to develop and commission scripts and to make them into films.**

- **To have a library of films from which the company receives income streams.**

Current Company SWOT Analysis

The company will need to carry out a detailed analysis of its strengths and weaknesses as regards achieving its stated aims. It will also need to look at the opportunities and threats that might help or hinder achieving these aims. In doing so, the Pompous Film Company might find their analysis reveals the following:

Strengths:

- **We have a clear understanding of the film genres we will be working in.**

- *We have contacts with a growing number of talented screen-writers.*

- *The scripts that we are currently developing are genre specific and have strong story lines.*

- *We have found and secured the locations for the first of our films, Fen Fever.*

- *We have full ownership of the rights to each of the screenplays we currently have in development.*

Weaknesses:

- *No box office talent has committed.*

- *No secured finance*

- *No distribution deals*

Opportunities:

- *More people going to see films.*

- *The target markets for each of the genres of our films, are expanding more than other film markets.*

- *Films similar to ours are being developed by the studios, but none has gone into production.*

Threats:

- *Films like ours are being developed by the big studios and may go into production with A list talent and studio resources being applied for marketing and distribution.*

- **There is a trend in the UK cinemas to show only Hollywood studio produced films.**

The Product

It is good to state clearly what the product is. This helps to focus the thoughts of all those engaged in the enterprise. For the Pompous Film Company, this might be:

- **Films for theatrical release that are controversial, thought provoking, engaging and entertaining, and commercially viable.**

Marketing

Films that are conducive to a strong and effective marketing strategy can also reflect a unique vision. Having the right marketing ingredients in the film means you are more likely to get the resources you need to make the film. Therefore, the process needs to start at the script development stage. This might mean the company states its marketing strategy as:

- **During the script development stage, we will create the key art for each film and test it with selected focus groups.**

- **We will apply the Viability Threshold Analysis to each of our films during their script development stage. We will then extrapolate the relevant information from the VTA analysis, and use this data to ensure that each film contains elements that could form a powerful marketing strategy.**

- **The results of the pre-production focus group testing, along with the marketing potential score analysis, will** inform the development of the script. This will greatly assist us in our primary marketing aim of securing an international distribution deal for each film.

- We will have a detailed schedule that will allow us to submit each film to key international film festivals such as Sundance and Cannes.

- We will seek to have a comprehensive ancillary distribution strategy in place that will generate income post any theatrical release.

- We will have, no matter how limited, a theatrical release of each film in order to enhance the marketing potential of each film.

Finance

First you will need to establish an office and place where you can work. This can be your bedroom or another room in your house, or it can be a small office in Soho in London, or Paris, or Los Angeles. However, wherever it is it will incur certain costs to establish it and run it so that you can conduct your business as a filmmaker. All situations will be different. The following are what should be considered in terms of start-up costs:

BUSINESS PREMISES	Costs
Rent in advance or premium:	
Repairs and alterations	
Decorations:	
Security:	
Other:	
TOTAL:	

TRANSPORT	COSTS
Cost of Vehicles:	
Road Tax:	
Insurance:	
Leasing:	
Other:	
TOTAL:	

OFFICE	COSTS
Furniture:	
Computer:	
Stationery:	
Other:	
TOTAL:	

PROFESSIONAL FEES	COSTS
Company registration:	
Advice and consultancy:	
Company and Public Insurance:	
Accountant's fees:	
Other:	
TOTAL:	

DEVELOPMENT	COSTS
Product samples:	
Market Research:	
Expenses:	
Other:	
TOTAL:	

When finalised, the total of each of these headings will go into the first column of the cashflow. You will need to envision start-up costs as being all the expenditure before you "open the doors" of your company, or sit at your desk in the company's office, for the first time. From then on it is the running costs you need to be aware of and control.

Running Costs

Cashflows

Each cashflow will be different depending on the company's aims and objectives, and working patterns. Below are the classic elements that go to make up a cashflow, but feel free to change any headings that do not suit the way your company operates. What is vital is that the information displayed tells you exactly what is going on and therefore allows good financial management. Beware business start-up packages from banks and other institutions that give just one way of creating a cashflow, and include lots of complex headings that must be filled in. The only headings you need or want are those you understand and which are relevant to the sound financial running of your company.

You may wish to just put totals in the cashflow or itemise each expenditure. It's up to you, but do make sure that you have system of being able to identify all the items of expenditure. Then when you do your profit and loss calculation you can see where the money is being spent and where savings can be made.

Quarterly Cashflow

The quarterly cashflow is for three months, but should be expanded to create a one year and five year forecast. However, for good financial management you should do a profit and loss calculation each quarter. You do not want to wait till the end of the financial year to find that your overheads exceed your income to the point that you are bankrupt. Research shows clearly that start-up companies, who survive beyond five years and are successful, are those whose accounts are well maintained and frequently monitored. This monitoring allows the filmmaker to make changes in order to ensure the company is on a sound footing. As you can see from the cashflow chart below, there is a column for what is budgeted for and a column for what actually happened. All companies, large and small, use this kind of chart to forecast sales and profits. However, nobody can say with certainty what will happen in the future, so this kind of forecast is sometimes known as a "guesstimate", that is, a cross between a guess and an estimate as to what is likely to happen.

The **"budget"** boxes will contain what you predict will be the income generated, or the expenses to be paid. When you start trading you then enter in the **"actual"** boxes what you did actually spend or earn and compare this against your predictions. After each three months trading, you can then do a profit and loss account to ascertain exactly what the company's financial position is.

Cashflow Headings

The following are examples of cashflow headings you may wish to choose. But feel free to add or subtract from the list.

Income

It is safe to say that the filmmaker or producer who is building a film company or career, will find that most of the time their income is from fees for producing or other activities. It is very rare to be able to keep any equity in the film. However, this should be the long term aim; and if this can be created then it provides an income stream for the company that allows for financing the development and possible making of future film projects.

Fees/Sales

- Fee income
- Other revenue streams such as from equity in films.

Capital Introduced

Any money introduced to the company:

- Bank loans.
- From you, family, friends.
- Private investors.

Expenditure

Wages

- Do not pay yourself a set wage
- Estimate what the business can afford to pay in wages.

Premises

- Rent
- Rates
- Service Charges
- Maintenance
- Power
- Gas
- Electricity

Insurance

- Public Liability
- Premises/Studio/Locations

Repairs/Renewals

- Premises
- Production

Consumables

- Postage
- Data base marketing
- Office
- Printing/ Stationery
- Business Cards
- Letter heads or use computer

Telephone

- Land line
- Mobile

Transport

- Car and van hire
- Vehicle purchase
- Tax
- Insurance

Professional Fees

- Accountant's fees
- Trade or professional associations
- Performance fees

Capital Items

- Any large purchase

- Car
- Computer
- Machine

Loan Repayments

- To bank
- To private investors
- To yourself

This can then be put in tabular form:

	Budget	Actual	Budget	Actual	Budget	Actual	Total
Income							
Sales/Fees							
Capital Introduced							
Loans							
TOTAL INCOME:							
Expenditure							
Salaries							
Premises							
Insurance							
Repairs/ Renewals							
Consumables							
Telephone							
Transport							
Professional							
Fees							
TOTAL EXPENDITURE							
Net Cashflow							
Opening Balance							
Closing Balance							

Net Cashflow

This is the amount left after you subtract the total expenditure from the total income. Note that this figure can be a plus or a minus.

Opening Balance

The first box for this sum will be left blank. Then, in the second month, the closing balance from month one will become the opening balance for month two.

Closing Balance

This is the money left in the account after the next cashflow has been added or subtracted to the opening balance. This then becomes the opening balance for the next month. This pattern is then repeated throughout the rest of the year.

Financial Planning

The total of the start-up costs will give you the amount of capital you will need just to begin trading as a film company. It is wise to add an amount as working capital until the income starts to come in. Therefore, your start-up costs may be £5,000, and your running costs for six months are £1,200, and minimum wages for six months are £4,000, then you need £10,200 to start with to make sure you are still around in six months time.

This highlights the need for monthly and quarterly profit and loss accounts to ensure that the expenditure is being spent wisely.

UK based Between The Lines 5 year cash-flow

Film	Budgets	Film's Gross Income	Company's Gross Income	Company's Expenditure	Company's Nett Income
Fen Fever	£0.87m	£3.4m	£0.425m*	£0.120m	£0.305m
Ride The Wind	£2.2m	£8m	£0.700m*	£0.140m	£0.560m
Eden	£3.8m	£10m	£0.900*	£0.190m	£0.710m

* Income from producer's fees and from gross points in the film.

Developing A Time Plan

When creating a production company, be it for one film or more, you need to have a time plan. As previously mentioned, it is generally considered that a realistic plan would include 9 films at various stages of development, over a five or six year period. This will provide your company with a slate of films which will be both attractive to investors, since it will mean they are not putting all their financial eggs in one basket, and give your company options and the ability to take advantage of changing situations in the film market. Remember, all markets die; all markets change and this means new opportunities arise all the time. It is this unpredictability that allows the unexpected to happen. It is also where the independent filmmaker can score over the majors. The majors must generate big profits or else they will not stay in business for long, and so work to tried and tested formulas; whereas the independent film company can look to develop the unusual. They should also have more time than the majors to go around the festivals, and other gatherings of new talent, to search out the next generation of directors and writers.

Do Not Lie To Investors

If you lie to financiers or other entities, such as studios, who are investing in your project, at best they will take their money back, at worst they will sue you for fraud. If you are going to make films about saving the environment, say so. Do not say they are action movies. Or, if you are going into the soft porn markets, say so. Again, you will only fool people once: after that you will have a reputation for being dishonest.

Summing-up

The objective is to identify and acquire the skills you need to achieve your filmmaking objectives. And, whether you are trying to convince a studio or investor or distributor, you need to show that you know exactly what you want to achieve, that you have the abilities to attain your goals and that your product has market potential.

Business Model Data File

Define your short, medium and long-term goals.

Are your films being made for the right price?

Have you assembled the right team for the projects you intend to develop?

How are you achieving the synergy needed to make a success of the projects in hand and those in development?

Have you completed an honest and thorough SWOT analysis?

Are you able to provide for the readers of your business plan a straightforward explanation of what you plan to do?

Chapter 3

Film Projects

"The reason most beginning independent filmmakers fail is because they have little or no experience judging the quality of a screenplay..." Gregory Goodell – Independent Feature Film Production

"If you had gotten the script to work and cast it properly, then you had a chance for something of quality. If you had not, it didn't matter how skilful the rest of the process was, you were dead in the water." William Goldman – Which Lie Did I Tell?

"The three most important things about making films are the script, the script, the script." Alfred Hitchcock in conversation.

In this chapter we will:

Look at the importance of the script.

Look at the importance of genre.

Look at the need to have a portfolio of films at different stages of development.

Explain the need to see film as a product.

Define attachments and evaluate their value.

Introduction

There is no blueprint for making a successful film. You can have the best actors with the best director with an unlimited budget and a highly effective marketing and promotion campaign – and the film can still fail. However, as often said in this book, careful planning can help the producer avoid obvious mistakes and develop projects that are likely to appeal to film financiers and distributors, both of whom are crucial to the film's success.

Film As Product

Success in any business evolves around the product and how it is received within the market place. Film is no different. Many new producers and filmmakers balk at the notion that a film or movie can be seen as a product. They feel that film is an art form and so is above and beyond mere commercial considerations. But the truth is that while film can be a pure art form, it is at all times an expression of an idea that has been made into a tangible form that will be offered to a paying audience who will either accept it or reject it. This means that film has to operate within a defined market and as such is subject to the commercial laws that operate within that market. Of course, you could decide that you want to be a filmmaker who only makes films to be shown at film festivals in order to garner accolades, and that commercial success would only taint your artistic integrity. If so, then this book is not for you.

Since you are reading on I will assume you want your films to be seen and accepted by a market, so that you will be in a strong position to make more films. In order for this to happen, you must have projects that are story driven. There is no way to evaluate your projects and the overall potential of your company without good stories to tell. In a recent analysis of the Hollywood system, filmmakers such as Scorsese said that the tradition of telling a good story was what lay behind the success of Hollywood. He said that telling a story is what drives his films. Many films fail because they are simply a vehicle for sending a message the filmmaker feels the world needs to know or consider, and as such are polemic by nature. If sending messages is what you want to do, then writing a thesis or essay would perhaps be a more appropriate way of doing it. That is not to say that films should not have messages or seek to change the way people see the world or interpret past events or those likely to occur in the future. **Soldier Blue** dispelled many of the myths about how indigenous Americans were treated by white settlers and the **China Syndrome** warned of the dangers of unregulated expansion of nuclear energy. Another film in this category is the recent **The Constant Gardener**. The key is to make films that have something to say but say it in an engaging way that appeals to the audience's psychological and emotional faculties.

Script

The story should be genre specific, original and commercially viable in that it has the ingredients that will enable it to be marketed effectively. In following and applying established script writing techniques and formats within a specific genre, the chances of success are greatly increased. There seems to be an idea abroad that in so doing the writer or producer loses their originality. This is clearly nonsense. In the much more abstract and complex arts of music and literature, formulas are adhered to without any loss of freshness or originality. Shakespeare used the sonnet form, Beethoven the symphony structure with the basic four movements.

A short synopsis of each of the scripts is what is usual to include in this section of the business plan, so keep your plot summary brief. The longer version of two to three pages belongs in the appendix. Remember, you want to keep the attention of your investor.

The Projects

Having a good story is the start; you also need to be able to demonstrate you have good stories set within specific genres with realistic budgets to be made over a set period of time. Be as accurate as possible when outlining each of your projects with dates and time lines when you expect them to be ready for principal photography, when post-production is due to be completed and the most advantageous release dates and strategies. When outlining your projects be truthful and realistic. If you blow things out of proportion or fantasise, money promised can be withdrawn and promises cancelled. Don't be too wordy. You need to tell just enough to keep the reader's attention. Concentrate on each of the project's assets, that is components that may add commercial value to the project, such as an actor who is a household name. You should never use too many figures to express a point; whenever possible use graphs instead of figures, but be careful not to overuse them. Look at how economic data and forecasting is presented on TV. Whenever a news bulletin needs to say something about the economy it always uses bar charts, or graphs or pie charts or a mixture of all three. Most people are familiar with these forms for expressing data so make use of them. By doing so it not only makes your document look professional, but also user friendly.

Finding The Right Script

All too often scripts, and books, look great on the page but do not *translate* into great films. There are so many elements that go into making a good, or great, film that no fool-proof formula can be devised. And long may it be so, or else all films would be predictable and never reach the heights of true art, which surprises and creates its own original truth. However, there are models that stop producers or filmmakers making obvious mistakes. The major Hollywood studios know this and so they structure their film projects with the best components available in terms of script development, actors, directors, marketing etc., all within business models that are right for each film. They also work on the premise that of every ten or twelve films made each year by each studio, only one or two will make money.

A recent graduate from an MA course in scriptwriting in the UK, went to the US and compared the attitudes and working practices of UK scriptwriters with their US counterparts. One thing that became very clear was that US scriptwriters are aware of the filmmaking process and so are aware of the production problems, possibilities and pitfalls and so write for specific markets that have defined budgets.

Producers and filmmakers must learn to judge scripts not by what they see on the page, but how it will look on the screen. Sometimes it is better to turn down a great script because the difficulties of making it into a good film are too great. It has been said that good films do not need good scripts. The James Bond movies are often quoted as an example of formulaic scripts that make great films which the majority of the world want to watch. The Bond books and their interpretation as scripts may be formulaic but they conform to the strictures of a specific genre, meet the expectations of the target audience and are therefore successful.

Art-House And Specialist Films

The need to fit within an identifiable genre and meet potential audiences' expectations, applies equally to what are termed "art-house films" or "specialist films". Recently there has been a trend for substantive film companies operating outside the main Hollywood studio system, to describe their films as specialist rather than art-house. These companies, like Miramax or Sony Picture Classics, appear not to want their films to be restricted by the connotations of intellectual intensity associated with art-house movies. Specialist films are still seen as non-Hollywood in that they deal with complex human issues and themes in a subtle and sensitive way. The thing to keep in mind during the planning stage of a proposed art-house or specialist film is that it will have a limited appeal and so to be viable it will need to be produced on a low budget. Only by being produced on a low budget will it stand a chance of recouping its costs. Unless you have a rich benefactor who doesn't mind you losing lots of his or her money, you won't be a filmmaker for long if you choose projects that cost more than they can ever recoup. The odd art-house film does cross over to mainstream such as **My Beautiful Launderette** or **The Girl With The Pearl Earring**, but it is very rare.

In the UK and Europe you stand a much greater chance of making art-house movies, since there are public subsidies that encourage this type of film. However, if your aim is to be a mainstream producer and filmmaker, then you will need to ensure that you make films that make a return for the investors, be they studios or private financiers. Although the British Film Council, who control the public funding of UK films, are keen to invest in specialist or art house movies that reflect national and cultural issues, remember, as previously stated, they also want to see non-government investors on board before they will give money.

The Right Films At The Right Time

All filmmakers are the product of the spirit of their age. Their ideas are formed by the social and economic forces that have shaped the society they live in, as well as all the ideas and art forms they have come into contact with, and been influenced by. Along with this goes the filmmaker's or producer's own set of personal beliefs and experiences. This is what gives individual films their focus and often becomes the style attributed to the films made by the successful producers and filmmakers. If this were not so, the filmmaker could not create the films that have resonance within the society they function in.

As a filmmaker you are often on the cusp of creativity. You give birth to the new, but it has to be an identifiable species. The problem is to push the boundaries of creativity without losing your target market. Those who comprise your target market are also looking for fresh new ideas, new ways to be scared stiff, emotionally moved or on the edge of their seats with excitement. Research shows that as consumers we are becoming much more individual in our tastes and the way we express ourselves. As a filmmaker or producer, you have to balance your desire to be as creative as possible with the needs of your target market. It is like a love affair; you want to please your partner so you need to know what works, and past history helps.

It must also be remembered that at different stages of our lives we want different things. Over-the-top adventure and romance will be more appealing to under thirteen year olds than foreign art films that are subtitled. And, as long as sub-thirteen year olds want to part with their money, or their parents' money, to watch blockbuster movies while consuming mountains of popcorn and lakes of cola, then so will it be. The filmmaker who wants to make films with intelligent stories that are well acted and are beautifully and creatively shot, will have to wait till the children become discerning adults. As noted in the previous chapter, it could be said that over half the cinema going public want to see such films, so there is no longer an excuse that the exhibitors and distributors won't show this kind of film – you just need to show why the film will appeal to this half of the cinema going public. At present, at the beginning of 2006, there is a raft of good films achieving box office and critical success, such as **Brokeback Mountain** and **The Constant Gardener.**

High Concept

"High concept" is a phrase much used in the film industry and can mean different things. It is most often used to describe a script, film or idea for a film that can be described in one or two sentences and has an immediate appeal to a wide target audience. Often it encapsulates a new way of looking at everyday events, an intriguing idea that has broad appeal, an unusual twist that most people would find interesting. Often it can start from the notion of "What if...". As in a lawyer who has to tell the truth for 24 hours – *Liar, Liar.*

Low Concept

It is said that a "low concept" script takes a lot of explaining, and so high concept scripts are easier to sell because the first reader of the script can easily pitch it to the next person in the chain of command who can then pitch it to the executive who can say yes. If at any of these stages a lengthy explanation is needed, the script is likely to be dropped. That is not to say that scripts that are difficult to explain and indeed remain obscure after the first reading do not get made into successful films, but this is only likely to happen when the script is written by an established writer and has attracted top class talent. A good example is *Chinatown;* written by Robert Town, directed by Roman Polanski and starring Jack Nicholson and Faye Dunaway. For a full account see the book *The Kid Stays In the Picture* by Robert Evans.

Developing A Slate

As previously explained, a collection of film projects is called a slate. This part of the business plan allows you to expand on, and describe in detail, the various projects you intend to pursue and how they fit into your company's objectives. These might be:

- To have nine projects in various stages of development, with three projects to be completed over a time frame of 4 or 5 years.

Or:

- A single project on which you hope to build the company.

It is generally accepted that to be a viable independent production company you should have at least nine projects in various forms of development. Working Title can have up fifty or sixty films in development while making only five or six a year. They feel it is important to have this number in development because it allows choices to be made as to which films to make depending on the prevailing circumstances. They also feel their success, as currently the most important UK film production company, is due mainly to being able to write off development finance without it breaking the company. Creating this kind of situation is what independent filmmakers and producers should aspire to, since having nine projects in development gives you the chance to respond to the market when an opportunity arises. However, it should be noted that the New Line Cinema Company started with **Nightmare on Elm Street** and built their company into a major independent that specialises in horror movies.

Choosing The Projects That Suit You

As an independent producer you will receive a vast number of scripts each year, most of which will be underdeveloped or just badly written with no potential. However, it is from these that you will select those scripts you feel can be developed and which fit your company's goals and aspirations. You may also commission scripts from new writing talent. This is where going to festivals and observing what new talent is emerging is vitally important. It is also an area in which you can have an advantage over the established studios and production houses, since they often do not have the time or resources to spend days just looking at what is new on the festival circuit. Robert Jones, who until recently headed the UK's Film Council, speaks of how he was at the Sundance Film Festival in the US and became aware of the work of an aspiring director called Brian Singer. As a producer, Robert Jones built a relationship with writer/director Brian Singer and together they developed a project called **The Usual Suspects** whose success became a defining moment in both their careers.

Simon Franks who created Redbus, positioned the company in the teen market. ***"I am a lot younger than most of my competitors, so I have a natural instinct for what films appeal to young people."*** Redbus decided to specialise in comedy, horror and supernatural films aimed at 15 to 35 year olds. Launched 5 years ago, Redbus is now one of the fastest growing UK film companies and has to date 75 films in its library. It has also moved into production and acquired 80% of the management and staff of Polygram when it was sold off in 2000. When Redbus get what they think is a good script they hand it to a team of writers and editors who cut and change it until it is ready to be filmed. One of their early successes was to co-produce ***Bend It Like Beckham***, a script that had been around for many years before they got hold of it.

Selecting A Screenplay

There are no set rules for selecting what kind of film you should make. The first thing to consider is did the screenplay hold your attention – did it grab you and you were unable to put it down? Is it a story you want to be associated with, in other words a story you feel should be told, either because it will thrill, entertain, educate or inform? This emotional response will give you the passion and commitment to persevere when things go wrong and you encounter set-backs. If you truly believe in the project then you will fight to get it made into a film. Once you have chosen your script, you need to analyse it to ensure it contains all the elements to make it a success.

What The Screenplay Will Need To Contain

There are certain elements that are commonly found in all the successful Hollywood blockbusters. The fact that they are found in films with mega budgets does not mean that they cannot form the basis for low budget movies. The reason these elements can be applied to any film is because they are to be found in the script, which is why the script is so important. In keeping with the original metaphor, the script is the blueprint for the original design of the film, and if the blueprint isn't right neither will the film be. Therefore, the foundations need to be carefully laid so that what is built will be original, inspiring, entertaining and will last.

The building blocks of a good script are defined as:

Genre specific: The film needs to be set within one clearly defined genre. You can mix genres, such as comedy horror, but single genres are stronger. We will assume that you are developing scripts for the commercial cinema, and so they will be genre based. Mckee in his book **Story** says that *"Genre conventions are the rhyme scheme of a storyteller's 'poem'. They do not inhibit creativity, they inspire it."* It is fair to say that there are almost as many systems for defining the various categories of genre as there are genres. Even the giants of literature could never agree – Goethe was convinced there were seven main types, but Schiller thought this too few but was unable to name any more.

Whatever the number, genre classification is a tool that you will need to master so that you can position your film in the market place and, during the development stage, know what elements the script must contain to meet market expectations. We have already discussed the notion that the cinema going public are genre savvy and come to films with sets of expectations that need to be met. The filmmaker needs to be aware that not only must he meet expectations, but also he must go further and add twists and surprises within the genre framework that the audience were not expecting. So you must do a double act – what is expected and at the same time what is not expected.

Genres basically divide films into various groupings that have identifiable characteristics, even though there are no absolute barriers dividing genres. (For more on this see chapter six)

Dramatic tension: This essential basis for all drama is based on conflict, not to be confused with action or special effects. Dramatic tension means that within each scene, and throughout the story, a struggle of some kind is taking place. This struggle can be physical, emotional or be taking place within the hero.

Two Goal Structure: Hitchcock referred to this as the McGuffin; the thing that everybody thought was important to find, only to discover it is something else. This means that half-way through, or at some other point well into the story, the hero discovers that he or she has been chasing the wrong thing and they must change direction. This heightens the dramatic tension and ensures the film picks up pace and keeps the audience's interest. Single goal films tend to be predictable such as the **Star Trek** movies or **The African Queen**. As audiences have become more sophisticated so they have demanded non-linear plots such as the two-goal structure.

The vast majority of the top grossing films of all time have a two goal structure, such as **Ghostbusters, The Return Of The Jedi, Beverly Hills Cop, ET. The Extraterrestrial.**

Pace: One way of getting pace is to ensure that one scene follows another because it has to. We are propelled into the next scene by the first one and so the story moves forward. Pace is lost when the scene takes us nowhere. Often writers have favourite scenes, but if they do not serve to take the story forward then as Scot Fitzgerald said, you must "Kill the little darlings" There are many books on the art of screenwriting but one technique that addresses pace very well I feel is found in the **Techniques of The Selling Writer** by **Dwight Swain.** It expresses a technique that could almost be called binary – On/Off. There are two elements – Scene, followed by a Sequel to the scene. This creates a basic rhythm of Scene, followed by Sequel, followed by Scene, followed by Sequel. One follows the other and is a reaction to the other, so that a rhythm is set up.

Scene: Three elements: Goal, then Conflict (or opposition), which results in Disaster (setback with no remedy). The scene is often described as a "unit of time" or, as some call it, a beat. All these phrases are interchangeable; they can be a few seconds or 9 minutes (3 pages of a script). The aim is always the same – to heighten tension or create anticipation.

Sequel: Reaction: The character must react to the new situation. This could be a facial expression, one line of dialogue or an action. Whatever it is, it must be visual and apparent to the audience. This produces a Dilemma. The character is now between a rock and a hard place. The options open to him or her are all equally bad. **Sophie's Choice** is a classical example of a whole film premised on this one notion. It all revolves around the heroine having to choose which of her children to give to the Nazi murderers and which one to save. The third element of the sequel is Decision. This is when the character has made a decision to act upon one of the alternatives. When this happens it is the beginning of a new Scene because the character now has a new goal, and so the Scene – Sequel cycle begins again.

Casablanca could have been a plodding melodrama, but the pacing within it, as well as other key elements, ensured it wasn't.

The Three Act Structure

This involves three well defined acts – beginning, middle and end – all serving a specific function within the screenplay. This structure has a long tradition in delivering well crafted dramas. Aristotle is considered to be the first to attempt to identify how drama works and what can be considered good and what bad. It is said he was appalled by the "quick fix" at the end of many of the plays being performed in his day, whereby the Gods came down and made everything OK.

The three act structure ensures that the screenplay has a unifying form. This doesn't mean that you must stick rigidly to the structure, but having a format helps you identify key elements within the screenplay. These elements can be moved around, but they provide a basis from which to make changes. Before you can bend the rules it is worth understanding how they work.

The basic structure for a screenplay is therefore that it has three acts and two key plot points. There may be many other plot points, but the classical structure demands that two key plot points are identified and hold the story structure together. Although all stories have a beginning, middle and an end, you may wish to switch them around as in **Memento** where mixing the time sequence was an integral part of the telling of the story.

Act One: Act one explains the environment within which the story will be told. This environment can be composed of mental, metaphysical cyberspace, physical landscapes, imagined other worlds, moral or ethical landscapes or any other environment the writer's imagination can conjure up.

Act one is often said to "set the story up" in that it not only introduces us to the film's environment but also to the main characters. Also, at the end of the first act there is the first major plot point. This can be described as the ***first key plot point*** because it unlocks the rest of the story. It is at this juncture that the main character is forced to act in order to achieve their need. This must be a dramatic need of such importance to the main character that they are compelled to achieve it. The stronger the compulsion and the obstacles they have to overcome, the deeper and more engaging the film. This can be an emotional need as in romantic comedies, or a life and death need as in many thrillers. Hitchcock always said that a great film depended on a great villain.

Act one usually comprises 20 to 30 pages or 25% of the film.

Act Two: Act two, usually half the film, is when the character confronts ever-increasing obstacles that stop them from achieving their goals. At the end of Act 2 is the ***other key plot point***. This turns the story from the main character about to achieve all their goals to dramatically about to lose them.

Sometimes there is a plot point half way through the middle act which raises the stakes and imperils the main character from achieving their aims. This also helps to stop the middle act from sagging and so losing dramatic tension.

Act two is usually about 50% of the screenplay and runs for 50 to 60 pages long.

Act Three: The third act deals with the outcomes and resolutions of the main characters' needs. These might be left not fully resolved so that a sequel can be made.

Act three usually comprises 25% or 20 to 30 pages in length.

The above is the three-act two-plot point structure so beloved of Hollywood studios. There are many variants on this but they all stem from this basic form.

Characters And Ideas The Audience Cares About

This applies to any good film. In order to engage the interest of the audience you must have a screenplay about an issue they find interesting.

Emotionally Based

The story should appeal more to the emotions than to the mind. It is said by psychologists that we feel first and then rationalise our feelings. We often accept that we like things just because we like them without attempting to rationalise why. It is also the case that an emotionally-based action is far more powerful and sustaining than an intellectual one. This is why, if the characters on screen are acting from emotionally based feelings, even if they don't know they are, we automatically relate to them.

Not Derivative

The story and the way it was told is original and not a rehash of a previous film.

Familiar

The stories and characters are such that people can relate to them no matter what the setting, such as **Star Wars** or **Toy Story**.

Summary

Just having these elements in the script will not guarantee success, since you need to have the right casting, the right director, the right budget and the other key elements needed to realise the full potential of the script. But if at development stage you can ensure that the script has all the right elements you are building a secure foundation for the making of a good film. Also, if the script is good and well made you stand a much greater chance of attracting the other key elements such as finance, a distribution deal and box-office talent. Remember, the script is what is on the drawing board, the blueprint for the film, and unless it works as an integrated construct with all the vital elements in place, then the film will not succeed.

That is why you must do as many rewrites as necessary in order to ensure you have all the above elements. It is said that Richard Curtis made 27 rewrites for **Four Weddings and a Funeral**, and he was a top comedy writer at the time. Calling in other writers if the original writer cannot or will not rewrite is permissible. In the end, if the script no good, the film will be no good.

Check-list for evaluating a screenplay

- Is it high concept?

- Is the film's concept marketable and can you imagine the trailer?

- Is what is at stake, the aim of the central character, important enough for the audience to care?

- Is there a hook that makes the audience want to know the outcome?

- Is there a clear goal for the hero to attain?

- Is there pacing so that the story builds to a climax?

- Are the obstacles in the way of the hero achieving his goals challenging enough?

- Is the story worth telling?

- Are the main characters, especially the hero, people who we care about and are we concerned as to what happens to them?

- Is there a key scene that depicts the emotional crisis point reached by the main character?

- Does the main character have to make crucial choices that affect the final outcome of the story?

- Are there set-backs and reversals within the structure of the story and within each scene?

- Are these set-backs and reversals sufficiently non-predictable to make the telling of the story surprising and unique?

- Is the story filmic enough? Can it be told mainly with visuals, secondly aurally and last, dialogue?

Defining Your Projects

You could put the nine projects into three separate bands.

Band A

Three film projects that are ready to go with a final draft of the script, a business plan that includes a budget, finance plan and profit distribution strategy, a marketing plan and any key talent attached.

Band B

Three scripts that are near completion and are being actively developed. They should have a basic business plan attached and indicative talent stated.

Band C

Three scripts, or ideas for films, that show signs of promise and are being developed.

You may need an extra band, called **Band D**. This could harbour those projects for which you own all the rights. These projects may not have a clear opportunity at present to be made into films, but they do have merit. You could then put them in the vaults ready to be resurrected should the circumstances change, and one of them becomes the right project for the time.

Having A Framework

You will need to develop a framework that easily and clearly explains what market each project is aimed at and the financial viability of each project. You will also need to consider how these projects work together in terms of the company's aims and resources. Is there synergy between the projects such as all being set within the same genre? Are the individual and combined talents of the principals being used effectively? Are the company's resources being effectively used and planned in relation to each project and the time line for development and production? This is a critical part of your business plan since it will show you how all the elements fit together. Each project will have its own business plan with a full analysis of the industry, markets etc. and show how all the plans fit together in a time and resources framework. To assist you in formulating and controlling this process you may wish to develop a critical path analysis model. (See chapter 5)

This is not to say that having a slate of films is the only way to develop film projects. While it could be argued that if you choose to work with only one script or single idea for a film you are limiting yourself in a way that could mean you never get anything made, which is the plight of the vast majority of aspiring producers and filmmakers, it could also be said that by limiting yourself to one project, especially if it is one that is strongly genre based, you are able to focus on all the aspects of the film project and so possibly find a new twist for a defined film market. However, having done a SWOT analysis, as detailed in the previous chapter, and defined your long-term goals, you should be in a position to decide which is the best course of action for you and the company you are seeking to develop.

Killing The Little Darlings

Often the most difficult part of being a producer is to be ready to ditch scripts that are no longer viable. The problem arises when a film project has passed its sell-by date but the producer is so attached to it he or she is reluctant to let it go. The same can also happen within scripts, when writers or directors become attached to scenes and insist upon keeping them in the script or shooting schedule only to see them end up on the cutting room floor because they are not right for the film. Producers and filmmakers must learn to be objective and professional and be prepared to listen to and accept advice that runs contrary to what they want to happen, especially from distributors whose livelihood depends on correctly reading the market for films.

Yes of course, scripts and film projects can be hawked around for up to ten years, suffering continual rejection, and then made into successful films, but it is very rare. Those films that are made after a long period of rejection are those where the producer has major contacts within the industry and has built a track record.

Influential Elements

The main elements that seem to influence the successful or otherwise outcome of a film are: genre; stars; director; distribution; ancillary returns. Your aim should be to have some of the following in your film and so give it elements that can help sell it to distributors who can then effectively market it: box office stars, (if you have no box office stars then actors who are known to the domestic audience – domestic meaning national rather than US); a challenging and original script that elicits great performances from the lead actors; sex; nudity; violence; terror; unusual locations where audiences enter another world they knew nothing about. These are the main patterns within filmmaking that you need to be aware of that sell films. Of course, everyone is looking for the film that not only observes genre structures and has crucial marketing elements, but also bends the rules to produce unexpected twists and has original plot and story lines.

It is good if the hero is dealing with a big problem and none comes bigger than life or death. It may be life or death for whole worlds such as **Star Wars** or life and death for an individual or the one he or she loves or cares for as in **Casablanca**. As well as dealing with external problems, if there is also internal conflict this will add to the hero's needs and challenges. The hero can either be an ordinary man in an extraordinary world such as **Jaws,** or an extraordinary man in an ordinary world such as **Top Gun.** Or, an extraordinary man in an extraordinary world such as **Indiana Jones**. If the locations are grand and help tell the story, such as in **Last of The Mohicans** or **Dances With Wolves** or **Touching The Void**, so much the better, since it adds to the filmic values of the finished movie.

Evaluating The Elements

You need to create a model that gives weight to each of the elements in terms of how crucial they are in relation to the cost of the film and its potential revenues. This will give you a paradigm within which the cost of the production can be measured against likely returns.

One such paradigm, in the form of a marketing matrix, is outlined in chapter 6. The matrix shows how to give weighting to each of the elements within the proposed film and arrive at a score that will indicate the potential success of the film. It is an attempt to analyse how a distributor might evaluate the project when it is presented to him or her. A studio executive or distributor will be thinking about how the end product will be marketed, even when presented with a one line pitch, treatment or unfinished script. This means that the professional producer or filmmaker must also start with marketing and envision what the finished film will have that will make it a success.

Even the major Hollywood studios get it wrong sometimes. Having spent $15 million on a film, when they see the finished product they might decide it's not worth spending a further $15 million on marketing and advertising, because they don't believe it will be a success. You only need to look at what UK films have grossed in the past couple of years to see that somewhere along the line not enough thought was given to how the film would perform in the market place.

It is often said that it all comes down to the script. If you have a great script that is challenging to the actor then you stand a good chance of attracting a top box office star who is right for the role. Then, if they give a great performance because you have the right director, you are getting the basics right. This can mean waiting till the right director and stars are available at the same time. It is worth the wait since the wrong combination can store trouble for the future.

Do not use an actor just because they are a name. Use them because they are right for the part. Big names can and do have big flops. You must do everything from the start to make your film a box office success so that studios will come running to offer you more work. And the more you are a success, the more you can dictate terms and do the film you want to in the way you want to; but always with Joe Public in mind and why he should leave his home and go and pay £7 to see your film.

Finding A Catalyst

It is sometimes said that getting a film made is a lottery. Any one of the above elements could be the catalyst that is needed to get the film made. For instance, an A list Hollywood actor may be seeking a more demanding role to show his or her talent and so will accept the leading role in your film for a greatly reduced fee. This will have the knock on effect of attracting directors and other A list talent who want to work with the actor. It will also get distributors interested since the A list talent will have box-office appeal. However, you need to be aware of the influence A list talent can have on the finished film. A star will look at the script and read it and evaluate it in terms of how it can enhance or expand their career. They may demand many changes in order to make the role fit their aspirations to shine more brightly than the other stars in the galaxy. A good actor on the other hand is likely to be attracted to the script because they feel they can express the underlying creative vision of the writer.

The Competition

Always be aware of the competition. You will need to keep an eye on what films are being developed and by whom; also, what films are in post-production and will be released within the foreseeable future. All of this data is available in the trade magazines and papers and also, to an increasing extent, on the Internet. Remember, the film industry is product driven and films need to find an audience who want to consume what you have created for them. Like it or not, the success of your film depends not on whether the critics like it, or it wins obscure awards for its esoteric content, but on the cinema-going public. If they like what they see they will tell others to go and see it, and this word of mouth is the most powerful form of marketing and promotion for your film. Having enjoyed, been scared witless by or had a good cry because of your film, they are likely to wait eagerly for your next one.

Even if your film has been allocated funds for development, there is no guarantee it will be made. And if it is, when it comes to competition for exhibition space, your film has to compete with all the others that have been made by the other producers such as the BBC, Channel 4 and Working Title, not to mention films from the US and other foreign countries. Given that in the UK 5 films open on average each week, you have to make sure your film has the elements to attract an audience. In Hollywood it is even more difficult. The average Hollywood studio gets 50,000 proposals for feature films each year, yet can only make twelve. So, as someone once said, it is a miracle if your film does get made. Remember, up to 200 films may be given the green light by the studio boss, but still only twelve get made. And that is where a business and marketing plan helps to persuade the studio executives or UK production companies or distributors, to say yes.

More Than One Way

As said before, some producers do not work with completed scripts and business plans but simply pitch ideas to other producers or production companies to see what the reaction is. This is likely to work when you are an established filmmaker or producer with a track record of successful films and so producers and film companies are keen to hear what your next project is. But the conventional wisdom seems to be that if you are a new producer, then just going around pitching ideas is not likely to end with one of your pitches being made into a film. It can take a long time to arrange meetings with people who can make your ideas for films become a reality, and so, to make the most of these meetings, you should be as well prepared as possible and that means having a complete business model so that you can answer all the questions that arise.

Treatments, Pitches, Taglines And Loglines.

Working Title say a ***treatment*** is good enough for them to evaluate it as an idea, but then it needs to be developed. A treatment differs from a pitch in that it is a short synopsis of the idea for the film. The length and content of a treatment varies according to whom you read or speak to. Treatments usually are between 10 to 30 pages and tell the story in narrative form without dialogue. Some films have been given the go ahead with only the poster and key art being available. But the poster will be based on a full understanding of how the film will meet the needs of the target market.

At the very least you should be able to deliver a good pitch. Again this will vary and often depends on what skills the producer or filmmaker has. The first thing is being able to say exactly what the script or proposed film is about. The most powerful and easily comprehended form is to express the film in terms of its genre. ***"It is a (Horror-Thriller-War) movie."*** The producer or distributor or financier will then immediately have a set of assumptions about what he or she is looking for.

You will then deliver your pitch. This is generally considered to be best when it is no more than a couple of sentences. ***"It is a story about a scientist who goes in search of the killers of one of his colleagues and uncovers a plan to blackmail the US government with a new deadly plague"***. This tells the studio or distributor the spine of the story. His or her response will depend on many things including how many other films of this kind are in development; something the person delivering the pitch should know.

To help your pitch you should also have a ***tag-line*** prepared. The tag-line is often confused with the pitch, but shouldn't be or you will lose the confidence of the person you're making the pitch to. The tag-line is what usually goes on the poster and other key-art. One of the most famous is that for ***Jaws 2 – "Just when you thought it was safe to go back in the water"***.

The ***logline*** is also important in helping you define your film. Again the logline is often confused with a tag line or pitch. This must not happen. The logline is a very brief description of your film and is what is used in catalogues or TV guides to describe your film. It is said to originate from the practice of film companies, when receiving a script, to re-title it with a brief description of the story; it is then "logged" under this description rather than the title of the script.

It is important that you are familiar with all these forms of expressing your film since it will enable you to understand exactly how to sell the idea for your film to those who can help you get it made.

Secrecy

Some producers do not want to say too much to distributors or production companies about their film projects in case people steal their ideas. The thing to remember is that as soon as you write your ideas down they are automatically protected by copyright. It is true that ideas can be stolen, but you must tell investors or distributors enough to show that the projects are viable and will work within the time frame you have decided upon. All the executives I have spoken to in the film industry say that there is no point in stealing someone's idea for a film or script; inevitably they will be found out, with consequences which can completely derail the release strategy and cost the makers of the film a great deal of money. It has happened that Hollywood studios and independent production companies have obtained scripts only to find out that they have been misled as to who owns the rights. The studios always settle the claim quickly and the person who misled them has to find another career.

Timing And Sequence

Whether you are working on developing one or several projects you need to have an integrated time frame that makes sense. You need to be able to predict production and sales over this period. Many companies are based on multiple products, so you must have a framework for judging these different projects. Each project has its own purpose and its own strategic place within the five-year time frame. These details will help inform the projected cashflow in the financial planning section of the business plan.

As you become more experienced you might decide to make bigger budget films. But be careful. It is said the Coen brothers feel they are more successful at making low budget films than big budget films. In fact, it could be said that low budget films stand more chance of being successful in box office terms, since they have less to recoup before they make a profit. Always try to keep within your abilities and resources. All is relative. If you make a film for £1m and it takes £2m, you are a success and will be taken seriously. If you make a film for £3m and it takes £2m, your judgement is in question.

What To Include In The Plan

Electronic Press Kit (EPK): The distributor is thinking ahead and judging your film proposal on how well it can be marketed. Making films work in the market place, where supply greatly outstrips the outlets available for films, is extremely difficult and arguably the hardest part of the film industry. You must learn to put yourself in the place of the distributor and so learn to speak their language. Understand what they are looking for and so give yourself a greater chance of their saying yes to your proposal. It's too late when the film is made thinking back to what you should have done. The EPK is just one part of a list of items that need to be delivered once the film is finished. It is therefore advisable that well before the film starts shooting you devise a **Delivery List**. (See appendix 1 for examples and a full description).

Executive Producer: The attachment of an established executive producer will substantially boost the chances of a film being taken on by a sales agent. There seems to be some confusion about the role of an executive producer. In the US studio system it defines the person who finds or provides the money. Since Hollywood dominates the movie business world-wide we will also adopt this definition.

Cast: One or two well known stars are clearly an asset and, if you have them, include a filmography of each. If you do not have stars already committed you can include a wish list. This wish list will show clearly the type of character you judge best for each leading role. A summary of the main characters should also be included.

Crew: A brief filmography of any of the crew who have committed to the project and have a track record would be very helpful

Story: A one or two page synopsis or treatment is essential.

Budget: An outline budget, detailing the major costs of the production values in the film.

Explain The Film

Be clear about what the film does and doesn't contain. If there is violence and nudity, say so. Some investors will see this as a real plus, others may think it wrong. Be careful because if you mislead investors and the film flops, they may be able to sue. Also, they might find out just before the film starts shooting and withdraw the money. If you don't have specific scripts, state this up-front. It will be harder to talk about the projects, but some companies, like Working Title, appear to be willing to run with just an idea. You should be able to describe genre and notional budget of your projects and then they can be judged against other films within that market.

Attachments And Their Value

Be positive about any **attachments** that have perceptible value, but do not exaggerate to the point of being misleading. Remember, most potential investors want to see specifics to which they can attach monetary or personal value, or both. This may be a cashflow forecast showing potential revenues, or what are called attachments which usually take the form of:

- Options
- Books
- Stars and other talent such as a well known director.
- Money

- Below The Line Deals
- Negative Pick-ups
- Pre-sales or Distribution Deals

Options: This is a written agreement giving you exclusive rights over a project for a specific amount of time. While you, the producer, hold these rights, nobody else can make the film. The person who obtained the film rights to the first ***Harry Potter*** and all subsequent books, just after the first book was published and before it was a success, did very well.

The item may be a script from a writer. If it is your own, then you don't need the rights. Or it might be someone's true story. If you are dealing with real people, living or dead, you may need to get the rights. Check this out before you proceed. If you manage to raise the money to make the film, then before you start shooting you will be called upon to provide a **chain of title** detailing who owns all the various rights to the film project. You will certainly be asked for a complete chain of title before the film can be released. (See appendix Five for an example of a chain of title)

Books: A published book adds value to your film in terms of sales history. If the book has sold a fair amount of copies, then it has a natural target market, in that the people who bought the book, or even heard about it from a friend, are likely to want to see it as a film – even if it is to be able to say that the film is not as good as the book. Often it is a two-way process; with sales of the book increasing after the film has been made. So publishers and authors are keen to see their books turned into films.

If the book is aimed at a specialised market, such as horror or historical romance, this can provide a ready-made audience. It seems that if you have a passion for the book and its subject matter, this helps enormously when negotiating with the authors. If the author thinks that you are likely to be true to the book, and he or she likes you, you might get the rights cheaply.

Again, your rights take the form of an option, usually for a set fee for a period of time.

Stars And Other Talent: It would be nice to have Tom Hanks and Gwyneth Paltrow in your film, but since they cost upwards of $20m a film, and your films are pitched between $1m and $5m, then it seems fairly remote. Unless of course they like the script, which does occasionally happen.

Money: Any money, no matter how small, that you have for each project should be mentioned.

Any below the line deals: This might for example be deals with post-production houses or getting good technicians on board because they like the project and are willing to work for a deferred payment.

Negative pickups: See glossary for a full explanation but basically it is a promise, by a distributor or other agent, to meet the cost of the film once it has been completed, subject to an original agreement.

Pre-sales: This is where you sell the rights to distributors to screen the film in the various territories, film markets such as the UK, US, Asia etc., before the film is made. These pre-sales can be very important when raising finance for the making of the film.

Budgets

This is one of the reasons why a complete script is an asset. It enables you to assess accurately the budget. That is not to say the script will not change, but it allows "real budgets" to be attached to "real stories". Also, it allows you to trim the script to make it viable at the right cost. Once you have decided on location and special effects etc., you can cost them and change them according to the needs of the market and the finance available.

Successful Business Models For Filmmakers

Also, if you estimate your film at £1.2m ($2.1m) and you run out of money during shooting, often the investor will say you asked for £1.2m ($2.1m) and that is what you got. If the investor is a studio, they do have contingency funds for overruns, but only if they think it is worth it. They can, and do, close shoots down. The best thing is to collaborate with an experienced production manager and break the script down so that each cost can be itemised and valued. Valued in terms of how much it costs and how important it is to the film.

Devising A Business Plan For An Individual Film

Having found the right screenplay and other crucial elements that pertain to the film project in hand, you need to compose a business plan that is specific to the film. The business plan for an individual film should comprise four key elements:

- ***The product***
- ***The market***
- ***The company***
- ***The finance***

What follows is an illustrative example of an outline business plan for an individual film.

The Product

A feature film: ***Fen Fever***

Running Time: 90 minutes

Genre: Teen comedy/Action/Drama

Pitch: A teenager, in East Anglia in the late 1950's, dreams of escaping his rural life by forming a rock and roll band and heading for the bright lights of the big city, London.

Strap Lines:

- *The end of an era and all things are possible, if only you can make them happen.*

- *How many chickens does it take to form a rhythm section in a rock band?*

Synopsis: A teenager, living in the fens in East Anglia, dreams of starting a rock and roll group and heading for London. He befriends the son of a black US serviceman who gets him all the latest music from the US. The black serviceman's son is meant to be helping the band, but he seems more keen on the local females, much to the consternation and anger of the local men.

Things are further complicated by the fact that East Anglia was, in the 1950's, one of the most isolated parts of England and most people in the area had never seen a black person. Most residents had never been out of their village and functioned in a time warp based on a simple rural life and deeply held superstitions. During the middle ages more women were burned or drowned as witches in East Anglia than any other part of England, and the locals seem strangely proud of this fact, especially as the ponds they were drowned in still exist.

Because of all the conflicts, things get out of hand and Danny has many obstacles, both physical and cultural, to overcome if he is to achieve his dream.

Project Strengths

- Genre specific
- Strong script

- A list UK talent committed
- Locations found and secured
- We have full ownership of the rights to the screenplay

Note: At this stage there should be no need to list, as in a SWOT analysis, the weaknesses and threats to the film project, since they should have been eliminated or turned into strengths by this stage of the development process.

The Market

Commercial Viability

There is a large and growing market for teenage coming of age films. They are universally popular, and because much of the comedy in **Fen Fever** will involve sight gags, the film will have universal appeal and will travel well. Also, being a film that deals with issues faced by today's teenagers, and being based within a clearly defined genre, it has the potential to cross the line to mainstream.

It is normally accepted that films need to generate income 2.5 of costs in order break-even and make a profit. **Fen Fever** has a projected sales multiple of returning 4 times the cost of making the film, and therefore generating profits.

We believe that there is a need for films that challenge the way we perceive society's moral framework. Over the past few years, films such as **Train-spotting, Shallow Grave etc**. have opened up a market for films that deal with controversial themes in an entertaining way.

Although primarily aimed at the biggest market segment, 16 to 24 year olds, the films are likely to appeal to film watchers of all ages. **Fen Fever** has playability and it will not only do well in theatres but also in the ancillary markets. The film takes advantage of the unusual landscape of eastern England and its isolated culture to emphasis the strange behaviour of the locals.

The universal theme of teenagers trying to understand and fit into a world they feel they do not belong to is fully exploited in **Fen Fever**. As are the gross excesses, toilet humour and mistakes that accompany teenage sexual awakenings. This theme is highlighted and given a new twist by being set in modern rural England that is still in a Victorian time warp, and where the unusual locations lend credence to the new teenagers not fitting into their world.

The theme of the film, the clash of cultures between black and white and young and old, reflects many of today's issues as more and more people, especially the young, because of the weakening of respect for ethical and legal institutions, are thrown back on their own assessment of moral behaviour. These conflicts are heightened as unlikely alliances grow up between the characters in the film.

Viability Checklist:

Sex

- Lots

Bad Language

- Lots

Nudity

- Lots

Word of Mouth

- Certain scenes will undoubtedly generate 3rd party after-film conversations because of their subject matter regarding the sexual predilections, possibly involving farm animals and fish, teenagers growing up in an isolated rural community turn to in order to explore their sexuality.

- Talking points about whether or not lewd, obscene or strange superstitious practices did, or do, actually take place in isolated parts of rural England will be a good talking point. Especially if some people come forward and swear they witnessed it first hand. Perhaps **The Blair Witch** marketing strategy could be adopted as to how true the story is.

- A web-site for discussion about the film prior to, and post, its release will undoubtedly help with the selling and marketing of the film

Gimmicks

- The title

- The residents of East Anglia are likely to be upset and so may protest against the film and try to get it banned

Press Angles

- The film will upset/antagonise certain groups

Scandals

- There is undoubtedly great scope for generating rumour and scandal involving the cast, and possibly the crew, in the making of the film

Similar films:

FILM	PRODUCTION COST		BOX OFFICE	
American Graffiti	$0.75m	(£0.42m)	$115m	(£65m)
Grease	$6m	(£3.4m)	$181m	(£102m)
Porky's	$4m	(£2.27m)	$105m	(£59.6m)
Stand By Me	$8m	(£4.54m)	$52m	(£29.5m)
Dirty Dancing	$6m	(£3.40m)	$63m	(£35.79m)
The Commitments	Not Available		$15m	(£8.52m)
Sean Of The Dead	$6.6m	(£3.76m)	$12.24m	(£6.69m)

Fen Fever is inspired by *American Graffiti* and *The Commitments*

American Graffiti portrays the teenage world when it was about to change and usher in the modern era. *American Graffiti*, although reflecting universal themes, is very focused on the US experience, while *Fen Fever* will take the same universal themes, but place them in a UK and European context.

The Commitments saw the struggles to create a soul band in an unlikely setting, but ended on a downbeat. *Fen Fever* ends on an upbeat. There will also be more comedy in *Fen Fever* and the script will be nearer the edge of what is acceptable.

Current activity in the Film Industry

- The overall market for films continues to grow (give current figures)

- The market for "teen movies", such as *Fen Fever,* has always been buoyant.

UK Press Interest

The film has immense potential for generating press and public interest since it is generally accepted that the UK has failed to produce a really successful home grown "teen movie".

Box Office and ancillary markets (except DVD)

The film has a strong appeal to the teen market, which comprises the largest segment of cinema going audiences. If the film can be edited to be a 12 plus for theatrical release and most ancillary markets, then it can be target at the widest possible audience.

Because of the theme, use of sight gags and visual presentation of the comedic situations, the film will travel well in overseas theatrical markets and ancillary markets such as airlines and hotels and broadcast TV.

DVD

The DVD should be released in its original form, but also re-edited and released with a certificate of 18 plus. The 18 plus version to be the uncut adult version. Extra scenes need to be shot during the making of the film for this version.

Word of mouth and other forms of marketing, such as a web-sites, can be used to start rumours about what is on the uncut version and so increase the "must see" factor. Also, questions posted on the web-site, such as "can chickens actually give oral sex?", will help.

Marketing Potential Score

The Viability Threshold Theory for **Fen Fever** produced a score of 1023. This is way above the average for a successful UK film made for under £5 million. For a full explanation of the theory and how to calculate the marketing potential score of a film, see chapter 6.

The analysis shows **Fen Fever** will do well in major markets and targeted ancillary markets such as DVD sales. And, having playability, it has the real potential to become a cult movie. This means **Fen Fever** will more than cover the costs of production and distribution and make substantial profits.

Cast

Cynthia Eccleston is a well known character actor in two major comedies.

Michael Boomer was in **The Secret Life of an Ice-cream**, which had similar gross and lewd acts as in this film. This will be a positive marketing angle for the film and will create the halo effect.

Finola Daily, as well as being seen as a rising talent in the film industry, was voted "body of the year" by the top men's magazine.

Certification

Theatrical release for 12 plus. Usually lots of nudity will be accepted within this band and will be a big draw. However, we will be looking for an 18+ for the DVD and video sales. The sleeve or jacket DVD or video should make it obvious that it includes extra scenes of gratuitous sex and gross acts, that appeal to teenagers, but were not in the theatrical release of the film.

The Company

A limited liability company will be formed for the sole purpose of carrying out the development and making of the film.

Company:

- Fen Fever Limited

Company Directors:

- John Sweeney

- Marcus Goodyear

Production Executives:

- John Sweeney – Finance and marketing

- Alison Doolittle – Script and creative development

The Management Strategy

Aim:

To create an effective and appropriate management structure that will utilise the full talents of the human, technical and financial resources available.

Objectives:

- To create a crew that balances experience and suitability with wage costs

- To ensure that the shoot is managed cost effectively and creatively

- To implement an effective communication network

- To ensure that all members of the crew are able, and want to, multi-task

Wage Structure

The producers will be adopting a three-band wage structure that has already been used successfully by the company to produce two low budget films. Both films have proved to be critically and financially successful. This form of wage structure allows for multi-tasking and commitment from crew and talent in that it is premised on an equitable format.

It also ensures that the film will be brought in on budget.

Management Team

The main strength of any company is its management team. The key BTL management team have extensive experience in business, marketing and the entertainment industry. In addition, the company has relationships with key consultants and advisors.

The current management team comprises:

John Sweeney

- Chairman and Executive Producer

Edward Flung

- Film School graduate

- Award winning short film producer and director

- Experience in the development and marketing of screenplays

Nigel Bottle

- Extensive professional experience in film and TV design

- Winner of the Cannes Best Film award

We will be working with the following consultants:

John MacDonald Solicitor, Senior partner in MacDonald, Fogget and Ross

Kevin Watts Accountant

Richard Light Expert in film finance

Fen Fever – Budget Top Sheet

Cost Of Production:

Above The Line:

Executive Producer	£35,000	
Story & Script	£60,000	
Director	£43,000	
Producer	£64,000	
Principals	£102,000	
Total Above The Line:	**£304,000**	**($0.53m)**

Below The Line:

Production Management:	£46,800
Studio Hire	£60,100
Camera Crew:	£34,500
Sound Crew:	£10,000
Wardrobe:	£14,000
Art Department:	£21,000

Line Production:	£14,000	
Set Construction:	£8,000	
Locations:	£50,000	
Editorial Staff:	£19,000	
Hair:	£10,000	
Make-up:	£17,000	
Continuity:	£8,000	
Stills Photography:	£6,000	
Non-Principals and Extras:	£19,000	
Second Unit Crew:	£11,000	
Post Production	£79,000	
Lighting Equipment	£68,000	
Music	£6,500	
Camera Equipment	£48,240	
Film Stock	£21,400	
Total Below The Line:	**£571,540**	**($1m)**
TOTAL BUDGET:	**£875,540**	**($1.5m)**

Financing Strategy

Source of Investment	**% of budget**
UK broadcasters The film will have wide appeal for UK TV audiences.	**30%**
Film Council: Meets the Film Council criteria for UK films.	**34%**
East England Film Board: Reflects East Anglican heritage.	**10%**
Government Grant for UK film: Set grant given to all films made in the UK that meet the government's criteria.	**20%**
Deferments:	**6%**

Break-even Analysis and Projected Income Streams

These are estimated income streams based on the values in *Fen Fever* and how they relate to the market. If bigger stars are assigned, or a major international distributor picks it up, then this will increase the potential earnings of the film.

Break-even analysis for the film *Fen Fever*

Cost of film	£875,540
P&A and all other costs:	£2,188,850
(2.5 of production costs)	

Total: £3,064,390   ($5.39m)

Estimated income from all film sales:

Theatrical Box Office:	£4,113,000
DVD	£2,000,000
Cable	£200,000
Airline/Other	£90,000
Terrestrial TV	£100,000

Total: £6,503,000 ($11.44m)

Projected Profit for *Fen Fever*:   £3,438,610   ($6.05m)

The above example shows how a business plan might be set out and uses the format most often used in the business and financial world. This doesn't mean you cannot depart from this model, but be very careful if you do, and have a good reason for doing so.

Repetition

Do not worry about repetition in your plan, it is part of the building block formula for business plans. Some of the things that we have touched on here, will be dealt with in more depth later on in the plan. As the investor reads through, they do not keep all the previous things they've read in their minds. Also, different areas emphasise different parts, but are linked to all the various parts.

If you do not have scripts and budgets you can still pitch the idea and give an outline of the proposed budget, but this will not have the same force. You should at least have the below the line costs, or direct costs as they are sometimes known. These are the costs that do not include the "talent", but without which you cannot make the film. (More of this in chapter 8). Often a producer will not include the above the line costs, or variable costs, because they do not know what talent, at what costs, will eventually come on board. You could also have a wish list for the director and the acting talent.

Making A Trailer Or Speculative Short

The word trailer arose because it was an advertisement for an up-and-coming film that followed the main film being screened – hence, it trailed the main film. However, people had a propensity to leave the cinema once the main film had been shown so they moved the trailer and screened it before the main picture, but kept the name. It is not always the best strategy for a filmmaker to create the trailer before completing the feature film. This is because to make a good trailer you will need to spend a lot of money that could be spent on the feature film itself. Also, the trailer may not reflect the true potential of the film. But you do need to think about what will go into a trailer once the film is completed and ready for release. This is another test to see if the film can be marketed once it is made. According to received wisdom in the film industry, to market a romantic comedy you need three big laughs, while for a family film you need three big images that will overwhelm an audience and reaffirm their values. And so, the logic goes, for a thriller you will need three tense moments. For an Action/Thriller – two powerful action scenes and one tense scene. Think about how often you have gone to see a film on the basis of a trailer and you find that the trailer contained all the good scenes, and the film offered nothing new. You need to avoid this if you want to build a good reputation and be asked to make a second film. So make sure you are spoiled for choice as to what to put in the trailer, and you've saved the best bits for the movie, so that when people come to it, they are surprised and have an enjoyable time.

Presentation

Do not send the investor a ten kilo package that contains every scrap of paper you have accumulated about the projects. They will not read it. Do not put the complete budget for each film in the plan – put a top sheet in the appendix. If the investor is interested they will ask to see the budget. The same goes for biographies of stars or directors – just a brief description is all that is needed.

Try to avoid putting photocopies in business plans; they can make it appear non-professional.

It seems obvious, given that many sales agents receive 600 to 700 scripts a year, that competition for their attention and time is strong, so it is surprising that so many producers or writers do not take the time and effort to present their work in an attractive and professional manner.

If a written proposal is badly presented with a scruffy cover that looks as if has made the rounds of all the sales agents in Europe, it is not likely to be read or considered. Remember, sales agents, like many others in the film industry are very busy people.

It is likely that projects arriving in this manner will not be put on top of the pile for consideration for promotion and finance.

It is also important that if a script is being submitted with the proposal, then it should be in standard film-industry format. (See appendix 2)

Ready For Opportunities

You can never predict when the opportunity arises to get the film made. It is often said that success is 90% preparation and 10% opportunity. You may be planning a black comedy based in a university as your fourth film in 4 years time, but the recent success of a similar themed film means your project is hot and hopefully ready to go.

Investor Confidence

The investor, be they private, studio or distributor has the right to know as much as possible about your projects in order to make an informed decision.

Investors look for experience. So if it has a budget of £5m and you have never produced a film before, get an experienced line producer or co-producer. After all, it is the producer who runs the show and is the interface between the investors' money and the successful creation of the project. The investor wants to know he/she is in safe hands.

Script Development

A film script or screenplay is not considered a work of literature; rather it is a tool through which the work of art is made. It is vicarious in nature, meaning that it is a conduit, or medium through which the ideas of the writer pass in order to manifest themselves on the screen. The script is subject to many changes since it is the blueprint from which the film will be made – just as the architect's drawings and designs are not an end in themselves, but a means to create a building. And just as the architect will change his design many times, so too the writer must be prepared to make changes. Often you, as the producer or filmmaker, will need to employ new writers to work on the script if you don't think the original writer is able, or refuses to make the necessary changes.

There are two scripts – the first is the one that the writers prepare, which is known as the **submission script** or **final draft script**. This script should not include scene numbers or camera shots. If the writer feels that a certain kind of camera shot or angle is vital to the telling of the story then it should be included, but only if it is essential. The second script is the **shooting script** and this will contain scene numbers and camera shots, but this script will be composed by the director, often in collaboration with the DOP and the 1st AD. As the filmmaker and/or producer you must ensure this script relates to the Critical Path schedule and the whole management of the film project.

Summing-up

Film projects, like all products, need to be clearly defined in terms that can be understood and interpreted by the key people in the chain that leads to the film's release and success. Filmmaking is a complex process with many crucial stages. At each stage there will be a gatekeeper – key talent, financier or distributor – who will need to understand exactly what you are proposing and how it relates to their needs. It may be investors or a studio seeking to invest in the next big comedy, or a distributor looking for the films to distribute in key territories, or key acting or directing talent looking for projects that interest them or are good for their careers. What is important in approaching the investors and distributors is that the original script is definable

in terms of genre, and has the potential to recoup its costs. In terms of approaching key talent, the quality of the script is usually the most important aspect.

Business Model Data File

Have you a slate of film projects that have a detailed time line of approximately five years?

Have you ensured that each film project, at whatever stage, can be presented to a distributor or studio if the opportunity arises?

Are your films genre specific and focused on a specific market?

Have you allocated as much time as possible in developing a good idea into a viable script?

Have you ensured adequate planning so that the correct post-production pathway has been established?

Have you ensured that the underlying idea of the film is attractive enough to get people to cross town to see it?

Have the scripts/films the key elements to be commercially viable?

Can you demonstrate that the strategic management of all the available artistic, technical and human resources is planned for?

Have you ensured that the film's potential earnings are more than the cost of making and distributing the film?

Do you have a film synopsis and/or treatment for each project?

PART TWO

The management of resources both human and technical.

Chapter 4

Management Strategies For Filmmakers

"The art of good management is not to manage" Scanlon & Keys Management & Organisational Behaviour

"... production is conceived from the beginning as a lower budget film and designed to maximise the creative and practical potential of this way of working." The Relph Report

---

In this chapter we will look at:

The main management theories as practised and developed by successful corporations.

How focusing on the needs of all the individuals working on the film project can greatly enhance their motivation and dramatically improve their productivity, both in practical and creative terms.

How film production jobs can be changed or restructured to ensure they are carried out more effectively.

How to engender Creative Thinking in the whole team, talent and crew, to the benefit of the finished film.

How to create the right communication system for the film.

Introduction

The two aspects of management theory that apply most to a film project are logistics, having the right resources in the right place at the right time, and the management of people, referred to as human resource management. These two key aspects of management are inextricably linked together and form, along with an excellent communication network, the basis of a first-rate management strategy that will help realise the full potential of the creative and technical resources available.

We are all familiar with the classical management model found on a film set where the director is God, and shouts at everyone. On such sets there is a defined pecking order and everybody knows their place. Only the director is the keeper of the vision and all decisions must be referred to him or her, and only certain persons are allowed to approach and converse with the director. Those with access to the director are usually the first AD (assistant director), the DOP (director of photography) and the set designer along with the production manager. The producer or producers will also have access to the director, since technically they are the director's boss and can fire him or her. But if the director is considered vital to the shoot and has status within the film industry, even the producers will have limited access to him or her. This model of management is called hierarchical, and pertains on most film sets of whatever nature, low budget or blockbuster.

The hierarchical model of management is premised on the notion that the director already knows exactly what he or she wants before the shoot begins and in no way intends to seek or want feedback or ideas from the actors or crew. This method of management is also known as **Scientific Management**. It is scientific in the sense that it sees the system of management or methodology as the important factor, not the ability to be innovative and spontaneously creative which relies upon the exchange of ideas between the director and the actors and crew. Scientific Management was developed in the US at the turn of the 20th century by a man named Taylor, and so this form of management is sometimes referred to as Taylorism. It is premised on the notion that the job is important not the person, so you select people to fit the clearly defined needs of the job. This means that people are not seen as an end in themselves, but rather as a means to an end. An industrialist setting up a new factory to make cars in a more efficient way applied these new management principles. His name was Henry Ford and the rest, as they say is history. However, Scientific Management is considered by many to alienate individuals and treat them as objects, which results in dehumanising people. Film, as an art form, is there to reflect the human condition and Charlie Chaplin created a brilliant critique of Scientific Management in his film **Modern Times**.

It may be that most people who want to be directors do so because they want to see their original vision, and nothing else, on the screen. Yes, good movies are made under these conditions but how much better could the movie have been if the whole team pulled together. And how many bad movies, which are the majority of movies made, could have been greatly improved if intelligent discussion replaced dictatorial edicts. Limiting discussion and not exploring all areas of the shooting process, restricts creativity. Only by releasing all the creative energy available on set will the movie reach its full potential. You can have a star-studded football team but unless they work as a team they will win nothing. Often, as in the European football cup of 2004, the least favoured team wins. This is because they all worked for each other and acted like a team and had discipline and self-belief.

If a director or producer sets up the management structure that enables the full release of the creative energy of all concerned with the making of the movie, from pre-production through shooting and post-production, then they are not giving away power, but enhancing it. Lots of directors say they are terrified on set because they have to come up with all the answers. In reality nobody has all the answers and research shows clearly that when an enterprise or corporation of any size or nature adopts a participative form of management rather than an authoritative hierarchical one, then organisational effectiveness and outcomes are greatly improved. And that, after all, is what the filmmaker wants – to make the best film possible with the resources available. It is also the case that a non-hierarchical approach is less stressful for all concerned. It is a sad statistic that the majority of directors only direct one film and the fact that they find the whole process so stressful is undoubtedly one of the reasons for this state of affairs.

It seems strange that most successful enterprises spend a great deal of time implementing and refining the management structure to ensure success, yet the film industry seems to pay very little attention to this vital area. I would suggest that if the UK and European film industry paid more attention to how the film making process could be better managed, a lot more successful films would be made in the UK and Europe.

The other compelling reason for adopting a participative form of management for filmmaking is that it is far more cost effective and makes much better use of the resources available and so is likely to result in a film with higher filmic values. Inclusive or empowerment management techniques work most effectively when an organisation or enterprise relies for its success on motivated people. This is often referred to as **Human Resource Management** because the main resource at the disposal of those seeking to achieve set objectives is the human beings who are involved in the enterprise.

It is generally held that filmmaking, especially independent non-Hollywood produces and filmmakers would greatly benefit from adopting a professional management approach to the whole process of making films. Of course if you choose to be the kind of director who wants to exercise complete power and control, then that is your choice, and you can skip this chapter or read it for interest's sake only. Making a film is above all else team-work and the finished film is the sum total of all the individual creative processes that have been harnessed, both from the actors and the crew. Developing an effective management strategy could make a crucial difference to the filmmaking process if implemented in a thoughtful and creative way.

Creating The Right Management System

Clearly, you can't ask everybody on the film set for their opinion all the time, or there would be complete anarchy and the shoot would very likely run over time and budget and be an artistic and financial disaster. The secret is in employing the correct management structure for the purpose in hand and the first task is to choose the heads of department not only for their creative skills but their ability to work as part of team.

Human Resource Management

It is said that the art of good management is **to get people to do what you want them to do, because they want to.** In other words, they wake up in the morning and think, hey I can't wait to get on set. Or, they can't wait to explain their ideas about how to speed up the time when setting up the lights for the next scene, so that more time can be spent by the director getting the scene right. In other words, total commitment to making the film the best it can possibly be. With total commitment, no session is too long; unless they are so tired they are making mistakes that result in loss of productivity. The professional filmmaker, if she or he is to make the best film from the resources available, needs to co-ordinate the individual needs and aspirations of many committed people, to the overall aims of the film.

What the producer or filmmaker should seek to do is to empower the film crew and acting talent, so that they work as a team and fire on all cylinders using their flair, imagination, initiative and intuition. This is the opposite of a megalomaniac director, or producer, running a shoot, built on the traditional hierarchical model, where everything comes from the top down. Nobody, not even the most egotistical auteur, or tyrannical producer or director, can achieve the full potential of the script, actors and crew unless all are working as a team.

Motivation Strategies

The aim is to motivate people and build a team that has a shared vision and whose output is greater than the sum of all the members. Most people work at between 50 and 60 percent of their abilities and it has been shown that money alone is not a motivator for people to work above this percentage. This is good news for those making low budget movies, since it means that other considerations besides financial are more important in getting the team to give 100%.

What we are doing is looking at the classical forms of management strategies, used in corporations throughout the world, and seeing how they can be applied to filmmaking in order to make better films for less money. We will be looking at four areas of management theory that have special significance for filmmaking. These are:

- **Motivation Theories**

- **Creative Thinking**

- **Communication**

- **Job Design**

The first three theories are concerned with the individual while the fourth is concerned with the structure of the work and where it will be taking place such as in a studio, on location or elsewhere.

Motivation Theories

There are four key motivational theories for the producer or filmmaker, and they are:

- Needs theory

- Herzberg's Dual Factor Theory

- VIE theory

- Equity theory

Needs Theory

This is premised on the assumption that we all have basic needs and they are satisfied in various ways, depending on our economic situation and physical well being at any one time. The first person to fully explore this area of human activity was Abraham Maslow, who in 1943 published a paper called **A Theory of Human Motivation** in which he claimed that humans have set needs that they seek to satisfy. He claimed that these needs are satisfied in a hierarchical order so that as one need is satisfied so the person moves on and attempts to satisfy the one above it.

Maslow was the first person to really attempt to identify and evaluate what needs humans have at any one time and how they go about satisfying them. His theories have been used not only by sociologists and psychiatrists but also by modern management strategists and analysts. Companies and corporations world-wide are very interested in finding out what motivates people, since they can then attempt to meet these needs and desires in individuals and groups in the hope that it will improve their productivity and so benefit the company. If the producer or filmmaker can successfully identify the needs of the actors and crew then he or she can construct a strategy for satisfying them which will result in greater motivation and commitment which in turn will benefit the enterprise of making the film.

Maslow believed that human needs are based on a hierarchy, in that certain needs must be met or satisfied before we can move on to higher ones. He identified five needs which he thought were vital for human beings. These are:

- Physiological needs
- Safety needs
- Love/Belonging needs
- Esteem needs
- Self-actualization

Physiological

If a person is standing naked in a rain swept wilderness they are not likely to be looking to satisfy some creative need. Their thoughts are much more likely to be concerned with shelter and food, since the first need for the body is to get enough warmth and nourishment to stay alive.

Security

When somebody has enough to eat and sustain life they then look for shelter and safety. They usually look for somewhere to settle and make a home for themselves and their immediate dependents, that is safe and secure.

These first two basic needs are often described as safety needs. Unless a person can satisfy these basic needs, they are not going to survive. Perhaps survival needs is a more appropriate definition. In modern societies these two needs are most often met by wages earned from work. If you have an adequate wage then you can buy or rent a home for shelter and purchase food for sustenance. Once these two basic needs are met the individual moves on to satisfying the next need in the hierarchy, social.

Social

Once the individual has a place to live and enough to eat he or she looks to be part of a community and so have a sense of belonging. This may manifest itself by being an integral part of a wide related family, and/or playing a part in a defined local community by being a local politician or volunteering to help to run a community organisation.

It is claimed that all humans look to be loved and needed and to be part of a group; that we are social animals. This love can manifest itself sexually or non-sexually, but the basic need is the same. Often, workplaces can provide a social framework that replicates the family and friendship networks.

Esteem

Once the social need is met the individual is likely to want to feel important within the community or other structure such as the work place. It has been observed that many doctors could have more lucrative careers but study medicine because they want to feel they are esteemed within the community. By the same token many people are driven to work hard to rise within the modern corporation so that they are seen as important members of the business community. National politicians are often said to be driven by this need.

Self actualisation

This, the final need, is considered to be the highest. This is when the individual is using all of his or her skills and firing on all cylinders. When this need is being expressed the individual is acting upon the world, rather than the world acting on them. This is when the individual is doing what they do because they want to do it, rather than because they have to do it. It could be said that the poet and the painter and any other creative activity falls within this category.

It should be the goal of the producer or filmmaker to have all who are associated with the filmmaking process to be motivated by, and working to, this need. Maslow says *"If this need is not met, a person will feel tense and restless and unfilled."* *"A musician must make music, the artist must paint, a poet must write, if he is to be ultimately at peace with himself. What a man can be, he must be. This need we may call self-actualisation."* **(Motivation and Personality, 1954.)**

Modern corporations often seek to incorporate the higher needs into their management strategies and this takes on the notion of worker empowerment. This strategy seeks to take power from managers and give it to those who are performing the work. It rests on the notion that good managers do not manage because they do not have to. This is because, if self-actualisation through empowerment is functioning effectively, people do the work to the best of their abilities because the want to, not because they have to. This is the crucial factor.

The theory claims that once the basic needs are met they stop being motivators, while the self-actualisation needs continue to shape one's life.

Applying Maslow's Needs Theory To The Filmmaking Process

As each need is satisfied so the individual moves to satisfy the next one in the hierarchy until, if possible, they are functioning at the highest level.

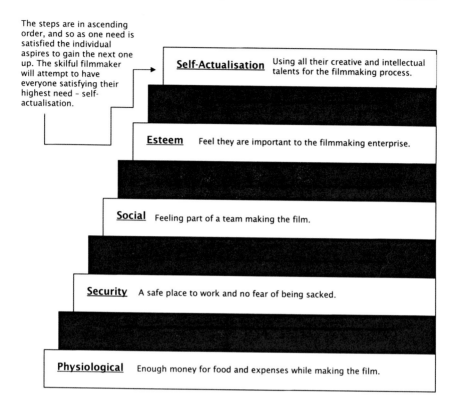

The steps are in ascending order, and so as one need is satisfied the individual aspires to gain the next one up. The skilful filmmaker will attempt to have everyone satisfying their highest need – self-actualisation.

Self-Actualisation Using all their creative and intellectual talents for the filmmaking process.

Esteem Feel they are important to the filmmaking enterprise.

Social Feeling part of a team making the film.

Security A safe place to work and no fear of being sacked.

Physiological Enough money for food and expenses while making the film.

Clearly most of these needs, especially the higher ones, are not met through money and this is good news for the producer or filmmaker since it means that a highly motivated workforce can be assembled without having to resort to financial inducements. However, the **Equity Theory** plays a vital role here as do the other theories dealing with creating a highly motivated, creative and integrated film crew and other personnel vital to the success of the film project.

As with all the motivation and other management theories, the filmmaker or producer must choose those theories, or parts of theories, that best suit the business model being formulated.

Herzberg's Dual Factor Theory

The crucial idea behind Herzberg's research is the finding that those aspects of the work process that result in job **satisfaction** are not the same as those that create job **dissatisfaction** – hence the notion of dual factors. Below is a list of those aspects of the working environment that lead to either dissatisfaction or satisfaction. On the left are those aspects of the job that were most often cited as leading to dissatisfaction, while those on the right were most often mentioned as motivational.

Dissatisfiers (Demotivators)	Satisfiers (Motivators)
Company policy.	*Personal Achievement*
Administration	*Recognition*
Supervision – Technical	*The work itself*
Salary	*Responsibility*
Interpersonal relations – supervision	*Advancement*
Working Conditions	

Dissatisfiers

What is important to realise is that the dissatifiers can only cause or prevent dissatisfaction. That is, if they are present then people will feel dissatisfied, but if they are not present then people will not feel dissatisfied but neither will they necessarily feel motivated.

They will have reached a neutral point. Not happy and motivated but also not unhappy and dissatisfied. Factors that can bring about this state of neutrality are wages, fringe benefits, physical working conditions and overall company policy and administration. When these things are adequately provided for, dissatisfaction will not be present, but neither will motivation. It has been found that on average a person works to 60% of their capacity. When they are given a pay rise to boost their productivity their work rate increases to about 80% of their abilities and then after three months returns to the norm of 60%. It appears that we soon get used to the new spending power and soon see it as simply adequate and nothing special. It should be noted that dissatisfiers relate directly to the first two steps of Maslow's hierarchy of human needs, those concerned with physiological and security needs.

Satisfiers

If we remain on Maslow's hierarchy, then Herzberg's satisfiers are those that relate to the higher human needs of esteem and self-actualisation. These include such things as recognition, feelings of accomplishment and achievement, opportunities for advancement, personal growth, responsibility, a sense that the job is important, a feeling of individual importance, new experiences and challenging work. This theory implies that weaknesses on the dissatisfiers' side can be offset by factors being present on the satisfiers' side. So, if you are unable to pay the standard rate for the job of a first AD or skilled cameraperson, then the fact that they feel the project is important and they feel they are making it happen because they are playing a crucial role in the process, will mean that the lack of money will not be a dissatisfier.

Relevance Of Dual Factor Theory For Filmmakers

What is important to the producer or filmmaker is that this opportunity to increase efficiency and productivity, and therefore the filmic values contained in the completed film, do not need extra financial resources. This is extremely important because the financial resource available for the whole process of creating movies is often what determines the quality, and therefore saleability, of the finished film. This being so, then a method of maximising the financial resource is of crucial importance to the whole filmmaking process. It is also important for producers and filmmakers to realise that these factors that result in greater motivation are more available in the film industry than in most other industries. It is therefore vital that the producer or filmmaker avail themselves of these opportunities for greater efficiency and productivity and a happy and motivated film-set.

Valence – Instrumentality – Expectancy Theory

A terrible mouthful for a very simple theory. It is usually referred to as the VIE theory. This theory has been developed in many forms over the years with perhaps the most important work being done by V.H. Vroom, L.W. Porter and E.E. Lawler. What follows is the general form of the theory.

Valence

This simply means reward and in a work situation this usually means a wage increase, a bonus, promotion, new office or in the case of filmmaking a special credit, position or opportunity. However, when offering this to someone on your team it has to be perceived by them as being of value. It is no good offering someone on a low budget film £5 a week extra when you are paying them £200 a week. What you need to find out is what your crew or talent perceive to be of value to them. It might be that you will offer them points in the film, either gross or from the producer's net profit. Or they may be more interested in a special credit for their services and want to be billed as the production designer rather than the set designer. It may be that they would like the scheduling to be altered so that they have set days off. What is important is that you as the producer listen to what the talent and crew say, and this means having a good communications system operating.

Often, very talented people will work on a low budget film for very low wages. In fact, in some cases, for no wages at all. This is because they perceive other things, besides money, to be of greater value to them. It might be that an actor likes the script because the role allows them to act against type – a comedy actor doing a gritty drama, a Shakespearean actor doing slap-stick comedy. Or it could be a talented theatre designer who wants to move into films, or a TV cinematographer who wants to show what he or she can do in film. What is vital is that these people are right for the film in terms of the skills they can bring to the project and at the same time what you are offering them is what they feel they need or want.

You will need to tailor these rewards to meet the needs of each person involved with the filmmaking project, especially the key actors and crew. The art is to find the people who are right for your film and, without endangering the original vision for the film, structure the key processes to suit, and bring out the talent of, all those involved.

Instrumentality

If people perceive what you are offering them to be of value to them, they must also feel confident that there is the means to achieve the reward. If you are going to spend all night at one location and then return next day to base next morning and give everyone the day off, then there must be the means to achieve this. That means there has to be a clear schedule within a thought-out time-frame; the transport must be available and reliable; the talent must be fully prepared; the crew must have all the lights and equipment they need without having to come back to base. In other words, the planning and logistics must be carefully thought out and implemented. If the shoot is badly organised and, because of poor scheduling, key scenes that an actor would die for have to be cut, then people are not going to believe that you will, or can, deliver in the future. Likewise, if a highly original but complicated shot was agreed to be part of the film and a talented cameraman committed himself on that basis, if that shot is then dropped from the schedule they are not likely to believe you can deliver on other promises.

Expectancy

This aspect of the theory is concerned with the process of how the reward, or need, is going to be delivered. People must feel confident that the actions they have agreed with you will result in them getting what you have promised them. What is important is that they feel that they can trust you to make good on the promises you have made. If the reward you have offered is what they want, then they must also feel that their actions will be instrumental in getting the reward. So, if they agree to a series of night shoots followed by three days off as a reward, this must happen. If you don't deliver the reward as promised you damage, often irreparably, your relationship with your team and they will not be likely to trust you in the future and so not give you the commitment you seek.

Likewise, if you say that you are going to enter the finished film in a series of festivals, make sure you have the resource set aside to do this. Even if the film is not accepted for the festival, or if it is and it doesn't win anything, it doesn't matter. What matters is that you have kept your word and in doing so built trust. This often means you can call upon their services in the future and also it means that you are getting a reputation in the film industry as someone who keeps their word and knows how to manage a film project effectively.

Multiplicative Factor

In order for the VIE theory to work, all three aspects of the theory must be present. If one is missing, such as the belief that you will deliver on the agreed promise, or if there are doubts about the production co-ordinator's ability to create the right logistical framework, then your offer will be rejected. If you impose it, then you run the risk of losing key members of the crew, or creating a demotivated work-force. The key, as always, is planning.

Applying The VIE Theory To Filmmaking

- Make clear what is expected

- Make clear what activities achieve what results

- Listen to the crew's or talent's suggestions

- Make sure rewards are what people want

- Remember, most people on a film set are not there just for the money

Equity Theory

This theory is premised on the notion that people dislike negative feelings and that people want to be treated fairly and equitably at work in terms of:

- Their inputs
- The outcomes they receive or gain

Inputs These are what the individual brings to the job. It may be skills or work rate.

Outcomes These are the rewards, money or otherwise, given to the individual for their contribution.

Wherever human beings gather to apply their skills to a creative endeavour, there is always a risk that they will feel that they are undervalued in comparison to what others are receiving. This is something that filmmakers and producers need to take very seriously, since it has a direct effect on how committed people are to the project. If people feel they are being treated unfairly, or not appreciated, they will have negative feelings and so feel de-motivated. This is a complex issue, especially as regards a creative activity like filmmaking where monetary reward is often not the major consideration for those making the film. Often people are more than willing to accept very low wages in order to be on a film set and they don't feel negative or undervalued. What matters is what others are being paid. If say a runner (gofer), usually seen as the lowest form of life on a film set and often not paid anything except expenses, is being paid £400 ($668) a week and the DOP (Director Of Photography) is being paid £300 ($528), then the DOP is likely to feel that she or he is being treated unfairly, even if they had agreed to the £300 ($528) in the first place.

Research shows that people who feel they are being paid less than others for the same job work less efficiently. What matters is not the actual amount of money being paid as wages for the job, but the perception of being paid less for the same, or superior, work and the feelings engendered by the perception of being treated worse than others. So it's not the actual amount of money that matters.

Sometimes it is prestige that is the motivator or de-motivator. Job titles can be a spur that motivates some people. In Salisbury in England a group of bus drivers went on strike for a week and lost pay in order to be classified as salaried staff and not manual workers. In the film industry job titles matter, especially if the film goes on to be a success either artistically or commercially – or both – since it can enhance the standing of the individuals and lead to more work at the same grade or level. The thing to remember is that human beings are complex creatures and are motivated by many things and it is the job of a good producer, director, line producer or production co-ordinator to understand the needs of the crew and talent and so be able to offer the incentives that work.

On one film that I worked on as producer, the set designer would only do the job if she had the title and credit of production designer and not set designer. I wasn't sure there was much of a distinction between these two roles, since I came from a theatre background, and so was not fully conversant with all the job titles in the film industry. However, I agreed to the name change and soon found out that on a low budget shoot job titles and credits proved to be a much more important issue to people than money. Having said that, I was careful to devise a strategy of banding, so that each job fell within a certain band that had set rates of pay and expenses. This meant that everybody knew what each person was receiving. I also made a point of getting each person to read carefully the terms and conditions they were offered and signing that they had read the terms and agreed to them.

To sum up, the key points as regards motivational theories are:

- Treat people fairly.

- Be aware that money alone is not an incentive.

- Remember that people need to feel valued.

Creative Thinking

Creative thinking is not just for the director or the art department, but should be used as a management tool for all aspects of the filmmaking process – from pre-production through the shoot to post production and then marketing and promoting the finished film. It is often said that creativity and innovation go hand in hand, but like most abstract concepts there is no one definition. The following are considered the classic definitions for these concepts, and we will use them for the sake of this discussion.

Creativity: Bringing into existence an idea that is new to you.

Innovation: The practical application of creative ideas.

Creative Thinking: The relating of things or ideas which were previously unrelated

It is often said that our education system actively discourages creative thinking, the problem being that we are encouraged to look for the one right answer. This is premised on the idea that there is in fact only one right answer. The result is that we spend too much time thinking analytically, rather than creatively. When children were asked what a dot on a board was they said: a bald head, an eye, a tiny insect and of course a dot. When adults were asked they simply said a dot. Is this because as we progress through the education system and enter the world of work we are encouraged to look for the one right answer, because there is only one right answer? It seems we lose the ability to see that there are lots of right answers, although this is not to say that all answers are equally valid. What we have to be aware of is that there are lots of solutions or answers and that one of them is more appropriate or apposite than the others.

A story goes that a physics student, when taking an exam, was asked to state how he would measure the height of a building with a barometer. He said he would go to the top of the building and tie a piece of string to the barometer and lower it to the ground. He would then measure the string. Needless to say his examiners failed him. He appealed and re-sat the exam and wrote he would take the barometer and measure the pressure at the foot of the building, and then measure it at the top of the building, and the difference could then be calibrated to give the height of the building. When asked why he hadn't said this before, he said he was fed up with the system preventing him from using his creative abilities because there was clearly more than one correct answer. The student could have been just winding-up the examiners for the sake of it, or not, but the premise is correct in that the height of the building could have been arrived at either way, the only consideration being which method was the more suitable.

Another example is how we see things with our brain. Some people are visual, others not so, but it doesn't mean visual is more creative.

Where to put E?

M   H   K
  O U

We often assume it is vowels below the line and consonants above the line, then E goes below. But what if the dividing format is those letters made with **straight lines** and those composed of **curves** – then E goes above the line. What if it is **visual and symmetrical** – then to make an upside down triangle you place the E just below O U and in line with H. All these solutions, and many, more were proffered by various classes of undergraduates I have taught over a number of years. The conclusion is that there is no one right answer; all are valid but not all are appropriate to solve the problem.

Balancing The Two Forms

What we need is a balance between the two forms of thought processes; creative thinking and analytical thinking. Firstly we need to use creative thinking, often in the form of brainstorming, to produce many ideas and possible answers to a problem, and then analytical thinking to arrive at the most appropriate answer. Often it will also depend on the nature of the problem. If the problem is to do with logistics, such as how to get the crew and equipment to a location in the most cost effective way, it may be that you will focus more on the analytical side. If you want to create a shot or sequence of shots that not only tell the story but also use imagery as a metaphor to help tell the story, then creative thinking will come to the fore. It could be said:

Creative thinking produces *Ideas*.

Analytical thinking produces *Solutions* (from ideas)

The two sides of the process could be defined as:

Analytical	Creative
Logic	*Imagination*
Unique or Few Answers	**Many Possible Answers or Ideas**
Convergent	*Divergent*
Vertical	*Lateral*

Applying The Method

This method might be applied to a problem such as how to get a good underwater shot, and you are discussing it during the pre-shoot planning stage. First you would brainstorm to get as many ideas as possible. The secret of good and effective brainstorming is that no ideas are out of the frame of thinking. All should be considered. For this particular problem these might be:

- Being a low budget shoot, you could use runners to stay under water holding the camera until they pass out or drown and then send another one down.

- Create a glass wall separating the water from dry land and shoot through the wall.

- Send the cameraman down with a long hose attached to his mouth so he can breathe underwater.

No right or wrong answer – just which one is the most appropriate. Each answer must be viewed in context and *One* of the solutions is the *most appropriate*, depending on economic, aesthetic, moral and legal considerations. We must learn to use both forms of thinking at various stages:

Creative – To Think of as many options as you can. (Brainstorm)

Analytic – To Filter the options so you get the MOST appropriate one.

These two forms of thought processing are sometimes called **Divergent** and **Convergent** thinking. Some experts believe that people can be divided into *Convergent* (Logical thinkers) and *Divergent* (Creative thinkers). If this is true, then when assembling the management team for the film-project it would be beneficial to have both types on board, as well as those who have both attributes. Many corporations using modern management techniques and seeking to make the most of their employees' talents use psychometric testing. One such test used in management training seminars can be found in appendix 8. Do be aware that these tests and their results are part of applied psychology, which is premised on statistical analysis, and not clinical psychology based on cause and effect.

The following is a flow chart to show how these two forms of thinking can complement each other and take us from the problem to the solution.

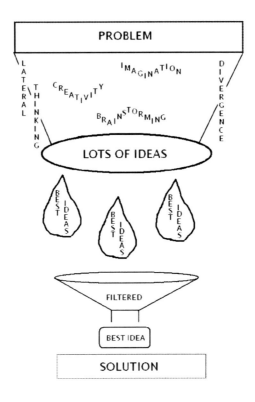

Barriers To Creative Thinking

Out Of The Box!

Most of us think within set structures, as if our minds and thought processes can only take place within a defined area such as a box with sides, lid and bottom.

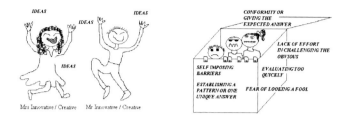

The aim must always be to think out of the box.

In order to improve our creative thinking ability, we need to know some of the barriers that hinder this thought process and keep us in the box.

1) Self Imposed Barriers:

This is when we assume things about a problem. There is a grammar of the kinds of shots that compose a film. Those who first broke the rules and used hand held camera techniques to add reality to police dramas were thinking out of the box. We all impose restrictions on our thinking and these self imposed barriers are the most difficult to overcome because we often impose them subconsciously.

2) Establishing a Pattern or One Unique Answer

Most of us look for ONE right answer and then stick to it and defend it. Many people feel that films will only succeed at the box office if they are composed with a three-act structure. Or, that the first plot point must come within the first 30 pages of the script. We now have successful films that have a five-act structure and some that have multiple plot points, the first of which is not always within the fist thirty pages of the script.

3) Conformity Or Giving The Expected Answer

Most people feel they have to conform to the patterns established by their colleagues or peer groups within the profession, such as thinking that directors must always have a master shot, medium shot and close-up shot of each scene. One successful UK based director only ever shoots master shots and close-ups.

4) Lack of Effort In Challenging the Obvious

This usually follows the path of those not wanting to do anything that might disturb the status quo. They may be happy in having found any solution at all and so want to leave things as they are. Is there another way of promoting the film besides posters? What about using mobile phones to send images?

5) Evaluating Too Quickly

"That won't work, we tried it last year" "That's a stupid idea" "Who ever heard of any one doing it like that?" Again, the first person to suggest using a hand-held camera to shoot a scene probably encountered this kind of response.

6) Fear of Looking a Fool

This is the biggest barrier of all. None of us likes looking a fool. The junior member of a management team will not put forward "wild" or "unusual" ideas in case he/she is thought of as a fool and therefore risks his/her chance of promotion. Likewise, senior members of a team are often reluctant to put forward new ideas since they feel they need to defend the status quo. There is also the reluctance to go against expert opinion and so be seen as a fool. This often happens when a new idea is radically different from the old one and experts say it won't work. On one shoot I was on, we were considering the idea of how to get a POV (point of view) shot from the lead actor whose head was spinning from a drugs overdose. We had few resources since it was a very low budget shoot, but someone put forward the idea that we tie the cameraman, holding a camera, and the lead actor together and let them spin around each other while the camera was running. Strange idea, but it worked.

All these barriers kill ideas. We must learn to suspend judgement. That is the essence of Brainstorming, which is one of the most powerful tools for generating ideas and solving problems.

A more comprehensive look at many of these ideas can be found in the books of those who developed and applied them such as Dr. De Bono. (See **Further Reading** for books on this subject and others raised in this chapter)

Communication

There are those who say that communication is the real key to any management strategy. Some go so far as to say it is the only management tool you need. Certainly with filmmaking, communication is vital, if for no other reason than to make sure that all who are involved with the shoot are making the same film. We will therefore look at specific communication strategies, which can greatly enhance the filmmaking process. These are:

- Communication models

- Information flows and communication networks

- Strategies for creating the right communications model

Communication Models

The different forms of contact between all who are involved with the development, making and marketing of the film, affect their performance and their sense of job satisfaction. The manner in which people communicate with each other is determined by the structure of the communication network. The number of communication networks you can choose from are practically limitless, but the three that are most apposite for the film industry are:

Centralised Model

Classic information flow on a film set

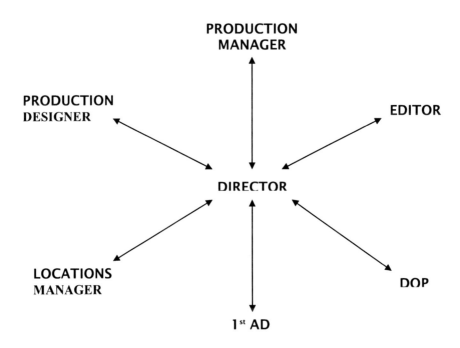

CENTRALISED MODEL

CLASSIC INFORMATION FLOW

With this centralised network all the information flows to a central person who is the decision maker. All too often this is the model used in filmmaking, with the director or the producer having to process all the information. The persons on the rim of the wheel are often the heads of departments such as DOP, Production Design, Production co-ordinator, First AD. On some shoots, these people hardly ever meet, guard their areas carefully and only communicate with the director. What if a lowly assistant in the wardrobe department had a brilliant idea about how to achieve a difficult shot, because either they had seen the problem before and new of ways to solve it, or they had a flash of inspiration? Could they go to the DOP or director and explain their idea? Or would the DOP and director feel that their authority or vision was being undermined and the film was being taken away from them?

Communication flows within centralised model

Within this hierarchical system the information flow tends always to go from the TOP DOWN in the form of directions or order, and from BELOW UP in the form of answers as to how and when the orders have been carried out. The head of department has to process all the information from the director and to listen to the information coming from below such as the first assistant or others in the chain.

The kinds of film projects that use these models rely very much on one person. In the preproduction or development stage it is the producer; during principal photography or the shoot it is the director; and then in post-production it is the editor who not only has to listen to the director but often the producers as well. Some film projects benefit from this system and many have to be run this way because of the people involved who want to keep power. With this system it would be unheard of for a runner to suggest something to the director, or producer, directly. Even if the runner had a brilliant idea, if the next person up the chain didn't like the idea, it would never get to the person who mattered. I once worked with an actress who had been in a movie directed by an A list Hollywood director. The director would sit on his own and would never speak to anyone, including the actors and actresses, directly. The director would send an assistant director to inform the key members of the crew or actors, what was required. At no time did the director seek feedback, except in terms of why his orders were not being carried out. Despite the multi-million dollar budget, that particular film was judged by the critics as being mediocre, saved only by the innate ability of the actors. It may be that this particular director lacked communication skills or felt insecure about discussing things with other members of the team. Or, perhaps he was just an egotistical maniac who loved to exercise power.

Decentralised Models

Of course it is the director who makes the final decision, since it is her or his vision that drives the film; but if all who are involved in the making of the film share the same vision, then a rich seam of creative ideas, that could complement and enhance the director's vision, is there to be utilised. Of course, this means that the director or producer needs to be secure enough in his or her own abilities to create the right climate and communication network to make use of this creative talent. Communication Models that will help filmmakers create good communication networks are referred to as decentralised networks.

The decentralised models most often used are built around the notion of committees, or quality circles. In fact, some analysts believe that the recent successes of the British economy have owed much to the implementation of working practices that empower workers and so release their creative energies. This had led to a greater commitment to corporate goals and therefore greater efficiency and productivity. I see no reason why these ideas should not help the film industry to achieve greater efficiency and therefore create better films.

The Decentralised Model

Peer group communication model

DECENTRALISED MODEL

PEER COMMUNICATION MODEL

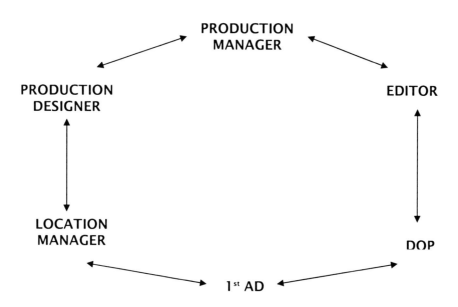

With this decentralised model you are talking to your peers doing jobs at the same level. So, it could be all the heads of departments, such as first **AD, production co-ordinator, production designer**, getting together on a regular basis to discuss issues and resolve problems. At the same time it could be **2nd AD**, the **wardrobe assistants** and the **set-designer and assistants** having regular meetings to discuss issues and tactics. The essence of this model is that you talk to your peer group to get the job done, and so all those concerned with an issue communicate and discuss the best way of achieving the desired result. It might be making sure that all the props, lights and extras are on set at the right time, so all persons who have similar levels of responsibility get together and work out a strategy. The aim is a collective act amongst peers, which relies on a clear understanding of what needs to be done, mutual support, a free flow of information and good communication.

Free-flow communication

<h2 style="text-align:center"><u>FREE-FLOW COMMUNICATION</u></h2>

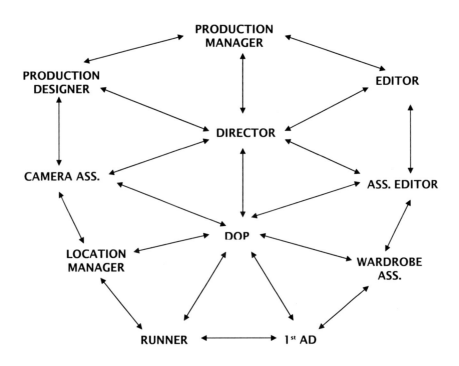

This model has the power to release all the creative energies within a film project. However, it can also be the most difficult to achieve and can be counterproductive if not properly planned and implemented. With this model you talk not only to your peers but also to those above and below you – in fact, all who affect the work in progress. The aim is to have a team composed of: top management (director, heads of department); middle management (second AD, gaffer etc.); and the shop floor (runners, drivers, clapper loaders etc.); all talking and or communicating directly to and with each other.

Of course this model needs careful planning and team building strategies, but it can be highly effective for independent filmmakers. If implemented correctly, this model could result in fewer persons being needed to construct the right set-up for each scene, but with each contributing fully to the outcome it can only be of benefit for the film. This model would undoubtedly lead to much greater efficiency of the use of resources both in financial and creative terms and so would increase the filmic values in the film.

Choosing The Right Model

Of course it would be ridiculous to use the decentralised models for all tasks. If the task is simple, such as unloading the props from the lorry then you do not need a committee to discuss it. The answer as to what model to use at any one time depends on the task. As far as filmmaking is concerned, the objective should be to choose the right communication model for the job in hand.

Simple Tasks

If the task is simple, the centralised method appears to be best, with all the information passing through one person at the centre who can absorb all the information and formulate solutions which he or she passes down the chain. If you want the runner or driver to take the dailies, the film shot that day, to the lab, you do not need a meeting of the heads of department and director to plan it. What could happen is that the production co-ordinator ensures it is done, but allows those carrying out the task to form a circle model to share the task and make sure it is done in the most effective way.

Complex Tasks

However, if the task is complex then the decentralised method appears to work best. The reason for this is information overload – the centralised person cannot cope with all the information and suffers information saturation, with the result that performance drops sharply. If the issue is to go on a key location for a complicated shoot that involves camera shots from cranes, and all the key actors are involved, then a structured decentralised model would undoubtedly be the best. If successfully implemented, all persons on the shoot would be focused towards coming up with the best solutions for achieving the aims of the director and DOP.

What is crucial when setting up decentralised networks is that the structures, such as peer groups, function properly, otherwise the performance rate will drop. Obviously, it depends on the abilities of the centralised member, such as the producer or director or production co-ordinator, as to when and how the centralised system becomes less efficient than the decentralised one. The reason why decentralised methods are likely to work better for film productions is because they engender job satisfaction and therefore people become highly motivated and so efficiency is greatly increased. This increase in efficiency can be in many forms, such as encouraging creative suggestions to production problems, as well as radically reducing absenteeism. If people are involved in the decision making process, in whatever form, they feel valued and that their contribution counts and that they have more status and control. This leads to greater motivation and also lessens feelings of stress.

Communication Channels

How the individual departments are set up in relation to the overall structure, shapes the direction and nature of communication within the whole filmmaking process. Information flows within organisations in four ways:

- up
- down
- horizontally
- diagonally

Often on shoots film departments become isolated from each other with each protecting their own territory. This can result in heads of departments and the director becoming isolated from what is really going on, which can be very damaging. The director, or the head of a department, needs to know the bad news even more than the good news. If the set-up for a scene is being delayed because the right electrical leads are lost, the blame game usually sets in with nobody wanting to accept responsibility for the delay. It is well known that people do not like to be the bearers of bad news, since they think it will cast them in a bad light. However, this news needs to known as soon as possible to the people making the key decisions, so that a strategy can be devised to ensure that it doesn't happen again. Only by having an open, inclusive model of management will people be encouraged to report problems immediately, so that that they can be quickly resolved and systems put in place to ensure no repetition.

Informal Channels

Amongst human beings, the need for information and communication is so strong that informal communication networks arise. If the film set is being run on hierarchical lines, more information will go through informal channels than will go through official ones. This informal channel is called the grapevine. It develops because it is natural for people to gossip and talk about work. People have a basic need for knowledge in order to make sense of the world around them. It also acts as a safety valve allowing people to express their views and anxieties and gain reassurance from others.

It is not, therefore, surprising that grapevines exist, but what is surprising is how accurate the information is that is conveyed on the grapevine. In a study it was found that 80% of the information carried on the grapevine was accurate. However, it was also found that the remaining 20% was highly inaccurate. This 20% could be very misleading and highly damaging. If a shooting schedule is falling behind, explain why and see if a collective discussion can resolve or help things. If certain shots or scenes have to be cut, explain why, do not let a rumour build that the production is running out of money and will soon fold. In all organisations rumours abound and never more so than on a film set. Squash rumours quickly, but do not deny them directly, since it may look as if you are trying to hide the truth. Release accurate information and get people to look at the facts. By simply denying the rumour you look defensive and some people will think you are simply lying.

Developing An Organisational Strategy

There are two crucial areas:

- Content.

- Organisational climate.

Content.

Two complaints often heard are that people don't know what's expected of them in their jobs and they don't know how well or poorly they are doing. Both these complaints could be dealt with by a greater downward flow of real information about the shoot and how well it is going. People need to be praised, especially when involved in a creative endeavour.

Creating a favourable organisational climate.

Get key heads of departments out of their offices and wandering around so they get to know what's really going on. Also, encourage a degree of informality. First name tags could help. Try to provide places for people to meet or congregate, especially on a spur of the moment basis. Create effective monitoring procedures to ensure that important information is communicated to all levels. Establish a true open door policy and create a time in the day when the heads of departments and the director can listen to complaints from those under them, or give praise and feedback to all levels on the shoot. Getting everybody involved with the film, from development through shooting to post-production, means they are more likely to be actively involved in the quality control, and processing, of each job. This will in turn result in greater productivity, enhanced creative input and a greater realisation of the film's full potential.

Summary

Through research, it is clear that communication networks do matter and can dramatically improve efficiency within an organisation, especially one belonging to the creative industries. Human Resource Management is a crucial aspect of modern management theory and could be applied very effectively to the filmmaking process. I think that if UK and European filmmakers were more willing to adopt modern management techniques, their films would be more likely to achieve their full potential within the constraints of the budget.

What needs to be developed is a management strategy that meets the needs of the individual film project. There is no point in just adopting set management strategies hook-line-and-sinker. They need to be adapted to suit independent filmmakers' cultural mores and economic conditions and need to be thought through carefully. The important thing is to be flexible, but models are there that would definitely enhance and improve the production values of any film. The aim should be to get the most creative and well wrought film for the resources, both financial and human, available. Recent reports such as the Relph Report have highlighted the fact that UK films cost more than in other countries. However, it is not just a question of wages; filmmakers, from whatever country, need to think long and hard about the best way of achieving the film project's creative goals.

Job Design

Job design, or job-redesign, attempts to make each task in the filmmaking process more appealing to those who are carrying them out. If this happens, then these tasks will be carried out more effectively and more efficiently and so enhance the quality and values within the finished film. When we looked at the definition of good management it was "to get people to do what you want them to do, because they want to do it". Redesigning jobs, such as those to be carried out during principal photography (the shoot), is another aspect of achieving this aim. The aim of designing, or redesigning, work practices is to build in more satisfaction from doing the task in terms of personal rewards, such as feeling that what you are doing is vital to the shoot or that you are using all your faculties and talents, as in Maslow's highest human need. It is also a motivational tool and so improves peoples' creativity and efficiency. What is important to understand about Job Design is that it looks at the person as well as the job. This is the opposite of hierarchical models often found on film sets, where everybody knows their place, and there is a definite pecking order. We will look at three models for re-designing jobs, which I think relate directly to the film industry. They are:

- Goal setting

- Job enlargement

- Job enrichment

These theories were developed in the 1960's 1970's and 1980's, with the idea of Job Enrichment being developed by Fredrick Herzberg.

Goal Setting

Goal setting is when those involved in creating the film strive to meet set targets within a time frame. Research shows that goal setting works; it is important that the tasks be difficult and challenging, but not too difficult so that they are rejected by those doing them. Therefore, gaining acceptance by those working on the film is crucial. One way of doing this is to involve those who are going to carry out the tasks and strive to meet the goals, in the actual setting of the goals. If, say, the goal or aim is to cut the set-up time for scenes to be shot, then you may need to talk to the gaffer, the make-up team, the first AD and assistants, and any other persons involved in the process to devise a strategy that ensures that the right piece of equipment is in the right place at the right time. To ensure this happens it may mean devising a Critical Path Analysis sheet that is time sequenced, so that each member of the team knows when each job should be done and the tasks that need to be carried out before and after each job. (Critical Path Analysis is set out in Chapter 5)

Just in time

The notion of having the right equipment in the right place at the right time reflects the successful Japanese concept of Just In Time. The Japanese revolutionised the efficiency and cost effectiveness of their car industry by using a strategy that ensured that the required component, be it an engine or a brake pad, was only delivered to the factory one hour before it was needed. This saved money on storage space and in not keeping stocks of components for months before they were needed. Money wasted in this way is referred to as dead money and on low budget films, expensive lights and camera equipment can waste precious financial resources by lying around for days before they are used. This can also happen when expensive equipment is hired for a specific location, then not used because of re-scheduling and then having to be rehired or the hire period extended.

Planning and effective communication are the key ingredients in ensuring that a Just In Time strategy is a success.

Feedback and Monitoring

When setting goals, feedback is crucial. You may have decided on the goals to be attained and discussed them with, and had them accepted by, the film crew, but in order for the process to be successful you must ensure that there is effective feedback. In one test where a goal of 95% was set and agreed with the operatives for satisfactory working practices, only 65% was reached when there was no feedback. When effective week feedback was introduced, 95% of the goal was reached. On a film-set, the crew need to be told not only how and why they should be doing the task but also how well they are doing it. It should also be realised that for goal setting to succeed as a strategy, it needs to have the full support of everyone working on the film, from the producer and director down to the assistants and runners.

It is often the case that low-budget films run out of money before the post-production phase is completed. This is usually the result of spending more money on the shoot than was envisaged or budgeted for. By adopting a strategy for setting clearly defined goals, and constantly monitoring proceedings to ensure they are met there is every chance the shoot will stay within the budget and so money set aside for post-production will be ring-fenced. Post-production can, and should, include not only the editing process but also the promotion of the film to distributors and festivals, since often low budget films do not have a distribution deal in place before the film is made.

Job Enlargement

One thing that characterises film-sets is the demarcation of work. Wardrobe assistants work in the wardrobe department, camera crew only are active in the setting up, running and breaking down the shots and those in make-up stay within their area. This means that lots of people are standing around doing nothing for long periods of time. Job Enlargement is a way of increasing the amount of work performed by individual members of the film team by increasing the number and variety of jobs performed, but not their difficulty. This is sometimes seen as horizontal job loading – that is, tasks are performed on the same level of difficulty. On a film set this can mean that make-up assistants can, when they have finished doing set tasks, help the camera crew and so speed up the set-up time for the scene being shot. The same applies to the art department. Also, when members of the camera crew have finished doing the set up for the next scene to be shot they could help the art department prepare the next day's set.

This multi-tasking not only ensures a much greater efficient use of scarce resources but also enhances the skills of the participants and often makes the experience of being on set more rewarding and fulfilling, since most people who work on low budget shoots do so to learn about the movie industry and improve their skills. This especially applies to those who want to be directors or producers, since knowledge of all aspects of the process of making a film is a real asset.

Job Enrichment

Job Enrichment is undoubtedly the most powerful, and at the same time most complex, of all the strategies that could be adopted to enhance the cinematic values and maximise the economic, technical and financial resources available to a film project. Job enrichment aims to give people, at all levels, more responsibility and control over their jobs. This is also known as **empowerment**.

The individual, or team, has more things to do of a more complex nature and is empowered to decide the best way to do it. This is different from Job Enlargement, which is more of the same kind of tasks. With Job Enrichment you may give people tasks that would normally be done by those below and above them. A person may have the job of 2nd assistant director and also be responsible for ensuring the dailies are correct. (For a list of all the jobs on a film set see Appendix 4)

Implementing Job Enrichment

Three factors need to be considered:

- **The physical layout of the set or location.** The extent to which changes can be made so that job enrichment can take place may be constrained by the aesthetic, artistic needs of the film, or a physical layout of the location that cannot be changed.

- **Human factors.** Who is implementing it? Do the heads of department support it? Do the crew want it?

- **Loss of power.** Some people will say no to job enrichment if it means giving away power and control over others. If they are ordered to comply, then they will not do it effectively and may well sabotage the shoot in order to be able to say the system doesn't work.

Job enrichment does work, but like the other theories it must have the full support of those it affects.

Core Job Dimensions

In order to understand how jobs need to be redesigned or enriched in order to achieve greater motivation and efficiency, a Job Characteristics Model has been developed. This has been described in J.R. Hackman and J.L. Suttle (eds) **Improving Life At Work,** and by J.R. Hackman and G.R.Oldham in **Work Redesign.** The model works on the idea that jobs could be considered in terms of their core dimensions. If we apply this to the film industry, we will need to look at what elements of a job need to be changed in order to achieve enrichment, and then devise a model for doing so. Within each role on a film set it is possible to identify core dimensions of the job, that have an effect on how the individual responds to the task. Five such core elements can be stated as:

- task identity
- skill variety
- task significance
- autonomy
- feedback

The first three, task identity, variety and significance could be considered as being the core dimensions that aim to make full use of the individual's talents, at whatever level they are operating.

Task Identity

This can be achieved by completing the task from beginning to end. Not just carrying the lights, but ensuring that at they are connected and positioned properly. Obviously deciding what the whole job is in terms of the needs of the film and the individual could be difficult. Should they be allowed to say what gels go on the lights? Undoubtedly not, since this is the province of the director and/or DOP. But maybe they should apply the gels to the lights and position them. In this way they are also improving their skill base.

Skill Variety

Wherever possible there should be a variety of skills that are exercised within a task. It could involve the physical manipulation of the lights and also reading the drawings of the set layout or story-board and suggesting the optimum position for the lights. The ideal would be to create jobs that exercise or use the individual's physical, intellectual and creative skills.

Task Significance

This involves the impact the job has on other people. If it is explained to the camera crew the importance a particular shot has within the film, the set-up for the shot becomes of significant importance. By explaining that their work is significant, people will try to achieve the goals of the director and DOP and will feel involved in the process and so responsible in some way for the outcome. Clearly, going off to get tea for everybody may not be seen as particularly important, but if it has been a long day and a break was promised, getting the tea and food to the right people at the right time could be crucial to morale. On low budget shoots feeding the crew well is of vital importance.

Autonomy

This involves the freedom to use one's own skills to get the job done. This means that the individual must be able to make decisions about the best way to do the job. Autonomy results in a worker feeling he/she is responsible for the job, and so accountable. This could mean that a person is told that it is their responsibility for making sure that all the right cables are functional and ready to be used for any shot. Or, a boom operator, the person who ensures the microphone is in the right position to record sound, might be given access to all the planned set-ups and so be giving the responsibility of ascertaining where the optimum positions were for recording sound. By discussing these options with the sound recordist and the 1st assistant director and possibly the director, the boom operative is using his or her initiative and getting job satisfaction. At the same time the efficiency of the shoot is enhanced since sound problems are hopefully being solved before they arise.

Feedback

As with other aspects of implementing management strategies, good and effective feedback is important. This allows all those working on the film project to know what the effect their work, or effort, is having and how it relates to all the other aspects of the film project. This makes each person feel empowered through knowledge.

Significance Of Core Dimensions

If the five core dimensions are present, then it is said that they result in three psychological states in those working on the film project:

- Meaningfulness
- Responsibility
- Knowledge

These three states go to influence the workers' feelings towards themselves and the work they perform. If these states are present, people feel motivated and so make greater efforts to give a high quality of work performance and it also results in lower absenteeism and staff turnover

Crucial Factors

The aim should be to attempt to ensure that all the jobs, at no matter what level, are perceived to be of value. If they are not then, wherever possible, they should be restructured so that they are. This will make people feel they are firing and functioning on all cylinders. It could be said that if this is achieved, then person is operating at the top of Maslow's hierarchy of needs. Their talents are being fully utilised and they feel they are acting upon the world rather than being manipulated by it.

Clearly it will be up to the producer and director to arrive at a structure for human resource management and logistics that meets the needs of the film and is at the same time within the capabilities of the individuals charged with carrying out the task. Major and not so major corporations and organisations are appointing human resource directors with departments that seek to maximise the full potential of individuals. It would be interesting to see the results of such a strategy on a major Hollywood film-project.

Job Diagnostic Survey

Hackman and Oldham also developed the idea that having analysed the jobs you can then set up a full diagnostic survey which will give a motivating potential score (MPS) for each task. The higher the MPS, the more likely it is that people are experiencing motivational work. We can analyse a job to see if it has the characteristics necessary to make it an enriched job. We do this by carrying out a job diagnostic survey and assign values to each task to be performed and then applying a formula that will give us a Motivating Potential Score. The method is as follows:

$$\frac{(task\ identity \times skill\ variety \times task\ significance) \times autonomy \times feedback = MPS}{3}$$

The job of the person designated to carry the lighting cables to where the scene is being shot might, on a traditional film set that is run on hierarchical lines, translate into:

task identity=3
skill variety=2

task significance=2
autonomy=1
feedback=1

This would then be expressed numerically:

$$\left(\frac{3 \times 2 \times 2}{3}\right) = 4\times1\times1 = 4$$

So the job diagnostic value will be 4.

When seeking to increase the MPS of the job, you might combine the carrying of the cables with connecting all the cables together and checking them and helping to set up the camera to achieve **job enlargement;** you could then include being involved in a discussion about what gels to use and where to position the lights to obtain **job enrichment;** and then, you could also give a relative amount of **autonomy** and **feedback**. If this were done, then the score for the job could be increased to 120. Of course the enlargement and enrichment of jobs, and hence the work being highly motivating, depends on the skill of the person running the project, be they the filmmaker, producer or director.

This system in no way claims to be a universally accurate method or fool-proof system of analysing jobs. As with all systems and theories involving human resource management, their effectiveness always depends on the people formulating and applying them. The other thing to remember is that you can assign any numerical values you wish, as long as you are consistent. The numerical values you use to first analyse the job must be consistent with those you use to monitor the changes.

Possible Problems In Implementing Job Enrichment

Obstacles to implementing job enrichment could be that the work processes makes it difficult to implement a meaningful programme. Possible obstacles are:

Technology Only one person is trained in the use of a particular piece of complex equipment.

Agreements There may be long standing agreements, especially with unions, about how the job should be done and by whom.

Control systems People might object to their control and therefore their status being taken away.

Summing-up Job Enrichment

It appears from research that that job enrichment really works and that it creates internal motivators in people. This has the effect of people, both talent and crew, seeking to work to their full potential, which in turn leads to much greater creative and cost effectiveness within film projects. It also results in lower rates of absenteeism and staff turnover, which again lead to greater efficiency. These improvements are most apparent if the enterprise relies on people, the making of a film is primarily people driven and so would greatly benefit from human resource management techniques.

Business Model Data File:

Do you have a good Human Resources Management strategy in place?

What are the main management theories as practised and developed by successful corporations?

How can focusing on the needs of all the individuals working on the film project greatly enhance their motivation and dramatically improve their productivity, both in practical and creative terms?

How can film production jobs be changed or restructured to ensure they are carried out more effectively?

How to engender Creative Thinking in the whole team, talent and crew, to the benefit of the finished film?

How to create the right communication system for the film?

Chapter 5

Critical Path Strategies For Filmmakers

"A journey of a 1000 miles begins with a single step." **Old Chinese proverb.**

In this chapter we will:

Outline the critical stages through which the filmmaking process must pass.

Demonstrate that each stage off the process must be allocated the correct amount of time for its completion.

Identify those aspects of the process that must be completed before the next stage can commence.

Cross reference each of the key elements in terms of cost, time available and value to the film.

Introduction

The CPA matrix will identify the key, or critical, aspects of the process of making the film within a set time frame that relates each of the key elements to each other and determines the order and time within which each needs to be completed. By doing this you will be able to assess the length of time to be allocated to each area and the sequence for each. This will enable you to identify those elements that need to be completed before a new stage can be begun, and those aspects that can run concomitantly or in parallel. The business plan is a detailed analysis and exposition of the aims and objectives of the management of the film project. The Critical Path Analysis (CPA) matrix is the strategy by which these aims and objectives will be realised within a set time frame.

Step Sequence

The following CPA uses a step sequence that shows what elements need to be finished before the next can start, and how much time is needed for each step. The amount of time for each stage will of course depend on how much time you actually have for completing the film project. It is generally accepted that in the UK and Europe producers and filmmakers do not allocate enough time to planning the film project and developing the script. This is sometimes due to factors beyond the control of the producer or filmmaker, but more often than not it is because there is no structured planning process in place. Two years is generally held to be the minimum time to be spent on developing and creating a film, with eighteen months being spent on development, three months shooting and three months editing.

Critical Path Steps

You will need to:

- Identify all the core elements that are contained in your film.

- Assess each of these elements and give it a weighting according to its importance in enabling you to create the kind of film you envision.

- Cost each of these elements.

- Cross reference each element in terms of cost and value to the film.

- Develop a time frame for achieving each of the above elements.

For the purposes of this model for developing, creating and delivering a finished film, I have identified twenty steps. These steps are not, as they say, written in stone and will vary with each project, but the essential principle is that no film ever suffered from being too long in development.

1) The Script

All films start with the basic idea for the film. This can come from a variety of sources: an idea; a published book; an unpublished book; an original script; a remake of an existing film. It doesn't really matter where the impetus for the film comes from, what is important is how the script is developed. Tim Bevan, co-chairman of Working Title, says that you cannot spend too much time in script development. Certainly for independent filmmakers and producers, the more time spent on the development of the scripts, in terms of how they relate to a shooting schedule and distribution strategy, would ensure many more successful films – not just in terms of box-office, but also in creating better films, and so, ones that have a greater chance of being around for a long time.

This is not the place to go into the details of script writing. We will assume that you, as the producer or filmmaker, have found a script that you feel has the potential to make a great film.

Work the script and re-write it, so that it is:

- Clearly structured within a popular genre.

- Tightly written, with original twists that are well structured.

- Budget orientated, so that all the potential values contained within the script can be realised within the financial framework.

2) Research Similar Films In Terms Of Revenue Generation

List income from films that were made for a similar budget to yours.

List income from films that were made within the same genre as yours, but for a higher budget.

3) Define The Budget In Terms Of The Cost Of Production In Relation To Potential Earnings.

The breakdown of the script should be in terms of:

- Speaking Parts
- Extras
- Locations
- Special Effects
- Firearms
- Stunts
- Prosthetics
- Music
- Period Pieces

Not all the above elements will apply to all films, but by analysing each of the above requirements, and judging how vital they are to the film, the producer or filmmaker can rework the script in order to ensure that the aims of the film are met, within the constraints of the budget. The key members of the team, the producer, the director and the script writer, are only constrained by their imaginative abilities. Often, by reworking the script in this way, it is improved.

Time costs money, and most independent shoots do not have an unlimited amount of time, or a studio to bail them out if they go over budget. Therefore, each element of the script needs to be analysed and costed and then judged against all the other elements.

4) Establish Key Marketing Elements Within The Script

At this stage you need to try to envisage what the final film will look like and why it will appeal to a target audience. Good films reach their full potential by being marketed correctly with the right marketing strategy. Bad films can make a profit by being marketed well. However, what is crucial is that there are elements within the film that can form the basis of a marketing strategy.

One way of testing the marketing viability of a film is to see if, from the script or treatment, you can create a viable trailer. It is said that any film to succeed must have three good scenes to hook the audience.

5) Detailed Analysis Of Script In Terms Of Main Cost Centres And Locations

Production Values Cost Ratios

You need to build a framework for each of the key areas in which the production values can be measured and assessed against costs and marketing potential. You need to give values to the various aspects of the film so that trade-offs take place that maximise the overall quality of the film. Directors and producers do this all the time, both during pre-production and when shooting the film. Usually it is done verbally and at very short notice. However, covering all the key areas during pre-production, and creating a model with values, will give you a range of informed choices. This also means making the most of your projected budget in terms of production values.

Locations

Once you have made a list of all the locations you can then assess the value of each of them to the film. For each location you can cost:

- Travel time and distance from main location
- Crew and resources needed on the location shoot
- Time spent on the location
- Hotel costs
- Food
- Special insurance
- Other costs

The project

- Genre
- Crucial generic elements

Locations

- Studio
- Internal – Non Studio
- External

Special Effects

- Crucial
- Not crucial

Stunts

- Crucial
- Not crucial

Format

- 35m costs. Values to the film
- S16 costs. Values to, and detractions from, the film
- HD costs. Values to, and detractions from, the film
- Digibeta costs. Values to, and detractions from, the film
- DVCAM costs. Values to, and detractions from, the film

The style and look of the film

- How each format/medium affects the look of the film
- Special effects
- Control of light in crucial locations

NOTE: If you know the film will eventually be cut to 90 minutes, then plan the shoot accordingly.

6) Create An Effective And Appropriate Management Structure.

Have in place the right team

- Experience and suitability versus cost
- Managing the shoot cost effectively and creatively
- Effective communication network
- Multi-skilling and tasking

Communication

- An appropriate system that allows a flow of information, not just from the top down.

Job Design

- Each job uses human and mechanical resources to the utmost
- Each job is viable and efficient
- Each job, where possible, involves multi-tasking

Motivation factors

Ensure people are satisfied with:

- Food
- Pay
- Status
- Artistic reward – not taken for granted
- Credit on film for work done
- Equally treated

Status and Remuneration

- Create a pay and status model that is open and transparent and accepted by all concerned
- Ensure that everybody feels they are being treated fairly

7) Acting Leads And Key Crew

- What they bring to the film and why
- Cost and availability

8) Crew Structure And Remuneration

Number of key crew and affect on costs:

- Payroll
- Catering
- Transport
- Housing

Cost and value of each key crew member.

Value of each key crew member to the film as a ratio to finished film and its marketing potential and the values each brings to the production.

- Director
- DOP
- Set Designer
- Line Producer
- Special Effects

9) Financial Plan

- Devise a financial plan that is realistic and suits the needs of the filmmaker and investors

10) Create Shooting Script

- Devise a shooting script based on the most effective use of time and resources

11) Recruit Acting Leads And Key Crew

- Research for actors to play lead roles
- Create list of prospective actors
- Audition and test in roles

12) Create Storyboard

- Devise a detailed storyboard
- Integrate the storyboard with shooting schedule

13) Create Shooting Schedule

- Calculate length of shooting schedule
- Itemise each day's shooting
- Arrange locations

14) Rehearsals

- Devise a rehearsal schedule
- Block all the complex moves
- Integrate final decisions with storyboard

15) Script Rewrites

- Test rewrites with rehearsals
- Give all key actors and crew up-to-date scripts
- Ensure all rewrites are integrated and tested with budget, shooting schedule and storyboard

16) The Shoot

- Decide how long the shoot can be in terms of cost
- Decide on the best management structure and job sharing
- Ensure time is allocated for re-shoots
- Ensure that shooting corresponds with the eventual length of the film

17) Post Production Pathway

- Decide if your film will be shown in a cinema or will go to DVD or video
- How long the editing should take
- When the music should be ready

18) Promotional Material

- Promotional material needs to emanate from the script and the shoot
- Stills to be taken
- Interviews arranged
- Screening to be organised

19) Edit Film

- Arrange for dailies
- Hire edit suite
- Decide on re-shoots

20) Complete Film

- Compose delivery list
- Negative for master print

Applying The Steps

The content of the above steps needs to be analysed and evaluated and put into a time frame. The different elements of each step need to be accurately placed within the time frame. For example in step 19 there is the need to arrange for the dailies to be delivered and viewed and this will need to be planned and finalised before the film starts shooting. The same goes for various elements of the promotional material in step 18.

Summing Up

The preceding model does not claim to be comprehensive, but it could be a good starting point. All models, and indeed planning, depend on the needs of the specific film project being developed and the social and economic conditions prevailing at the time. The more planning that results in informed choices, the more it is likely that a good film will be produced. At the very least, detailed planning that results in a coherent business model, will greatly enhance your ability to attract funding. It will show you are taking a professional and business like approach to the project.

Critical Path Data File:

You will need to:

Create a defined time line matrix built on a calendar of days, weeks and months with headings for each key process.

Describe in detail the key critical stages through which the filmmaking process must pass from the start of development through to the delivery of the completed film.

Allocate the correct amount of time for the completion of the film, from the start of development through to the delivery of the completed film.

Identify those aspects of the process that must be completed before the next stage can commence.

Cross reference each of the key elements in terms of cost, time available and value to the film.

PART THREE

The Marketing, promotion and distribution of films.

Chapter 6

Marketing For Filmmakers

"Know your audience, understand your market. Without this, any attempt to create a sound basis for film production in Europe is doomed." **Mike Downey – The Film Finance Handbook**

"We need to be led by demand, not pushed by supply" **Building a Sustainable UK Film Industry – Keynote speech by Sir Alan Parker as Chairman of the Film Council.**

In this chapter we will:

Show why marketing begins with the first idea for the film.

Show how to understand and define film markets.

Explain how films are positioned in the markets.

Outline the likely revenues for English Language Films in the worlds markets.

Show how to segment the market.

Explain how to develop a marketing strategy.

Introduce and describe the Viability Threshold Theory

Introduction

European and UK filmmakers have not fully appreciated, and taken advantage of, marketing as a key component of the filmmaking process. Indeed, it has been said that UK filmmakers have been at a disadvantage because of a lack of marketing expertise and knowledge. In recent years, the top twenty films in the UK were American. UK contemporary filmmakers cannot even compete in their own country. It seems that the US filmmakers are better able to predict what the British would like to see than the Brits themselves. Maybe this isn't true, and it is just that the UK producers lack the skills to find the financial resources to make their films. This is what I believe, and that is why this book has been written. Marketing is the key to releasing funds so that many more great films are made and shown. There is no limit to the demand for good films.

Therefore, the aim of this chapter is to give film based enterprises, of no matter what size or in what country, a clear understanding of the importance of marketing to the success of their careers as filmmakers. It also aims to enable filmmakers and producers to build their own marketing strategy to suit their business. From popcorn filmmakers to pure art house filmmakers, all need to know who is their market, what are their needs and how to reach them.

Essential Part Of The Business Plan

Marketing, undoubtedly, is the most important part of the business plan. In fact, many would argue that 80% of a business plan is a Marketing Plan. The major Hollywood studios certainly act on this premise, as do most consistently successful independent producers and distributors. Independent exhibitors, when not backed by a distributor, live or die by their marketing abilities.

There are those in Hollywood who say that the only thing that matters in the film industry is marketing. Of course by marketing they do not mean what many people think it means – advertising – but rather the whole process of creating a product, film, and developing it into a commodity that can be promoted to an identifiable market. This means that, as Nick Powell, producer of **The Crying Game**, said in his Masterclass For Producers: ***"You begin marketing your picture from the day you start developing an idea."***

So, from the very moment you have an idea for a film, or you read a script you want to make into a film, you need to ask: who is likely to want to see this film? What would such a market expect from the film? What scenes are likely to be in the trailer? What will the poster look like? What will be the strap line on the poster?

It is said that **The Usual Suspects** started off as an idea and a poster. The producer then went to a major Hollywood studio with the idea for the film and the key art for the poster. There was no script, no budget, nothing – just the poster and an idea for the film. The major studio commissioned the film to be made on the strength of the marketing potential of the film as expressed in the poster. However, the studio only provided some of the budget, the producer then had to go in search of the rest. To do this, the producer needed to provide a lot more information in terms of finance and marketing potential. Eventually all the money was secured and the film itself went on to be an international success.

Marketing People Will Often Refer To AIDA

- AWARENESS
- INTEREST
- DESIRE
- ACTION

What you want to achieve is that the target audience become **aware** of the film, either through promotion or word of mouth. You want this awareness to stimulate **interest**. From this interest you want **desire** to emanate. And you want this desire to be so strong as to make them take **action** and cross town, even if it is raining, and pay good money to see your film.

One possible way of measuring the film's potential for being marketed effectively, is to evaluate each of the elements in terms of their likely impact on the target market. You can score each of these elements, and from this score you can see if the marketing potential for the film is high or low. The following pages demonstrate how the MPS could be arrived at. A full description and illustrative example of how the Marketing Potential Score can work is found later in this chapter. This model makes no claims for being fool-proof or not open to improvement. But it could offer a start and is likely to impress a distributor.

Marketing

Marketing, as a business tool, has grown dramatically in importance over the past thirty years, and is now seen as the key ingredient in any business strategy in all industries. None more so than in the film industry. So, what is marketing? If you ask most people they will reply "adverts", "posters or TV commercials asking you to buy things". Well yes, this is part of marketing, but only a small part and it comes under the definition of promotion. In the movie business, this would be the advertising part of the P&A budget, spent by the distributor in order to promote the film to the target audience. However, marketing is far bigger than that and far more comprehensive.

Here are a few definitions:

- **The Management Process Responsible for Identifying, Anticipating and Satisfying Customer Requirements.**

- ***To Know and Understand a Customer so well that the Product Sells Itself***

- ***To Make and Keep a Customer***

Let's have a look at each of these definitions.

The Management Process Responsible for Identifying, Anticipating and Satisfying Customer Requirements.

If you apply this definition to the film industry, you first identify and anticipate what a modern film-going audience is likely to want to see. A film usually takes three years to complete and so, when you first have the idea for the film, you must imagine how it will be received in three year's time. You attempt to satisfy those projected requirements by finding the right script with the right talent to be made at the right price to be released at the right time with the right promotion and advertising strategy. Clearly, this encompasses the whole process of filmmaking, creative, technical and financial. That is why marketing should be seen as the engine that drives the filmmaking process.

To Know and Understand a Customer so well that the Product Sells Itself

This again does not mean writing to a set formula, but you do need to understand the requirements of the target market and how they are changing. You must be aware of social and economic trends, and how they affect your target market, so you can create the films they want to go and see. This is especially true for genre based films. If you are making a horror film, then your audience comes to view it with a specific set of expectations. Just as you are changing and developing as a human being in terms of the social and economic landscape in which you find yourself, along with your personal and emotional experiences, so is your audience. The issues that concern you, or the things that make you laugh or scared, are likely to be the same for a specific audience – this then gives you empathy with that audience and the ability to connect with them. The films of Woody Allen are a case in point. You cannot please all the people all the time, but if you master your genre, and refine your filmmaking techniques, and stay close to your audience, you will stand a good chance of building a successful career within the film industry.

To Make and Keep a Customer

This must be the ultimate goal for filmmakers. If achieved, it means that you have developed a fan base who appreciate the films you make and wait eagerly for your next release. Very few directors and producers can work effectively in many different genres. You can of course aim to become a jobbing producer or filmmaker and thereby take whatever comes along, but if you do it is unlikely you will master a particular genre and build a reputation for making films with a unique vision. Inside each individual is a set of attitudes and a vision of the world that if expressed creatively through film can be original and engaging and entertaining. If you achieve this, your audience will find you. It will also mean that you are true to yourself and so you will be able to continually connect with your fan base. It is also likely that you have a deep affinity with a certain genre; if so, you need to master the needs of this specific genre and deliver, in an original way, what your target audience is looking for. This does not mean being "product led" and only making what films you want, but rather choosing or commissioning scripts that you have an affinity with and which are commercially viable. It could be said that this is what Hitchcock did. It will also mean that when studios or independent production companies or even major distributors are looking for a filmmaker for a specific project, if it is a genre in which you have shown your abilities, your chances of being commissioned are much higher.

Marketing And Creativity

As argued in earlier chapters, there is no conflict between marketing and creativity as long as they are kept in balance. If you create purely for the market, then yes, it can be too formulaic and predictable. It could be said that **The Temple Of Doom** and some of the later **Star Wars** films, fall into this category. Sequels are prone to this blight. But the original films, from which the sequels came, were genre specific and made for a specific market and at the same time highly original, creative and successful, otherwise there would be no sequels.

So, creating contemporary films that sell doesn't mean filmmakers have to lose their creative integrity. The aim of the filmmaker is to create the **marketing match**. This means ensuring that your creative films match the needs of the markets. We all go to films with expectations and if they are not met we are highly unlikely to give the director or producer another chance.

People Buy Benefits

In the final analysis, people do not actually buy products, such as a film, they buy benefits and experiences. People do not buy an ice-cream or chocolate. They buy pleasure, indulgence or comfort. Just look carefully at the ads for ice-cream or chocolate. People do not buy a drill bit – they buy a hole. If they could go to the shop and buy a selection of holes instead of drill-bits, then that is what they would do, because that is what they want.

It is the same for film. You buy emotional, intellectual, mood-changing benefits, not the latest video. You buy tears – because you like a good cry. You buy an intellectual or emotional mood change into another world, not the latest Art House release. When going to see the latest horror movie, you buy fear. The best films are artefacts and therefore life-enhancing and possibly life changing. There is no finite market for good films; the more that are made, the more people will go and see them.

Understanding And Defining Film Markets

Markets are created by exchange of value, and this is expressed in terms of volume of sales (100,000 DVDs sold, 200,000 admissions), or the amount of income generated from theatrical release and ancillary sales. The total market for horror might be, say, £400m world wide. This is the total market, but it is highly unlikely that your film will appeal to the whole market. This figure needs to be broken down into the income generated from each territory and ancillary market. The figures can then be analysed in terms of how different film values and characteristics, influence sales in the various markets. For example, it might be that slasher/horror goes down best in the US and Japanese markets. Gothic horror might do better in the European markets.

DVD sales of horror might do best when it is certified as an 18, but not do well at the box office because it limits the target group. The general consensus is that 18 certified films do better as DVD's, than they do as theatrical box-office. All of this will inform how you can create a film that balances production costs with potential sales, and therefore put forward a viable business plan for a feature film.

You could say that the 3 billion adults in the world are your potential market. However, you cannot make films that appeal to everyone. You need to narrow down your target market in the form of genres and style. You should aim to make a film with a new way of looking at a universal theme. There are many successful producers who believe that a film project must start with an investigation into the potential market for the film, i.e. be market led, not product led. Market led is when you analyse the market and spot trends and then devise a film that fits that trend. This always happens after a new film is an unexpected success, such as **Shallow Grave, Four Weddings and a Funeral** or **Trainspotting**. After these films had been released and became unexpected successes, the studios were inundated with scripts that were identical in format and story to these films. Needless to say, the vast majority were poor imitations of the original films and therefore rejected.

Market Positioning

This is vital. You cannot be all things to all men. You must have a clear idea where your film fits into the market. Each film carries a set of values within it in terms of talent, locations, set build etc. Certain genres demand certain values, such as lavish sets in historical dramas, or lots of special effects in science fiction films. By having a clear vision of the potential market for your film, you will be able to devise a viable finance and marketing plan that will engender confidence in your abilities, and so make the financing of the film more likely.

When thinking about where your film should be positioned, it might help to think of films as being in one of three categories.

Product Led	Crossover/ Breakout	Market Led
Art House and specialist movies. Limited release.	Mainstream but limited release. Potential for crossing over into a wide release.	Mainstream with a wide release strategy.
Low budget – Up to £1.5m.	Low Budget – £2-£3m.	Mid budget – £10m plus.
3 Colours *Fool for Love* *Letter To Brezhnev*	*4 Weddings and a funeral* *The Full Monty* *East is East* *My Beautiful Launderette*	*Nottinghill* *Charlotte Grey*

Market Expectations

You will need to have a clear idea what values are in your film and how they relate to the expectations of your target market. Marketers often use the concept of the Pareto effect. This basically argues that a small number of people will account for most of the activity within a given market. It is sometimes known as heavy or light users, or the 20/80 effect. What it means is that 20% of consumers in any given market, from films to chocolate, will account for 80% of the market share. That means that 20% of the filmgoers who like horror films will account for 80% of all tickets sold for horror movies or horror DVDs purchased.

Again, this reflects the fact that your target audience is well versed in the kinds of film genres they like. Never underestimate the intelligence or sophistication of film audiences. They know what they like, and often they know why. This is why if you create a film that sits within a given genre and has something fresh and original about it, the distributors will have a clear idea how to market it and they will beat a path to your door. Even if you don't secure a distribution deal before the film is made, if your film is genre specific and uses the conventions in a surprising way, when you take it to the festivals, or you arrange a private screening, you may end up with a bidding war for your movie.

Meeting The Target Market's Needs And Expectations

Independent producers, who do not have big budgets, need to use ingenuity, creativity and originality to ensure that they meet their target market's needs. As said before, people go to see a film to engage on different levels and you must understand the needs of your target group. They will ignore low-budget production values, but will not forgive being bored or cheated out of what they were led to expect.

Target Markets

It is a good idea to create what in marketing terms is known as psychographic profiling. This is the creation of a model of the kind of person who will want to see your film in terms of demographics (where they live, size, growth, density, distribution, age, class), sex (gender) age (teen movies or mainstream) personal preferences (horror, thriller etc). This kind of information not only allows you to estimate the size of your market and therefore sales, but it also allows you to build a promotion campaign and this will enhance your ability to secure a distributor.

According to the Motion Picture Association of America (MPAA), the US market can be segmented along the following lines. There is reason to think that the UK and European markets are not too dissimilar. Although the French market is often considered unique, it is changing and becoming more mainstream.

Segmentation By Age

> **_Persons aged twelve to twenty four are 41% of all admissions._**
>
> This audience is sometimes known as the Teen Market and coming of age films are clearly aimed at it. It is the largest style market group and the UK has not produced a teen comedy to rival those made in the US, yet there is a clear UK and European market for them.
>
> **_She's All That, 10 Things I Hate About You, Clueless, Porkie and sequels_**

Persons aged twenty five to twenty nine are 12% of all admissions.

This group tend to see the same films as the teen market, but they are starting to change and develop a broader taste in the movies they want to see.

The Matrix, Terminator, Godfather. Skilful

Persons aged thirty to forty are 18% of all admissions.

This seems to be when cinema watching attitudes really change. Perhaps it is because this group are looking for new experiences, or explorations of themes and ideas that concern them.

Bladerunner, Mulholland Drive, Blue Velvet

Persons aged forty to fifty nine are 21% of all admissions.

This group have clear attitudes and tastes, and want good stories told in a sophisticated way.

Chinatown, Casablanca

Persons aged sixty and over are 8% of all admissions.

Very eclectic tastes

However, be careful. Because of increasing economic security and wealth along with healthier lifestyles, people are living longer and refusing to grow old or be categorised. It has been said that those currently in their sixties are behaving like people used to in their forties. This is happening to all the age groups. Also, these admission statistics change from year to year so check the latest figures.

Opportunities For The Independent Filmmaker

What these figures show is that cinema audiences aged thirty and upwards, constitute nearly 50% of the market. The characteristics of this group show that 50% of film goers will go to see films that are well made with interesting stories. Also, the UK and Europe have a long tradition of making this kind of film. This means European filmmakers, and others throughout the world who work within this tradition, are working to their strengths. Also, this kind of film has a long shelf life and will generate income over many years in the ancillary markets such as cable TV and DVD and video sales.

Tracking Markets

This is when you track a generation through its life cycles. All those cinema goers in the 70s and 80s who went to see **Teen Movies** are now part of the 40-59 group. What are their attitudes, preferences, needs? We saw that the 30 plus group now make up 50% of the cinema going public, and that their needs and preferences change as they get older. This ties in with the marketing concept **To Make and Keep a Customer**.

Finding The Data

Every Tuesday the **Hollywood Reporter** and **Daily Variety** publish a list of the 60 top-grossing films in the US and Canada. **Screen International** is another good source for data relating to cinema attendances. In the film business the US and Canada are considered the **domestic market** since they comprise the biggest, and therefore the most important, market in the world. Over the past few years 30 of these top-grossing films have been classed as independent movies. There is a growing propensity for the major studios to partner independent filmmakers by providing up to 50% of the budget. Some feel that this blurs the distinction between what is truly a studio movie and what is not. However, the key is distribution and, as Working Title in the UK has found out, to be a successful independent producer you must be able to ensure that films made are seen, and so linking with the majors is an important strategy.

However, it is clear that studios are concentrating much more on the blockbusters which can almost guarantee an income, and are looking to the independent producers to supply medium and small budget films which they will then distribute. The studios will often invest up to 50% of the budget for these films. In the US a low or small budget is considered less than £15m.

British Films

The British Film Institute also publish a year book that contains a vast amount of relevant data.

In 2003, the British Film Institute released a report called: **Producing The Goods? UK Film Production Since 1991**. It contains all the facts and figures for the UK film industry over the past 13 years.

The magazine **Sight and Sound** is also worth consulting.

Other Territories

This can be difficult, but **Weekly Variety** and **The Hollywood Reporter** cover the top 10 grossing films in various territories. Also, **The Hollywood Reporter,** prints the "The Going Rate" in their American Film Market and Cannes Product Editions. You can also subscribe to the Show Biz Data Web-site

Estimating Revenues

This is always difficult, but there are published tables that show how well or badly films have done in the various territories. These should be used as a guide only. Nobody knows how a film will perform once it is out there and there is plenty of evidence to show that critics often get it wrong and they are meant to be the experts. However, by looking at the figures and what genres and films do well in each of the territories, you can build a picture that will help you build a marketing strategy. Having a strategy will show that you have adopted a professional approach to your filmmaking and so studios and investors are much more likely to want to do business with you. Also, you will be speaking the same language as the distributor which is the key to success.

English Language Films

You can also use historical performance data from the main film territories. By using an historical framework, you can then project the probable sales for the various territories. This prediction then becomes your Marketing Objectives

Theatrical   In US $000s

Territory	Max	Min	Probable
UK	130	23	
Holland & Belgium & Luxemburg	29	12	
Canada	60	22	
Germany	520	180	
Italy	152	90	
Spain	90	25	
Scandinavia	60	20	
South America	124	40	
West Indies	12	4	
Hong Kong	20	8	
Korea	70	35	
South Africa	40	12	
Australasia	147	50	
USA	300	40	
Japan	90	20	

Of course this is just an overview, and you will need to refine the above figures in terms of genre and styles. But it is a start. Be careful, it is not a good idea to inform your investor of the details of each territory and what you expect to earn in each one. They might expect you to keep to these figures.

These figures are based on the historical average advances from distributors; they are not sales. Remember, the distributor buys the rights to distribute the film in certain territories and will expect to keep all the income from sales. After all, they are taking the risk and putting all the money up for the promotion of the film in their territories. Various deals can be made, but it is often the case that distributors will only pay you a maximum of 10% of the film's budget. But, there are many ways to do a deal, so nothing is written in stone.

Developing A Strategy

Building The Base

You might decide that you are going to specialise in one genre and build your expertise. Working Title have developed an expertise in romantic comedies. It could be said they started with a low budget **Four Weddings and a Funeral**, and built to the multi-million **Bridget Jones Diary**. I am reluctant to quote any figures, since it is notoriously difficult to get a definitive costing for any film, but it is generally accepted that Four Weddings cost about £2.2m and has to date taken over £150m world-wide.

You will need to clearly identify the market genre your project falls into. There are no universally agreed criteria for what defines each of the film genres. But there are sensible definitions that are generally agreed upon. Also, as you develop your ideas about what kinds of films you want to make, so you can decide how you define the films you want to make. But be careful, make sure that what you mean by a romantic comedy or thriller is what other people also think it is, especially distributors. As you build you strategy you will wish to break down the genres into their sub-genres, or in marketing terms, segment the market.

Genre

It is notoriously difficult to allocate a specific genre to every film because often they contain elements of more than one genre. Therefore, the British Film Council allocates, in various degrees, up to five genres to every title. The BFC states that "The list of genres is based on conventions commonly used by published sources including the Internet Movie Database and the British Board of Film Classification (BBFC) website. The final list was decided following consultation with the UK Film Council Production Funds and other industry representatives."

Action
Adventure
Animated
Biopic
Comedy (including romantic comedy)
Crime
Documentary
Drama
Family
Fantasy
Horror
Musical
Romance
Science
Thriller

Hence, the genre classification for **Fen Fever** would be: *Teen comedy/Action/Drama*. The principle genre the film relates to is teen-comedy, with aspects that include action and drama.

It is important to define your genre as best you can because it then becomes a tool whereby you can define the type of theatrical experience the target market will have, and also where your film fits within the distribution and finance model.

Segmentation

If you take comedy as a genre you wish to specialise in, then you can segment it further, so that within the comedy genre you can have teen-comedy, black-comedy, spoof-comedy etc. You can then decide:

What kind of audience the film is intended to appeal to:

- Specialist

- Crossover

- Mainstream

What market is the film primarily aimed at:

- European

- International

- Audience under 25

- Audience over 40

Medium by which the majority of the target audience will be reached:

- Theatrical release (Cinema)

- DVD/Video

- Television

This kind of analysis could then give you

Film – Comedy

Style – Teen

Market – international

Target audience – under 25 year olds

Distribution medium – Limited theatrical release then sold via the internet on DVD format.

The Film's Revenue Potential

You will also need to carry out market research into your specific market for similar films:

Size – How much was the total world-wide revenue for the specific genre your film falls into.

Demographics – What were the percentages of each age group who went to see this kind of film?

Sales and territories – What was the specific box office and ancillary incomes from each of the territories?

You can then assess your film in relation to its potential revenues in:

- **Home market (Where the film is made and produced)**

- **Key or main territories,**

- **US market (Called Domestic Market even if film is not made in US)**

Assessing Production Costs

Once you have done this you can then ascertain the right production costs in relation to its potential box-office. When making your case for the film, you will need to look at as many areas as possible.

Although no two situations are alike, the common methods are these:

Like With Like

Once you have defined your genre, find as many films as possible that were made for the same amount of money. That is, the negative cost. The closer you can get to like for like, the more confident the investor will be. Make a list of these films, their budgets and their grosses – then extrapolate from the figures the low, middle and high outcomes in terms of investment in relation to income.

Your film should be able to make the same or better revenues. And, it should, hopefully, have the potential to be a breakout film, like the **Full Monty**, and **Four Weddings and a Funeral.**

Similar Film, Higher Budget

See if you can show that your film will tap into similar films, made on a low budget, that have done well. If so, then you are showing that the market is there. Also, the bigger budget will allow you to add more value to the film by having, say, a named director, star or bigger production values. However, you will need to show that this extra cost will greatly improve the film's ability to generate potential income, and also allow you to exploit more markets.

Project Market Revenue Scenarios

It is a good idea to project the film's potential earnings so that nasty surprises do not suddenly occur. One way is to project good, average and bad scenarios.

Good

- The scenario if everything goes according to plan

- The film reaches audiences who are not regular cinema-goers and becomes a "must see" film, such as **The Full Monty**

- This will give you the maximum revenues the film can expect to generate

Average

- Revenues if the film neither goes really well or really badly

Bad

- The estimate of the revenues likely to accrue if all goes wrong, such as no overseas sales and a limited home release

- If this happens you may need a plan B that focuses on ancillary sales, such as DVD and cable TV

What To Put In The Plan

There is a difference of opinion about mentioning exceptional films. When doing your assessment, take ordinary films as your parameter. You can mention **The Full Monty** and **Four Weddings And A Funeral** and even **The Blair Witch Project**, but state that these are exceptional. If you are conservative in your estimates it will reassure the investor and demonstrate that you have good business sense and are not just a dreamer. However, you can then say that although you are being cautious, each film does have the potential to be a breakout movie and we could all end up very rich. But, make sure that your plan is built around prudence and that you will husband the investors' money carefully and not take unnecessary risks.

You will get some producers who say that categorising their film is wrong or even demeaning. They say their film is exceptional and different and cannot be compared to any other film. OK, they may be geniuses who will redefine the cinema experience, but no level headed investor is likely to touch them with a barge-pole. You need to put yourself in the studio's or investors' place and ask yourself if somebody came to you with that kind of proposal, would you hand over hard earned millions to them?

Target Markets

When determining what markets a film could be aimed at, there are various strategies that can be adopted.

Market Penetration

This means aiming a film project into an existing market such as Horror, Drama, Thriller, Comedy or Action. This often appears to be the best choice, since the market and products are familiar and clearly defined. However, it does mean going up against established figures in the form of directors and writers. Why should a studio take a chance on you when they have established producers and directors who have shown they can deliver? It is thought that this is where a short film, showing your abilities in that genre, would help. However, it is important to keep in mind what skills you are trying to demonstrate.

Product Development

This means modifying the product in some way, such as a new slant on an established market. This is when you take an established genre and you stay within its structure, but you do so in a new and unexpected way. Everyone knows that in action movies the good forces will triumph over the evil ones. But it's the way that this feat is accomplished that matters. Low budget unexpected hits often emerge from this area. ***Thelma and Louise*** was a road movie that won an Oscar for the writer. ***Four Weddings*** was just another romantic comedy that followed the set pattern of boy meets girl, boy loses girl, boy gets girl. The script was re-written seventeen times and produced an excellent film.

Market Extension

This means finding new markets for existing products. You've made a great film, not just for the UK, but one that has the potential to be sold in other markets. Possibly a teen movie made in the UK that you think will do well in say the Asian market. If a drama concerning UK Asians does well in the UK, then maybe it could be marketed in India or to distributors specialising in Asian markets in the US and other places where there are large Asian communities.

Diversification

Diversification is sometimes known as suicide corner. This involves a new product being developed for a new market or a new genre for a new market. Perhaps a horror movie for people who like gardening and don't like being scared. I know, perhaps something lives under the earth, but why should gardeners like it. If you go down this road of seeking something totally new, then sales agents and distributors would need to make a leap of faith if they were to back you in any way. And being business people, they are not known for leaping into unknown territory.

Creating The Marketing Match

As we have seen, one of the definitions of marketing is: ***To know a customer so well the product sells itself.***

The Marketing Match is when the creativity of the filmmaker is matched by the needs of society and so both benefit. The filmmaker is paid for their labour and so can continue to film, and the customer receives the benefits that satisfy a desire.

Successful Health Food purveyors know how their customers think and what they want and, more importantly, what they don't want. It is the same for filmmakers. Film genres exist because they have identified the audiences' response to different types of films. Rather than the studios manipulating filmgoers, it is the audiences who determine what films are made by showing their support for them. The fact that horror movies only have 5% of the UK market is because only that percentage of people are willing to leave their homes and pay money to see them. That is a fact. And any filmmaker who wants to make horror movies must be aware of this fact, and so, when creating their business plan, they must ensure that the costs of production match the expected revenues.

If there is a market for 1000 wooden cars at £10 each, then the maximum return is £10k. You wouldn't make the cars for £20 since you know you would lose £10 on each car. Yet, film producers will go to finance and production companies with scripts and film projects that have no chance of making their money back, or, because no business plan has been created, no one has any idea of the potential cost and earnings of the proposed film. It may be that the old Hollywood adage that nobody knows anything in terms of what will be a definite success, still holds good. But, international distributors have very clear ideas about what will bomb.

Marketing Objectives

Defining markets in terms of audience admissions or income generated is useful for the filmmaker since they can then set themselves market objectives. The marketing objectives of a film company is also the top line of its cash-flow, in other words the estimated sales forecast, and this helps financial planning.

As an independent producer you cannot hope to make films that will appeal to everyone so you will be making films for niche markets. You will need to assess those markets and find out how big they are in terms of number of attendances. This then translates into ticket sales and is defined as your marketing objectives. These are expressed as volume of sales in terms of the numbers who have seen your film or box office gross, plus any predicted ancillary sales. All this is on a time line which may stretch over a number of years. We will look at this more closely in the finance section, but it is important to note that the marketing objectives determine the cash flow.

Respect For The Audience

Filmmakers need to have this. Too often you find independent wannabes saying it is "their" film and "their" vision, as if the audience doesn't matter. Obviously the film's concept will come from inside the filmmaker or producer, but the films that are created must have a resonance with potential customers. Filmmakers must not just make films for themselves. They must make films with others in mind. You wouldn't buy somebody a present just because you like it. You would, hopefully, buy it because not only do you like it, but you also think that the person you are buying it for will like it. Often we have friends because they think and act like us – we have a common empathy with them. Filmmakers must also develop this empathy with, and for, their potential customers.

After all, the true filmmaker is one who wants to share his or her vision with as many people as possible.

Trends

You need to be aware of socio/economic trends. Films, like drama and literature, express the pain, anxiety, joy of current society. They can be cathartic in that they give expression to a felt need or pain. Or they can explore complex, and possibly unresolved, moral, political, social issues. This is especially true in today's society when the certainty of religious or socio/political ideals no longer provide the belief systems they once did. This again is where film can become the 21st century's prime art form.

Tracking Trends

It is a misconception that there is somehow a contradiction between the creating process and having a marketing strategy. The truth is that there is no contradiction. The filmmaker needs to know the current needs of her target market and the forces that are influencing that market. Many companies, even large international ones, forget this at their peril. The success of the **Matrix** and the two sequels shows that a generation brought up on sci-fi and computer games was ready for such a film. It is the role of the producer to spot these trends and needs within the market place.

Film, like all art, reflects the times in which it is created. It is said that Joel Silver, a successful Hollywood producer, made the right films for the time when Ronald Reagan was president of the US. This period was thought of as very conservative and right wing, so films like **Die Hard** that are very macho with not much sex did well. Now we live in a different world where films like **The Matrix** appeal to "techno-literate, internet-savvy" audiences.

Trend Analysis

Genre such as action/adventure and comedy, in all its forms, always seem to be popular. Other genres often go through cycles. In the late eighties horror films constituted 24% of all the films made in the US. However, by the mid 1990s horror films captured less than 3% of the total US market. Many thought that horror was dead and it was very difficult to persuade investors and studios to make one. Then along came **Scream** and others such as **The Mummy** and **Lake Placid** and horror film climbed back to just over 6% of the market in 2000, where it has stayed. In the UK it is about 5% of the film market. This kind of analysis informs your predictions for the likely income streams that will be generated.

If a film is successful, it will immediately be followed by imitators hoping to cash in on the trend. **Chinatown** helped to bring back film noir, which is a term that defines the American gangster and crime movies made in the 40's. Then there was the remake of **Cape Fear** by Scorsese, released in 1991. Then came **The Usual Suspects** in 1994 followed by a long list of films that culminated in **LA Confidential** which won 2 Oscars. So, from being a niche, or cult market, modern film noir became mainstream. Of course, when a trend starts it can only survive until too many films are made and the market is saturated. The public become bored with the familiar and so turn to something new to stimulate and surprise them.

Art versus Speciality Films

If you aim to become an independent filmmaker, you need to decide if your film is an art-house movie or a speciality film. This can be defined in broad terms:

Art House has a very limited market and goes to an art house cinema in London, such as the Curzon, and then often to University towns.

Speciality films could be those that open in 1 to 15 and then expand to many more cinemas as audiences and critics give it the thumbs-up.

A critic referred to Jane Campion's **The Piano** as art house, but the distributors saw it as a speciality film. However, as it grew, and was awarded the Palme d'Or at Cannes, and got an Academy Award nomination, Miramax rolled it out and it eventually played in 500 theatres and won 3 Oscars.

What you need to do is, define what you mean as "speciality" and use whatever films and distributors come closest to it. This helps the investor see where you are positioning your company and the kinds of films you want to make. Remember, it is only the big budget movies that open on 2000 to 3000 screens.

Jurassic Park seemed to have something for most cultures. From China to the UK it seemed to have the values and story to appeal to most people. Then along came **Titanic** which to date is the top grossing film of all time £1.8 billion box office. What this means for the independent producer/filmmaker is that the major producers are concentrating on making the big budget films and leaving the low end to the independent filmmakers like Fine Line, Miramax, Working Title.

Viability Threshold Theory

I have developed the **Viability Threshold Theory** around the notion that the values and elements within a script, the talent and how these relate to potential markets, can be analysed to give an indication of the potential viability of a film.

The theory is built on ascertaining a **Marketing Potential Score**, which is an attempt by me to put into some quasi-scientific form how studio executives think and how major international distributors analyse the potential of films. I have also researched all the successful UK films made since 1991 which cost less than £5m to produce, and then created a matrix to analyse them in terms of 21 key marketing determinants. What I found was that the average cost of each film was £2.6m. The average earnings were £10.6m, which meant that earnings were 4 times the cost of production. The film industry usually uses a formula that says a film must earn 2.5 its production costs before profits are made.

Had eight independent UK companies each made 3 of these films, along with 6 other films that broke-even or flopped, then we would currently have 8 viable independent film companies in the UK, instead of, in the judgement of most people in the UK film industry, just one.

The matrix can then be used to break down the different elements within a film, before it is shot, to see if it contains the necessary ingredients to make it a potential success. I am not aware that this has been done before, and I'm sure there will be those who feel that art can only be understood in an intuitive, emotionally based metaphysical sense. This is a valid position, but so is the attempt to create business models for professional filmmakers.

Script Elements, Talent and Markets

The strengths of these three aspects, script elements, talent and potential markets, need to be evaluated and given a score. Each score is then added-up and the total becomes the MPS. In order to evaluate and score these aspects, the finished film needs to be visualised and its strengths and weakness identified and analysed. The weaknesses can then be eliminated or negated, and the marketing strengths can be built upon during the pre-production stages and during principal photography.

Script Elements

The script elements within each film will depend on the genre and story. However, it is generally considered by sociologists and psychiatrists that the two most powerful human drives are sex and power – and, being major expressions of the human condition, are therefore found in many successful films. Sex can also be expressed as love, and power as violence. Sex, sometimes in the guise of love, has often been the critical factor throughout history for wars, the gaining or losing of empires and the destruction or creation of happy human beings. Power has often been expressed through violence, and motivated fathers to kill sons and daughters, uncles to kill nephews, brother to kill brother.

Comedy is another major expression of the human condition and is again found in many successful films. Sex, violence and comedy, in their many guises and manifestations, are therefore often crucial to the creation of a successful film. The originality of the way these powerful, fundamental drives of human nature are creatively expressed will determine how well made the film is.

How these forces are expressed, whether through rawness and crudity or subtle sophistication, will depend on the story being told and the manner, often determined by genre, in which it is expressed. **Casablanca** has sex and violence, but both are underplayed. **Straw Dogs** expresses these themes in the opposite way. In both films, the hero eventually rises to external demands and uses violence to make an heroic stand for love and honour.

Talent

The producer needs to identify and ascertain the value of the acting and/or directorial talent that is committed to the film.

Markets

Once the producer has identified all the marketing elements contained within the script and evaluated the talent he has on board, he needs to choose those territories he has identified as being the ones in which these elements will be most successful. Within each of these territories, he can then give a score for each of the script's marketing elements.

By adding up the scores for all three aspects, you will arrive at the film's Marketing Potential Score. I have used the following set of co-ordinates, but you should feel free to adapt the model by reducing or increasing:

- *The scale numbers*

- *The number or type of script elements*

- *The number of territories*

If you do, you must reduce by the same percentage the viability threshold score.

You will need to exercise judgement based on careful research to arrive at the appropriate scale numbers, script elements and selected territories, for your film. When you are doing this, you are thinking like a professional filmmaker, and this will give you the edge when seeking finance or distribution deals.

Creating A Marketing Potential Score

I have used the following scale numbers:

High 10

Above average 7

Average 5

Below Average 3

Low 1

None 0

Individual Tables

There should be individual tables for each script element, talent strength and market.

Script elements:

- Story strength
- Story structure strength
- Sex
- Special effects
- Nudity
- Violence
- Unusual locations
- Original comedy
- Soundtrack
- Generating interest through word of mouth
- Gimmicks
- Certification strength
- Press Angles

Talent Strength:

- Director
- Cast strength

Markets:

- Video & DVD
- Pay for view
- Cable & Satellite
- Pay TV
- Free TV
- Internet

Territories

Very few films have universal appeal, and those that do are usually block-busters such as **Titanic**. I have used the notion that most non-Hollywood films have 8 key box office territories, along with ancillary markets. Of course, films made for the international art house market may have a different release strategy, but the following are often viewed as important territories for film distribution:

- US
- UK
- Sc – Scandinavia
- Eu – Europe
- Ger – Germany
- Fr – France
- Jap – Japan
- Aus – Australia.

Example:

Feature Film **Fen Fever** (See Chapter 3)

Synopsis

A teenager, living in a remote part of rural England, the fens in East Anglia, dreams of starting a rock and roll group and heading for London. He befriends the son of a black US serviceman, stationed in a nearby US air base, who gets him all the latest music from the US. The black serviceman's son is meant to be helping the band, but he seems more keen on the local females, much to the consternation and anger of the local men.

The following, the first of the 21 key marketing elements, is shown here as an example. You will need to complete one for all the other elements you use. I have used 21, but feel free to use more or less, and to change the territories or numerical values as it suites your scrip.

Script Element: **STORY STRENGTH**

Territory	US	UK	EU	SC	AUS	JAP	GER	FRA	Total
High		10			10		10		30
Above Average	7			7		7			21
Medium			5					5	10
Below Average									
Low									
None									
STRENGTH:			TOTAL MPS – FOR STORY						61

John Sweeney

Interpreting The MPS

As stated previously, in order to arrive at a framework for interpreting an MPS score, I have made a study of, and applied an MPS score to, all the successful UK films that have been released over the past 13 years, and which were made for under £5m. I started with the most reliable current figures for budgets and box office takings, 2004, and then worked back. Using this system, the highest MPS score any script could achieve is: 1,680. What my research showed is that all the films selected fell within the 600 to 800 score, which meant that the average MPS score for a successful box office film made for less than £5m was 44%.

It could therefore be construed that there is a score below which a film is not likely to be successful at the box-office. Of course, just because a film scores above this threshold doesn't mean it will be successful, but it does mean that the elements in the script have the potential for viability at the box-office. And this is what the distributors and investors are looking for.

Applying The Theory

There is no such thing as a foolproof formula. If there were, there would be no unsuccessful films. Whatever weighting and values are given to the script elements and the talent, and whatever markets are identified as potentially the most lucrative, will depend on the judgement of the producer. The Viability Threshold Theory is therefore only as good as the input from the producer.

It should therefore be stressed that it is for the filmmaker or producer to create the matrix within which the theory will operate. That is, the producer or filmmaker needs to select the films in terms of genre, potential market and budget that are most similar to the one he wants to make. He must then give weighting to each of the marketing elements contained in the films he has chosen, and this will then produce a viability threshold score. The producer

218

then calculates the Marketing Potential Score within his film and measures this against the MPS for similar films.

These scores should then be used for the creation of a detailed SWOT analysis that will analyse:

- **Arriving at the right cost of producing the film in relation to potential sales.**

- **Creating the key elements, within the film, needed to successfully market the film.**

- **Identifying the key markets that need to be targeted and where most resources should be used.**

Summing Up

It could be, and has been, said that marketing is all that matters in the film business. That the bigger the market, the better the film and hence the growth in blockbuster movies. However, although marketing, in all its aspects, is crucial to the success of all films, no matter what budget or genre, it should still be seen as only one of the key elements in a business model along side others, such as the need for a story to be told.

> ## <u>Business Model Data File:</u>
>
> **Identify the key marketing ideas for each film.**
>
> **Define markets for each film with estimated revenues.**
>
> **Be clear about the positioning of each film in its target markets.**
>
> **Be aware of the current revenues for English Language Films in the world's markets.**
>
> **Know what market segment you intend to exploit for each film.**
>
> **Have a marketing strategy for each project.**
>
> **Create an MPS that shows the viability of each of the film projects.**
>
> **Set target figures for all the main territories.**
>
> **Have a clear understanding of the size and structure of your potential market in terms of its turnover, how much money is generated and cinema attendances.**

Chapter 7

Film Distribution

"The most important thing to remember is that the market for the independent producer is not the ticket buying public, it is the acquisition executive" **Gregory Goodell – Independent Feature Film Production.**

In this chapter we will:

Show how the film distribution system works.

Explain what distributors are looking for in a film.

Outline the role of exhibitors.

Demonstrate film distribution patterns.

Discuss market positioning and release strategies.

Introduction

Without a distributor, the chances are that your film will never be seen, except at some festivals and by your immediate family and friends. For your film to have any chance of being seen by a wide audience, and so establishing you as a filmmaker, you will need a distributor. Securing a distribution deal is often the hardest part of the filmmaking process, and so you need to understand the needs of the distributor and be able to meet those needs.

It is worth remembering that the distributor gets only one shot at making the film a success, and so he/she needs to feel strongly that the film has the elements within it to be marketed successfully. That is why the studio system sees marketing as the core element in the filmmaking process, as discussed in the previous chapter. This often means compromise on the part of the filmmaker. If you want to be in complete control of your project from start to finish, and to stay absolutely true to your artistic vision, then you may need to think about another medium through which to express it. Once you cross the line from being artistically self-sufficient and ask for massive resources that involve the livelihoods of many people, and the sustainability of an industry, then you have a responsibility to create projects that are viable. Remember, the best films have artistic integrity and commercial viability, which in turn means they will be around for a long time and have the potential to become classics.

It could be said that making the film, that is developing it, shooting it and editing it, are the easy parts and that the real difficulties arise when attempting to get the film distributed. It is estimated that two thirds of all UK films made, never get a theatrical release – that is, shown in cinemas – and less than half get distributed in any form, be it DVD or TV. Therefore, distribution, like marketing, needs to be thought about in the development stage of the filmmaking process. Many professional producers see distribution as the key to the film's success.

Distributors

So who are the distributors? Distributors are the people who take your film, then invest their time and money in selling to:

Exhibitors. These are the people who own the cinemas in which your film will be shown. The cinema owners have many overheads that they need to pay in order to keep in business. Therefore, the distributor needs to be able to convince the exhibitors that your film will put bums on seats. The distributor will decide on a release strategy to suit the film – either a slow release and shown in only one or a few cinemas, or a fast release and shown on hundreds or thousands of screens at the same time. Often the production values within the film will determine what strategy is to be adopted. The slow release often works if market research shows that word of mouth, rather than big names in the leading roles within the film, is likely to create a "must see" buzz and so draw ever larger audiences. This happened with **Leaving Las Vegas**, **Four Weddings and a Funeral** and other crossover films.

The media. The distributor's aim is to get the media to print stories, reviews and articles that will hopefully give the film a buzz and create a "must see" bandwagon. However, if the film doesn't contain any original or marketable elements, then the distributor's task will be all the more difficult.

Marketing partners. This often involves fast food outlets, or other providers of mass market consumer goods, who might want to be part of a joint campaign if the target audience for the film is the same as theirs. **Harry Potter** is such an example.

The public. Remember, in London, as with many other European cities, each week five new films are screened. Therefore, the aim of the distributor is to create a compelling reason for the cinema-goer to choose to see your film, rather than one of the others.

Respecting Distributors

The selling of the film by the distributor will take time and money and the full use of available resources, so the distributor should be seen as a person who will be investing directly into your film. It therefore follows that you need to treat them as an investor.

According to the MPAA the average cost of releasing a US film in North America in 2004, had risen to $39m. If you add in the average cost of production, $63.8m, it makes a grand total of $102.8m to make and distribute a US film. From these figures you can see that a huge expenditure is needed to distribute films, nearly two thirds of the cost of production, and so the distributor needs to be sure he can sell the film. At the same time distributors are eagerly looking for the hot script or new low budget film that is right for now. Your role as producer is to have the right film, in the right place at the right time for the right price.

Often, the distributor is as involved in the film as the producer or director – and it becomes her/his baby. The distributor will invest time and money, often scarce resources, in the hope of making your film a success. It is just as important to the distributor as to you the producer, that the film is a success. If it is not, then the distributor loses money, and if that happens too often then the distributor goes out of business. Therefore, during the development stage, producers and filmmakers need to be thinking about what elements can be incorporated or enhanced within the script to make the distribution process a success. There was an instance when a distributor was paid from public funds to distribute six films at a US film festival. However, the distributor was heard to say that he was grateful to be paid for his services, but he didn't have a clue how to promote and sell the films since they did not fit any genre and did not contain any marketable elements. Needless to say, the films died a quiet death. Whether we like it or not, film audiences have expectations and distributors know what they are and so are attracted to films that contain these elements.

UK Distributors

UK distributors get a lot less of the box office receipts than in other countries, and so they are reluctant to take chances with new directors or films with no stars. In the UK it is the exhibitors who get a higher proportion of the box office split. This is usually explained because in the UK, rents and rates and other overheads are higher than in other countries. However, all deals are different, and the split between the distributor and the exhibitor often depends on how marketable your film is. Obviously, the income earned by the distributor directly affects how much money you, as the producer, will receive.

Because of the difficulties in making a living as a distributor, there are very few independent distributors, and in recent years there has been a consolidation of distributors. It is estimated that there are now only about twenty major distributors in the world. For a list of current world and local distributors and sales agents, such as for the UK, see the relevant web-sites and yearly publications. In the UK there is the Year Book published by the British Film Council.

Being Professional

Before going to meetings with distributors, sales agents or financiers, always be prepared. If need be, rehearse the meeting with friends or colleagues so you are sure you know what you want or need. If the film is still at the script or treatment stage, then you will need to have a clear idea of:

- *The length and cost of the development stage.*

- *The below the line costs. (Those costs that do not include stars and director or writer)*

- *Who you think will play the leads.*

- *What markets you think the film will appeal to.*

- *The elements within the script that you feel could be used to successfully market the film.*

- *In what stages you want the payments to be made.*

- *What you are selling the rights of each territory for.*

It is worth bearing in mind that the distributor is just as important to the creation and success of the film as the investors. Therefore, much thought needs to go into targeting the right distributors for your film project. Often, if you get a major distributor on board early on in the process, the raising of finance for making the film becomes much easier. There is no set time in the process when it is right to approach distributors; the received wisdom is that the sooner you acquire a distributor the better. Of course the reality is that most films are unable to acquire a distributor and most finished films are hawked around the festivals in the hope of finding one.

Involving The Distributor

In order to ensure that the finished film will be commercially viable, distributors sometimes get involved in a film long before it gets the green light for production. In exchange for an element of control in the making of the film, and/or for certain rights, the distributor may be willing to invest in the making of the film. Remember, if they come on board just as a distributor, they are often committing to spend as much as the cost of most European films. So, if they are also willing to invest in the making of the film, they will expect a major say in how the finished film looks. It is important to remember this and to judge just how much control you really want to give away.

But also remember that the distributor is at the sharp end of the process and their skill, judgement and enthusiasm for the film will often be the difference between a film being successful and it being left on the shelf or, if it is lucky, going straight to video. It is often said that there are three films:

- The one that is written

- The one that is shot

- The one that is edited

Because filmmaking is a dynamic process, the notion of what the film is saying and how it is saying it will change during the process. This is when the advice and knowledge of distributors can be invaluable. They know what will sell, and therefore what, and how, they can promote as the finished film. Also, during the filmmaking process, and especially during the shoot, there will be certain marketing elements, such as the taking of photographic stills that the distributor will need in order to promote the film once it is finished and ready for distribution. Remember, the cost of distributing the film can be more than the cost of producing it, so the distributor's voice matters.

Deals And Calculating Revenues

Generally, the amount you get from each distributor, in each territory, is the same as what the distributor can expect to make in return. For example, if 8% of a film's revenues might be calculated to come from Japan, therefore you would seek to get 8% of the cost of the film from Japanese distributors. If the film costs £2m to make, then you as the producer would want 8% of £2m for the sale of the Japanese distribution rights. The Japanese distributor would expect to get 8% of £5m. Remember, they calculate a film as successful when it grosses 2.5 of its negative costs, the final cost of producing the film ready for distribution.

The US is where the producer or distributor could expect to receive 40% of the final revenues for the film, and this makes it the most important market for the distributor. For example, Miramax might give you 40% of the cost of the film in exchange for the US rights. You then work out a deal to share the profits once the distributor has recouped his initial payment to you. However, all deals are different and, obviously, the more successful you are as a filmmaker the better deals you will get. The distributor will be calculating his/her percentage from the global box office and ancillary revenues; you, as the producer, will be calculating yours on the negative cost of the film.

Sales And Marketing

The sales and marketing strategy is unique to each film. The thing to remember is that the film must have elements that are marketable. We have already discussed this, but I make no apologies for repeating it since it goes to the very heart of what many people believe is the problem with European filmmakers. That is, they do not fully appreciate that filmmaking is primarily a marketing exercise, and that this goes for art films as well as pop-corn films or blockbusters. (It is said that the term Blockbuster comes from the fact that if a film was a big success then the queues to see it would stretch round and beyond the block, therefore busting beyond the block). Even though as a producer or filmmaker you are not trying, or want, to make a blockbuster, you should be attempting to have the right film in the right market at the right time at the right cost.

The Hot Project

The distributor, at their best, is the mirror of the market. The distributor does not acquire or finance films for distribution because she/he likes them, but because she/he believes they have market potential and will generate sales. Remember, a distributor lives or dies by his/her ability to find and distribute films that do well in their chosen markets and thereby generate profits. Your film, therefore, has to reflect what the market needs. You, as the producer, must learn to see what the distributor sees in the mirror.

The objective is to offer the distributor a "hot title" that is clearly going to be the next big breakout movie. This means you have the right film ingredients in terms of script, director and cast and crew. The more of these ingredients you have, the more readily the distributor will be to take on the project and back it financially. And, if the UK film industry's future lies in it being "distribution led", as declared by Alan Parker in his speech as the newly appointed Chairman of the BFI, then UK producers must learn to develop effective strategies for securing their services.

All Singing From The Same Sheet

Despite distribution being seen as the most crucial aspect of the filmmaking process, it is also the most unpredictable. If the distributor does not sell films that make money, he/she will soon run out of money and go bankrupt. This causes a major problem for independent filmmakers, since it is far easier for the distributor, and the exhibitor, to have a film that has been produced by the majors and has clear market potential. All films have a potential market from one (your mum), to 300 million who have seen a James Bond film. As we saw in the last chapter, all film markets, like all other markets in a free market and democratic society, have characteristics in terms of size and trends. If you learn what these are then you are speaking the same language as the distributor. Remember, it is a common language and the same words and concepts that you use to sell your film to the distributor, the distributor will also use to sell your film to the exhibitor, the public and the press.

The distributor is making a major investment in your film, even though they may not have invested up-front at the pre-sales stage. As discussed before, the investment can sometimes be greater than the cost of making the film and that is why in the US, even though a film may have cost up to £30m to shoot, the studios may decide not to distribute it because they think it will not recoup the original amount spent on it, so why waste more money. Often, these films go straight to video or DVD or just lie on the shelf.

The Distribution Process

Once the distributor accepts the film they must then try to do a deal with the exhibitors. It is often the case in Europe, and especially in the UK, the distributor's cut of the box office receipts is only 25% and so they must be absolutely sure the film will be a success. Once a distributor decides to distribute your film, they must then invest in the prints and advertising of the film and so

– given that each 35m print costs approximately £1k – then you can see that opening in hundreds of screens will entail a large investment. Also, there are the astronomical costs of advertising the film through posters, media, screenings, events etc. Given all this expense, then the distributor must be sure she/he can make a profit or she/he will not be in business for long.

In the US $30m is the average spend on prints and advertising for a run-of-the-mill studio film. The spend on blockbusters can be up to $200m. Given that the average UK film in 2004 cost £2.2m ($3.87m) to make, you can see what UK and European filmmakers are up against. **Four Weddings** cost £2.2m to make, but the prints and advertising was a great deal more, especially in the US.

Distributors' Slates

Overall profitability for distributors usually comes from a small number of the films in their slates. As in other countries, the UK has a small number of major distributors who are affiliated with, or associated with, the major Hollywood studios. This means they get their films direct from the majors.

Always keep in mind that as a producer or filmmaker you are asking people to invest their hard earned money in you and your ideas, therefore you need to be able to show that they will not be throwing their money away. Production companies and distributors are often amazed at filmmakers' responses to being rejected. Lots of filmmakers seem to think that they are doing the distributor or production company a favour by offering them their project. Think what would your response be to someone who comes and asks for £50,000 ($88,000) because they have an idea for a film. You could raise it by re-mortgaging your home, and it would be worth it if you knew for sure that the investment would, at least, get you your money back, and, at best, make you a profit. The same goes for distributors and exhibitors; they want to stay in business and that means minimising the losses and maximising the profits.

You, as a producer or filmmaker, need to be aware of the needs of both distributors and exhibitors alike, and so, help them as much as possible to say yes to your film. So, let us have a more detailed look at what the distributor or sales agent is looking for.

A Hot Script

Most producers and directors feel that there are very few good scripts being offered to them. It is often heard that good scripts, dealing with contemporary issues that are expressed through a well structured story are very rare. That is not to say that all good scripts are immediately recognisable, but the vast majority of films that do well are those that have been identified as potential winners at script level and then script developed through many rewrites. It may be that like **Lock Stock and Two Smoking Barrels**, the film's full potential won't be seen until the editing stage.

Cast

Most major film producers will want to see who you think will play the lead roles. If box-office names are already committed then that is a big plus in getting the money to make the film. However, even if no named actors have committed to the project, state who you think would be good to play the lead roles. If you believe in the script, then as a producer or filmmaker make sure you contact the acting talent you feel would be right for the lead roles. It is surprising how many big stars are willing to work for a lot less than their normal fee because they like the script or want to work with a certain director.

Director

Lots of production companies are swayed by who the director is. It is felt that the director can bring an extra quality to the film and make a good script great by using creative insights, and/or coax good actors to give great performances. Also, if you have a hot director then you are likely to attract top actors who want to work with the director.

Remember, making and producing a film is very much a team effort, and all really good films are the sum of their parts. If all the parts are good or great, then the finished film reflects this. This is what is what many believe makes **Casablanca** the best film ever made. It had a great script, great acting, not only from the leads but also the minor parts, great sets and great music. Also, Hal B Wallace made sure all the costumes and props complemented and augmented the sets. Try to imagine if the film would have been as good with other people playing the lead roles, such as Ronald Reagan who turned it down; or if the director had not been skilled in ensuring the film had pace, without which it could have been just another slow melodrama.

Distribution Pattern

Under English law, the maximum period a distributor can ask an exhibitor to book his film for is two weeks; therefore, if a film does get to the exhibition stage, then the distributor is only guaranteed two weeks in which to make an impression. In the UK 60% of cinema attendances take place on the weekend from Friday to Sunday. This means that over a two week period 60% of sales will be made in six days. The distributor hopes that during these six days the film will develop "legs" and start to run, and that word of mouth will create a "must see" buzz.

A distributor needs to be fully convinced that a film can be sold to its target audience. One of the main gripes of the UK film industry is that they cannot get their films distributed. Indeed, the Film Council is now investing money into subsidising UK film distribution. However, a film must deliver what it says it will. Target audiences are just that. They have a collection of needs that allows them to be an identifiable group that can be targeted. A friend of mine went to see **Young Adam** on its opening night. It had been billed as a dark, erotic thriller. When he went to see it he was dismayed that there were only 5 people in the audience. He was even more dismayed to find that it was not what he had been led to believe it was. He didn't think it was dark or erotic or a thriller. Clearly word of mouth had meant that a lot of other people thought the same, hence the small audience. In the end, no matter how much marketing and promotion has taken place, the success of the film will rest on the response of the audience. If it is well received, then it will be spoken about positively amongst peer groups, a "must see" climate will be created, and anybody not having seen it will feel out of the loop.

Market Positioning And Release Dates

When developing your project, you must bear in mind the time of year when you plan to release the film. This is of vital importance and the release date will be informed by the genre and type of film and where it is positioned in the market.

How and when to release the film always needs careful consideration. Each year over 300 films are released and so the market-place is crowded. With today's average spend on a Hollywood studio movie being $35m, with a further $10 – $20m on prints of the film and advertising, and the fact that most theatrical releases do not make a profit, then you can see that even before the film is made the marketing people are thinking long and hard about how they will launch the film.

This is where the problems arise for so many independent films. The marketing strategy has to be developed after the film is made. It's a bit like making a car and then taking it to the showrooms to sell it without having first thought about what cars are being made currently, what models have recently been sold and what are the trends. Making a big gas guzzling Cadillac for the UK market is not likely to sell well. Yes, you might get lucky, but no showroom is going to stock your cars if they have no idea who to sell them to. Think about it – there are family cars, sports cars, prestige cars etc., all of which have defined markets and no carmaker will invest millions in developing a car for which there is no clearly defined market. This is the same for filmmaking, yet filmmakers often approach film financiers or production companies or producers and expect to be given millions on the strength of an idea for a film for which there is no clear market.

OK, it could be argued that because of trying to track the market these days all cars tend to look the same, and some critics could say this about studio films. But the vast majority of filmgoers flock to see studio films, just as they flock to buy off road 4 wheel drives.

European Films

There is a growing audience in Europe for films produced in Europe. In 2004, a network of cinemas known as Europa Cinemas has been showing European films across the EU. The films are not just shown to a national audience within the film's country of origin, but right across the EU. The top films were: from Spain *Talk To Her* (30,771 screenings in 19 countries); from Germany *Good-Bye Lenin* (28,074 screenings in 20 countries); from Finland *The Man Without a Past* (21,512 screenings in 20 countries); from France *The Pianist* (21,487 screenings in 20 countries); and also from France *Etre et Avoir* (21,106 screenings in 11 countries).

Europa Cinemas currently dedicate 33% of screenings to European films which in 2003 resulted in 19 million people going to watch a European film.

Source: CG (documentation: Europa Cinemas & Media Desk Belgium)

Essential Elements

When a distributor considers accepting a film, either at development stage or the finished product, they have to consider:

What kind of genre does the film fall into?

- Horror
- Comedy
- Action/Adventure
- Thriller
- Romance
- Drama
- Other or mix of genres
- Is it an event film – blockbuster?

Should it be released at Christmas or Summer? What other blockbusters are there in the pipeline – what will the competition be?

Is it a niche market film?

- What territories can it be sold in.
- If a slow release, then how many cinemas could it open in and at what cost.
- How to promote the film to a small discerning market. Does it have the right obscure, extreme, thought provoking, taboo-busting elements to make it appeal to minority groups?

If a sequel or franchise film such as Harry Potter

- What has the new film got that distinguishes it from the original.
- What new twists or plot. (**Terminator Two** swapped the protagonist with the antagonist).

Is there a seasonal pattern when particular genres do well?

- Certain weekends in the year
- Christmas
- Summer

Is this film a potential award winner – Academy or BAFTA?

- If so, it will be released in the UK between January and March, a period known as the "awards season".
- In the US – Summer and Autumn.

The cast and any star power

- How were the leading cast's last couple of films received both critically and commercially?
- Are they available for national and international publicity?

Release dates

- Which films are other distributors planning to release at the same time as this film?
- Are the most appropriate screens available?
- Will this film lead the reviews of that week's film releases?

Buzz Factors

- Directors or stars
- Book or script
- Controversial theme
- Controversial scene/s
- Bandwagon

Reaction from release in other countries

- Web sites
- Word of mouth

British Film Board Classification

- Does it match the film's targeted audience
- Does it match the film's genre

Clear Target Market

- The distributor will have a good idea if the proposed film has a target market
- There are "break-out" or "cross-over" films, but these are very rare. Most successful films are made with a specific market in mind
- The UK market is broadening as the general population ages and cinema attendance continues to increase, but the core groups are still aged between 15 and 24
- It is a shared experience with an average of 3 persons per party

It is no good thinking about these things after the film is made; by then it is too late to go back and incorporate them since it would cost too much money. The major studios do carry out pre-release screenings and then make any necessary changes to the film to increase its chances of success, as with **My Best Friend's Wedding**, but they have the resources to do it, and very few independent producers or filmmakers will have this luxury. It did happen with **The Crying Game**, when the initial investors agreed to invest more money so the ending could be changed, but that was considered a lucky one-off break. Therefore, is essential that during the pre-production planning stage all these post-production issues are considered.

The Exhibitors

It is worth the producer or filmmaker understanding the role of the exhibitor since the language and concepts used by the producer to bring the distributor on board, will be the same as those used by the distributor to secure an exhibition deal.

An exhibitor is the company, or individual person, who owns and operates the cinemas in which the films are shown. The exhibitor earns his money from percentage of the box office receipts, but also makes a lot of money from selling drinks and sweets. Therefore, the exhibitor is more likely to accept large blockbusters and a lower percentage of the box office, if he is convinced that a major promotion campaign will bring lots of people into his cinema, especially if they are children who will spend lots of money on soft drinks and sweets. This is where the modern term "popcorn movie" comes from – it defines a middle of the road family film that will ensure lots of soft drinks and popcorn are sold when it is screened. When these films are screened, more profits are often generated by the sales of soft drinks and popcorn than from the sales of cinema tickets.

Exhibitors are like any retailer; they must be convinced that by stocking your product they will make sales. Each deal between the distributor and the exhibitor is strictly confidential and will vary from one exhibitor to another.

As previously stated, under English law, the maximum period a distributor can ask the exhibitor to book his film for is two weeks. This protects the exhibitor who might be "leant on" by the distributor to book it for longer periods or, if it is a major distributor, be threatened with not getting the blockbuster that is coming up. After two weeks it is up to the exhibitor to decide if the film is doing enough business to warrant it being kept on. Because of this, the distributor must be sure that the product he is trying to sell is a marketable product. If he cannot persuade exhibitors to buy the product then he will go out of business.

The distributor therefore needs to have a product/film that has the qualities the target market is looking for. People do not turn up at a multiplex and then decide what film to see. They arrive, having decided what film to see, with expectations based on past experiences. Those expectations, often based around genre, need to be met. The distributor will be well aware of what the target audience expects and he will need to see those elements in the script or film.

An example is **The Cable Guy** starring Jim Carey. It was promoted and marketed as a comedy, which is what Jim Carey is best known for, but in fact the film was a horror movie. Jim Carey was attempting to do something different, but because the way the film was sold to the public they turned up expecting a comedy and were disappointed and the film did badly at the box office.

Distribution Markets

The UK now has more than 3,000 cinema screens, mostly in multiplexes. This is nearly double what was available in 1992. So in 10 years there has been nearly a twofold increase. Along with this has gone a rise in cinema attendance, from 103 million in 1992, to 156 million in 2001. However, the growth in screens has outstripped the growth in attendances. There is therefore scope for the market to develop.

London accounts for 26% of all annual visits to the cinemas in the UK. This offers a real opportunity for independent filmmakers to devise a strategy for low budget films to be slow released in London, and then' if well received, to be rolled out gradually in art-house or local cinemas in the rest of the country and Europe.

Although the production values in UK films are rising:

- 1995 – 33 films made with budgets of £2.6m

- 2002 – 56 films made with budgets of £3.2m

Yet, there is a decrease in the number of UK films that get shown in the UK. The most significant increase in film funding came from the US Hollywood Majors.

The time a film spends in cinemas is usually four months, but most of the money is made in the first few weeks. In the US the opening weekend box-office is seen as an indicator of what the film will eventually make, and is therefore watched with great interest and fear. The fact is that a film can only be launched once, so the pressure to "get it right first time" is immense. Once the weekend sales figures are in, distributors hold meetings, usually on a Tuesday morning, with exhibitors to discuss the "holding over" the film beyond the current 2 weeks. This of course depends whether or not the film has done well in box-office terms and what are the up-coming new releases. The exhibitor has to make commercial judgements about the potential sales of new releases, compared to current sales. Again, it's a business, but a very unpredictable one.

Marketability And Playability

It is important to get these concepts right.

Marketability focuses on the different ways to sell a film to a target audience.

Playability looks at how the audience perceived the film – did it grip them? Did it meet their expectations?

As the release date nears, the marketing strategy gains momentum. This is when it is important that the film has elements within in it that allow a good marketing campaign to be created. Once the campaign has started, distributors will hire people to track awareness about the film amongst its target audience and what elements the public find appealing. You can have a brilliant campaign that exploits all the must see elements within a film, but if all the "good bits" are in the trailer, then when the public see the film, they will go away disappointed and will pass on this disappointment to their peer group. It is estimated that one person will tell seven other people of their viewing experience, and these seven will pass it on – so, exponentially, it is not long before word is out and the whole target group has formed an opinion.

Films compete not just against other films, but against other leisure activities such as staying at home and watching the TV, or renting a video or DVD and buying a pizza. Whilst great marketing cannot save a film the public do not want to see – word of mouth being the crucial element as to whether or not a film is really successful – poor marketing can bury a good film. Distributors have limited budgets, and so must decide how much to allocate for each of the films they will release. The budget for each film will vary, depending on how well the film is expected to do, and what returns the distributor can expect.

Many producers, especially those whose films do not do well, complain that they were not marketed properly. However, good films invariably eventually find their audience. It is said that **Leaving Las Vegas** was released in just one cinema in the mid west. The rest is history. You also need to be aware of the different needs of different markets. A film might need to be marketed differently in different territories. The poster may need to be different for the UK market and others, as opposed to the US market. (See **Shallow Grave** and **Terminator** posters).

Box Office Is King

In 2003, the Hollywood majors kept back completed films that were due for release in the autumn. They did this because the blockbusters being shown in the summer had not generated enough money over the usual release dates. Blockbusters are crucial to the cashflow of the majors, and so they kept the blockbusters in the cinemas longer because over time they would generate more income than more serious films. Although the films kept back cost an estimated £500m ($880m) to make, they were considered to be "art house", and so would not take the money that blockbusters would. The reasoning was that although they might be good quality films, they were not necessarily profitable.

Therefore, Hollywood executives decided to keep the blockbusters in the multiplexes for an extra month – till September. The reason given for holding back the "non-blockbusters" was that box office receipts were down 4%, and the executives calculated that by keeping the blockbusters, many of which were sequels *(From The Matrix Reloaded to Terminator 3)*, they could make more money because more people go to see blockbusters than any other kind of film. So, although the number of people seeing the blockbusters were down on previous years, it was calculated that more people pro-rata would go and see them, than would go and see the art based films, especially if nothing else was offered. *"If you show blockbusters and little else, the audiences will come"*, said one studio boss.

So the films, such as Meg Ryan's *Against The Ropes,* that were scheduled for late August and September were "dumped forward" into next year when many would be killed off or released only on DVD or Video. These are quality films that many say would attract Oscar nominations, but nominations are usually in by December 31st when voting starts and it is therefore considered by industry insiders that Spring releases, no matter how good, rarely receive Oscars. Critics have said that Ryan's performance in **On the Ropes** was brave, startling and unexpected, but that is not what the studio executives wanted to hear. They want her to be "charming and cute" as in **When Harry Met Sally** and **Sleepless in Seattle**.

There are those who say that audiences are suffering from "sequel burnout", but studio bosses seem not to buy it and reports say they plan to release another batch of sequels next year.

This gives perspective to the independent UK distributor negotiating with the exhibitors. Both need to earn a living or they won't be in business for long. But what chance do UK made films with micro-budgets have? If Hollywood films, some costing $47m to make, were held over, then what chance the average UK film made for £2.2m ($3.8m)? So, competing with Hollywood is perhaps not the best strategy for European filmmakers, and a different kind of business model is needed.

In the long run, some films that bomb at the box office, such as **Waterworld**, which it is said cost $200m to make, do eventually make their money back through ancillary sales such as video and DVD. But it often takes up to 5 years to do so. So profit is the bottom line, and has to be so or there would be no film business. Positive cashflow is as important to the film business as it is to any other business.

US System V UK And European System

The big difference between European and US films is the manner in which they are financed and distributed. The Hollywood majors develop, finance, create and distribute. They have deals with exhibitors. They make between 10 and 12 pictures a year. They hope for one or two immediate successes and the rest to earn a return over five years in terms of TV, Cable Video DVD and other ancillary markets.

These majors are all owned by conglomerates and so have vast sums of money to invest in the pictures. It is generally considered that the cost of entering and becoming a studio would be prohibitive for the UK as it is estimated that entry costs for first year of trading would be £300 m.

This also gives the US enormous marketing advantages. By the time an initial version of the script is in place, the marketing departments are already putting together a marketing strategy and campaign. This may even happen when the film is just an idea. Maybe all they have is the poster – now let's create a script and make a film.

It is now accepted in the US that overseas markets are vitally important to financial success of the film. Sometimes, the overseas distribution arms of the Hollywood majors will be asked to make comments about the script, potential stars, director and genre to ascertain the film's likely success in the various overseas territories. This is because the earnings from overseas markets can often be more than the home, "domestic", market. Therefore, the majors will often seek the advice of European distributors before a film is given the green light. The executives are attempting to forecast the film's potential earnings in the various territories, based on the track records of the genre, stars, director and production values of similar films previously released in those territories. It is a simple marketing exercise; and it could be said that the exercise is market-led, not product-led.

Selecting A Distributor

It may not always be possible to fully negotiate deals with distributors, but if you have a hot project that more than one distributor is interested in obtaining then you should check them out to determine which one is best for you. Things to keep in mind will be:

- What is the amount of advance, cash, being offered?

- What rights are being handed over to the distributor – North America and the rest of the world; ancillary rights such as TV and DVD?

- Is your film part of a group of films being cross-collateralised?

- What is the size and extent of the guaranteed marketing commitment?

- Does the distributor have a good track record distributing your kind of film?

- What monthly or quarterly accounting statements do you get?

- What is the marketing strategy? Does it accord with your idea of who the target market is? Be careful on this – if it is a well known and respected distributor who has agreed to take your film and he disagrees with your ideas about the target market, then you are probably wrong.

- Is the distributor currently handling films similar to yours, which will be in competition with yours? If so, make sure there is no conflict of interest.

- Can you regain distribution rights easily and quickly if the distributor withdraws your film from distribution too early?

- Is the deal the best you can get in the circumstances?

The Sales Agent

Although not as important as they used to be, sales agents can still play a vital role for the new filmmaker. It is the agents who have the contacts with the major studios and distributors. Also, given the way many small distributors have ceased to exist, and only large ones are operating now, it is helpful to have the advice and guidance of a sales agent who can act as an intermediary. Sales agents select between 6 to 12 scripts per year. Their selection is based on the projects potential sales revenue, pure and simple. They make their money from films being made and distributed and then earning box office returns.

Summing-up

The distributor plays a key role in the success of a film. It is the distributor who will know what territories to promote the film in and how to do it. Distribution is a high risk business and so the distributor needs to be sure that he can market the film effectively or he stands to lose a lot of money. The filmmaker must choose carefully which distributors to approach, so they find the right one who has a track record of marketing the kind of film made. This means the filmmaker must start out with a clear idea as to how the finished film will be received by individual distributors and what they are looking for. The aim should be for filmmakers and producers to build up a relationship with distributors so that projects can be discussed at the development stage and, if possible, distribution agreements entered into for the finished film. This will make raising the finance to make the film much easier.

Business Model Data File

Have you got a list of all the distributors and what kind of films they specialise in distributing?

Is the script well written and does it express contemporary issues and concerns? Or, does it possess other equally relevant strengths?

Have you identified and fully analysed the territories where the film is likely to do best?

Have you identified the release dates when the film stands the most chance of success?

Have you ascertained that the predicted sales will meet the cost of production and distribution and should create profits?

PART FOUR

Financial planning to acquire funding for film projects and to generate income and profits.

Chapter 8

Film Budgets And Financial Management

"Money talks...but all mine ever says is good-bye" **Anonymous**

"Money isn't everything... but it ranks right up there with oxygen" **Rita Davenport**

In this chapter we will:

Introduce zero accounting as a radical method of ensuring the budget realises the film's full potential.

Look at the importance of cashflow forecasting and working to a time frame

Look at some examples of how recent films were financially packaged

Look at what to put in the financial plan

Introduction

The more you can eliminate the chances of the film failing financially, the more you are likely to get the money. Investors are, or should be, well aware that investments in films are high risk and there is no certain outcome or guarantee of success. However, building a strategy that avoids making foreseeable financial, management, tactical or strategic errors, helps the investor to feel confident in you and that you will deliver the project as planned and therefore the projected revenues are likely to happen. If an investor or studio or distributor is interested in the project, they will expect it to come out as they envisaged it, which is why the finance and business plan must state exactly what is being offered.

The finance section of the business plan contains the sales projections and income statements for the time frame within which your business plan is being formulated. The main thing to do is to list the crucial elements of the forecast. These are likely to be:

The Capital You Need

This will be the overall total for all the films you intend to make, including the costs of development, production and post-production. Also included will be the costs of running your company. You will need to keep these to a minimum until the revenues start to flow, but they should be included since you will need to eat and live while you are attempting to get your projects off the ground. Remember, planning plays a crucial role in the success of a business enterprise, and financial planning is a vital part of it.

You will need to make a business and marketing plan for each of the films you want to make, and each of these plans will include an element of costs related to the overall running of your company. It may be that you want to include these costs, sometime called **on costs**, as part of your producer's fee for each of the films. But whatever method you choose to use, it should include these costs. They are easily forgotten.

Where The Revenues Will Come From

This is often of most interest to the investors. After all, you can have a less than perfect business plan, be rather poor at management, but as long as the revenues are flowing into the company, money can be spent fixing the other things.

The investors will look very closely at this part of the plan to see if you have made sound judgements as to the likely source and amount of these revenues. Do be open to critical analysis of these figures. Too often new producers and filmmakers talk up revenue figures, and base projections on unsound, or unsubstantiated, predictions. Investors and studios appreciate sound business acumen, and this usually comes in the form of being conservative when projecting revenue streams.

Who Gets What

As said before, the finance plan, in fact the business plan itself, is basically about how the money is raised and how it is distributed. You need to make sure that all the investors are aware of how the revenue streams are distributed amongst the various parties. This is especially true regarding the distributor's and exhibitor's fees. The amount taken by both is often a shock to new investors in the film industry. You will need to research and be very clear about how the revenues from the film are distributed, such as in the US the distributor takes less then in the UK.

The Time Frame

You need to explain carefully the time frame in which films are developed and produced. You have a thousand and one other things to worry about as the producer or filmmaker without the investors demanding to know why things are not happening. Make it clear to the investors that it is a creative process and that things do go wrong and that schedules are only a guideline.

You should also explain, written into the plan, when you expect the revenues to come on stream. Explain that these revenue streams vary from film to film and there is no set pattern. Get examples from other films of a similar nature to yours. Also, show that it is a rolling programme over a number of years in terms of ancillary income from TV, Cable and so on.

Ridley Scott's **Blade Runner** was released in 1982 and was a critical and financial flop. It cost $28m (£16m). However, ten years later in 1992, a director's cut version was released and became a hit both financially and with the critics.

The Costs

Explain to investors new to the film industry that the budget for each film usually only covers the actual cost of shooting the film, and the post production phase. Once the film is at the point when it can be shown in a cinema, in whatever format, the distributor comes into the picture. OK, but not literally, just in terms of meeting the costs of the prints to screen the film, and the costs of advertising and promoting the film.

The Basis Used For Revenue Projection

You will need to show that the films used in the tables to show revenues from similar films, are a fair basis for projection. Also, that any one of the films on your slate has the potential to be a breakout film and generate immense profits. Indeed, if you have created a viable slate, you may be able to show that one of the strengths of all your films is that they have this potential.

Conservative Estimates

Always try to deliberately set the costs of making the films on the high side, while keeping revenue expectations low. This is good financial management on your part, and will impress the studio or investor. If you manage the process well and bring the film in under budget, the likelihood of being in profit is even greater. However, it is never a good idea to cut costs during the shooting stage unless absolutely necessary and cuts will not harm the look of the finished film. Remember, it is very costly, and often impossible, to go back a re-shoot once the film is in the post-production stage.

Distribution Fees

As previously discussed, in the US this is usually based on 35% of the distributor's gross revenue, whereas in the UK it is much higher. There is no typical deal, so all deals are based on negotiation and it often depends on your standing within the filmmaking community. So, if you are a new producer you may struggle to get a good deal, but then you are building your career so obtaining any distribution deal is likely to be a bonus.

Protecting Crucial Interests

Make it clear to the investors that you will husband all the resources carefully, and that you will not enter in to any deals, whether pre-sales, negative pick-up or ancillary rights, unless they are in the interests of the investors.

Financial Management

Again, reassure the investors that their money will be well looked after according to prudent financial practice, and that all funds will be deposited in an interest bearing account and only drawn upon when needed. Also, remember to speak about the **ESCROW** account, (see glossary) which ensures that no monies will be spent until all the funding is in place and the projects can go ahead. It is often the case, to protect all the investors, that you will be asked to set up an escrow account. After all, if you are looking for £10m and one investor puts in £2 m and then you are unable to raise the rest, but you have been dipping into the £2m to fund development an other costs, the original investor will be never be able to get his/her money back because the film will not be made.

Net Producer/Investor Income

The income going direct to the investor and the producer is usually termed net. This is because all the other expenses have to be paid first. Make sure that the investors realise that this is the projected profit after the exhibitor's and distributor's expenses and fees have all been deducted. The net income to the investor and producer will depend very much on what kind of deal you have been able to put in place. If the money, due to the producer and investor, looks like it will take a long time in being realised, make sure the investor is aware of this. Remember, you are building a career and you want to be able to return to your investors for projects in the future.

Cashflow

Time Frame. Usually a film will take from eighteen months to three years, from pre-production through to post production and the creation of a master print.

You must make it clear that the release date of the film cannot be precisely predicted since it will depend on the distribution deal and the release strategy, which might be slow or fast. However, you can state that you anticipate that the release date will be within six months of the completion of the film.

Revenues. Again, you can state that with most films the majority of the revenues will come back to the producers within two years from the date of the release of the film. However, bear in mind that some of the ancillary revenues, TV, Cable etc, are likely to take longer and will depend on the film becoming known.

The cumulative totals. Explain that you will not be paying out money as it comes in, but rather as staged payments, since distributors usually make payment to producers once every six months or a year.

Completion Bonds

Explain that you will try to secure one. (See glossary)

Risks

Do make sure that you apprise the investors of the fact that the film business is a highly speculative one, so that, just as the rewards can be higher than other investments, it also contains risks not encountered in other enterprises. You can cite that even the Hollywood majors cannot assure the success of any film.

Make it clear that like all products, films depend for their revenues on finding a market that wants to buy what they are offering. First, a distributor must be found and then the film must be skilfully targeted and promoted to the right audience. The risk of failure therefore lies not just in the film itself, which might be really good and have real potential, but is let down by the distributor or the fact that there is too much competition when the film is released. It may be a good idea to hold the film back until a suitable release window becomes available. This may not sit well with some investors who are looking for a quick return.

To avoid problems in the future, when you are assembling the package, make sure that all the investors and interested parties are aware of not only the potential gains, but the risks as well. Do not be afraid to do this, since it will show that you have your feet on the ground and that you are a serious player with long-term goals.

Financial forecasts are just that, and like the weather forecast, can change at short notice.

Cashflow Forecasting

What holds the whole plan together is a positive cashflow. In other words, money flowing into the company in greater quantities than is flowing out.

All business plans, not just for films, are based on this premise. Nobody is going to put forward a business plan that shows the investors will eventually lose money. However, forecasting is an art, not a science, and therefore it is not precise. It is somewhere between a guess and an estimate, and so the word guesstimate is often used. This is because you can reasonably ascertain the costs of your film, but you cannot know what revenues it will generate, no matter how big you are in the film industry. Hollywood is just as capable of creating turkeys as the small independent film company. The problem is that when Hollywood creates a turkey, it is so big that when it crashes, it often crushes its creators, especially the studio executives, underneath it.

Some say that part of the buzz of investing in films is likened to gambling in that you can win the jackpot or lose your shirt.

Make sure your investors know this. But, the better informed the forecaster, the truer the prediction will be.

One of the most important things about creating a business plan, is that it will help to highlight any obvious mistakes. Is there a market for the film? What size is the market and is it big enough for us to recoup our investment? A good plan makes you ask the right questions, and so, used intelligently, stops you making ill-informed mistakes. It cannot guarantee success, but it can help you spot obvious failure. Also, it helps stage and guide the decision making and so allow you to make informed choices at various stages of the filmmaking process.

Estimating

If you have a budget of £1.5m, then using films from £500k to £3m is OK, and will give you a much wider selection of films to use as comparisons. Also, the production values in films between £500 and £3m are likely to be the same, and so comparison is valid. However, by careful planning and creating a well-structured business model you can show that your film for the same price will have greater production values.

It is only when you go over the £5m mark that you are looking at elements you cannot match in terms of production values, costs of prints and advertising and promotion, and quality of cast and other talent.

What To Put In The Plan

In order to inform those whom you are asking to invest in your film, you will need to show the "position" your film will occupy in the market place in comparison with other films. There is no database that includes all the films ever made, so you cannot have a truly "fair" comparison. Also, there is plenty of debate about what constitutes each genre and so what should be compared to what. In the end, what you put in is up to you, but be careful and try to compare like with like. Also try to put in a fair spread of films, not just the successful ones. If you just put in films like, **Four Weddings, Fargo, Blair Witch Project, The Full Monty,** then you are cherry picking and this may raise expectations that cannot be met.

Investors will carefully evaluate your business plan and the data you use. If they think you are trying to pull a fast one you will not only not get any investment money for your current project, but you may also damage any future relationship. Remember, your investor or studio may not want to take up your current offer because the script is not suitable for their slate, or because they are already have a film in development similar to your one, but they may be impressed with the way you bundle the package and so leave the door open for future projects.

Zero Accounting

Zero accounting was developed during the 1960s by the US government to try to control the costs of defence spending. The US government would place a contract for an item of defence equipment to be developed, such as a surface to air missile, and then find that there was considerable overspend on the original price they were quoted. The defence companies would rationalise the overspend by saying that the exact amount of monies spent researching and developing complex items such as new rockets could not be forecast in advance. The US government countered that the problem was money being spent on research and development that was not crucial to the project. Hence, the US government decide to impose a zero accounting methodology that is premised on the notion that there is no money for any of the activities to be undertaken unless they are shown to be crucial to the development and creation of the project. This is the opposite of ascribing set amounts of money to budget heads. This does not mean that there is no budget, but rather that no monies are allocated for items until they fulfil essential criteria.

If we transfer the notion of zero accounting to filmmaking then expenditure is on a need to spend basis rather than on the traditional method of setting each department, such as wardrobe or locations, a fixed budget. If using the filmmaking model shown in this book then money should only be spent on what is needed to achieve the key elements as identified by the Marketing Potential Score. (See Chapter 6 on marketing)

Of course, if it is a Hollywood blockbuster and money is no object in order to achieve the desired effect, there is less need to ensure that all money is spent efficiently. However, the average spend on a Hollywood big budget film is often upwards of $200m and a low budget US film $15m. If you compare this with the average spend on a UK film of $5m, you realise that if Europe and independent filmmakers are to achieve high filmic standards for their movies they need to husband their resources in the most efficient manner. The objective is to make films for £700k or £2.2m that look like £5m or £10 films. This can be done, but it needs careful planning, sound management techniques and good financing strategies.

Methodology For Zero Accounting

Each aspect of the film is analysed and given a weighting in accordance with the importance of its role in achieving the full potential of the script and attaining the highest Marketing Potential Score. You, as the producer or filmmaker, will need to do the necessary research in terms of genre and market needs in order to ascertain the value of each aspect of the proposed film. You will then apply the MPS matrix and see which aspects have the highest score. These then become the key elements of the film and this is where the expenditure needs to be focused.

These may be four key areas such as:

Locations: Two key locations that are part of the major plot points.

Special Effects: A special effects sequence that is essential for telling the story and adding filmic values.

Sex: Sex scenes that are not prurient but are necessary to show adult themes in a new and more complex way.

Talent: Having this particular actor will ensure box office success in certain territories.

You may then need to decide that within these four key elements some are more important than others. Once this is done, you analyse the needs of each of these areas with a detailed time frame for each, and detailed analysis of the resources needed to achieve the required result. Each unit of costing is judged in relation to what it can contribute to the end result. For example, if the landscape is a metaphor for what is happening within the story, as in **Dancing With Wolves**, detailed planning is required to ensure that enough footage is shot so that that the full potential of the metaphor is achieved. If because of poor planning this does not happen, it is possible the film will fail as a movie. The editor can make reasonable footage into a better film, but if the footage is not there because it has not been shot in the first place, it cannot be created in the editing suite. The opposite is also true, and large amounts of irrelevant footage end up on the cutting room floor; or, worse, end up in the final cut of the film because there is nothing else to fill the gaps. This is when zero accounting based on the marketing potential matrix can be vitally important in ensuring that all resources, including what is scheduled to be shot, are used to their full potential and not wasted.

Model Budgets

This model was used to create a 90 minute film shot on Super16 and then blown up to 35m. A detailed breakdown of this follows by way of illustration. The shoot took place over eight weeks in the UK in London in 2003/4. The crew were divided into three main bands and each person knew what band they were in and so were aware what others in the band also received. Each person was shown the remuneration scheme before they were offered a contract.

The total is shown as:		
Above and below the line:	**£688,651**	**($1.21m)**
Blow-up:	**£27,000**	**($47,000)**
Sound mix:	**£4,880**	**($8,588)**
Total:	**£720,531**	**($1.26m)**

However, in actual fact a large section of the actors' and crew fees were deferred in exchange for points in the film and special deals were done on equipment hire and editing facilities. This meant the actual cost was a great deal less. So, it can be done, but the crew and actors have to believe in what you are doing and feel they are being treated fairly.

Above The Line

Story & Script	£30,000
Director	£43,000
Producer	£64,000
Co. Producer	£30,000
Principals	£60,000

Sub: £227,000-00

Non-Principals and Extras:

41 X £64-50	£2,644-50
13 X £100	£1,300-00
1 X £20	£20-00
4 @ £20 per day	£200-00
2 X £86	£172-00

Sub: £4,336-50

Below The Line

Model Crew Structure and Remuneration

The crew were divided into three main bands. Each person knew what band they were in and so knew what others in the band also received. What was vital is that everybody was shown the scheme before they were offered a contract. Since all the money was spent in the UK, and rates will vary in other countries, the amounts shown are in UK pounds.

Crew A	Remuneration
Production Co-ord:	£15k 1 Gp.
DOP:	£15k 1 Gp.
1st AD:	£15k 1 Gp.
Make-up:	£15k 1 Gp.
Wardrobe:	£15k 1 Gp.
Production Designer	£15k 1 Gp.
Sound:	£15k 1 Gp.
Editor:	£15k 1 Gp.
Choreographer:	£5k ½ Gp
Music:	£5k 3 GP

Crew B   Remuneration

Gaffer: £10k ½ Gp.
Continuity: £5k ½ Gp.
Focus puller: £5k ½ Gp.
Locations Manager: £5k ½ Gp.
Choreographer Ass.:   £5k ½ Gp.

Crew C   Remuneration
To receive, on a pro-rata basis, a share of 2% of net profits.

Clapper Loader: £3k
Boom Op: £3k
2nd AD: £3k
Costume Assistant 1:   £3k
Hair/Make-up Assistant 1:   £3k
Office Manager: £3k
Set Design Ass. 1:   £3k

Runners

To receive food and travelling expenses.

3rd AD
Costume Assistant 2
Hair/Make-up Assistant 2
Office Assistant
Set Design

Studio premises and Locations

Studio Base

There was one main building used as a location for interior shots, and also as a base for the production offices and storage of equipment. It also had a canteen facility.

Locations

Seven interior locations.
Five exterior locations.

Sub: £132,000

Lighting

	PER DAY	
2x 2.5 Flicker Free HMI 3 weeks		
4 x 1.2Kw FLICKER FREE H.M.I.	£160	£4,800
4 x 2Kw Tungsten Fresnel	£40	£1200
6 x 1Kw Tungsten Fresnel	£48	£1440
4 x 650W Tungsten Fresnel	£26	£780
4 x 300W Tungsten Fresnel	£24	£720
4 x Blondes	£56	£1680
4 x Redheads	£32	£960
Stands and distribution for 13A	£18	£540
4 x Polecats	£16	£480
Smoke machine + refill	£15	£450
1 Super windup Stand	£15	£450
2 Single wind up	£10	£300
4 x Master stands	£10	£300
3 x Backlight Stands	£4.50	£135
6 x Y cord splitters	£12	£360
12 x 13a Cables	£48	£1,440
2 x .2 BAC Cables	£9	£270
2 x .2 BAC Cables	£7	£210
2 x Tails Cables	£6	£180

Flag arms & Assorted flags	£8	£240
Yashmaks	£12	£360
Finger and Dot Kit	£12	£360
MSR sungun, Batteries and charger	£35	£1,050
Tungsten sungun, Batteries and charger	£20	£600
2x 2.5Kw H.M.I.Stands	£30	£900
1 Lastolite	£4	£120
1 Circular Lastolite	£3	£90
10 Gaffer Clamps	£10	£300
6 X Turtles	£12	£360
8 x 4 Poly Reflector	£12	£360
Reflector Circular	£3	£90
Arri boom arm	£8	£240
Medium / Large Boom arm	£12	£360

SUB:£22,125

Camera and equipment

Camera

Super 16 SR3 Camera	Per week £1,280	£6,400
Video Tap B/W	Per week £585	£2,925
9' B/W monitor	Daily £52	£1,560
O'Connor Head	Daily £120	£3,600
Ronford Tall legs	Daily £21	£630
Ronford Short legs	Daily £21	£630
Hi Hat	Daily £18	£540

Sub: £16,285

Lens

*9.5 mm, 1.3		
*12mm		
*16mm		
*25mm	*Set Per week £460	£2,300
32mm	Per week £260	£1,300
50mm	Per week £260	£1,300

85mm	Per week £260	£1,300
50mm Macro	Per week £240	£1,200
8-64 Zoom	Per week £340	£1,700
4" Matte Box	Per week £168	£840
Lightweight Matte Box	Per week £140	£700
FF3 Follow Focus	Per week £200	£1,000
FF4 Folow Focus	Per week £160	£800
4 x Batteries	Per week £52	£260
Charger	Per week £52	£260

Sub £12,960

Filters

85B / ND & 81EF / ND set	Daily £22	£660
Blue Grad set	Daily £92	£2,760
Polariser	Daily 19	£570
Sepia Set	Daily £82	£2,460
Optical Flat	Daily £18	£540
1/8 and ¼ Black Pro Mist	Daily £30	£900
1/8 and ¼ Warm Pro Mist	Daily £30	£900
ND Clear Centre Spot Set	Daily £35	£1,050
4 point star	Daily £22	£660

Sub £10,500

Grip

| Chapman Peewee Dolly (3 weeks) | Daily £175 | £3,675 |
| Soft Wheels | Daily £35 | £1,050 |

Offsets

Set: World cup etc.	Daily £66	£1,980
6x lengths of track	Daily £30	£900
Curves (360 degree)	Daily £29	£870

Sub: 8,475

Editing:
During shoot: Mobile edit suite set: **£4k**

Post shoot: 14 weeks in edit suite @ £5k per week   £70,000

Sub: £74,000

TOTAL:

Above and below the line:	*£688,651*	*($1.21m)*
Blow-up(to 35m):	*£27,000*	*($47,000)*
Sound mix:	*£4,880*	*($8,588)*

Total: **£720,531   ($1.26m)**

Budget for UK film of £2.6m ($4.57)

Budget Summary	Main Budget
Story/Script/Development	77,250.00
Producer/Director	205,625.00
Princpal Cast	314,220.00
Salaries – Production Dept.	161,200.00
Salaries – Ads/Continuity	65,700.00
Salaries – Camera Dept.	82,500.00
Salaries – Sound Dept.	23,040.00
Salaries – Lighting Dept.	53,460.00
Salaries – Art Dept.	236,000.00
Salaries – Wardrobe/Make-up Dept.	111,090.00
Salaries – Editing Department	44,800.00
Salaries – Second Unit	25,600.00
Salaries – Related Overheads	92,366.28
Materials – Art Department	119,400.00
Material – Wardrobe/Makeup	26,650.00

Production – Equipment	176,250.00
Facilities – Package	24,250.00
Studios/Outside broadcast	60,000.00
Locations/ Production Facilities	125,700.00
Film/Tape Stock	53,041.00
Picture/Sound Post Prod. – Film	54,232.00
Picture/Sound Post Prod. – Video	48,850.00
Archive Material	64,430.00
Rostrum/Graphics	120,750.00
Music (Copyright/Performance)	3,500.00
Travel/Transport	85,465.00
Hotel/Living allowances/Catering	66,295.00
Other production Costs	18,800.00
Insurance/Financial/Legal	14,950.00
Production Overheads	34,575.00
Production Insurance/Audit Fees	23,810.00
Total	**2,613,799**

Summing-up

All budgets will be different and will depend on the amount of money available and the artistic vision of the director in terms of how it should be spent to achieve the full potential of the script. However, the guiding principles should be that each financial outlay needs to be measured against its potential to realise the maximum Marketing Potential Score.

Business Model Data File

Have you analysed each budget heading, in terms of zero accounting, and have identified and costed those elements that must be in the film if it is to be commercially and artistically viable?

Have you created a cashflow for forecasting which monies are to be spent and when?

Have you arrived at a formula for distributing any profits that might accrue?

Have you started to develop a time frame within which the monies will be needed?

Do you have examples of how recent films, that are similar to yours, were financially packaged?

Have you decided what to put in the financial plan?

Chapter 9

Film Financing Strategies

"The Art of making films is the Art of getting money to make them". **Jean-Luc Godard**

In this chapter we will look at:

Defining the value of a film.

Deciding what is the best financial deal for you.

Selling the rights to various territories.

Estimating the value of non-financial considerations.

A business model for a film project.

Examples of financial packages recently used to make UK films.

Introduction

The main thing that investors are really looking for from producers or filmmakers, is that if they give them the money, the film will actually be made, on time, on budget and with the cinematic values that were promised. In other words, exactly like, or better than, what was envisaged in the original agreement when they decided to give you the means and resources to make the film. Why should anyone lend money to somebody who has never made a film before? And the irony is

that often these first-time producers or directors are asking for millions. It's a real dilemma, since you can't make a film until someone gives you the money, and nobody wants to give money to someone who hasn't a track record in filmmaking. Therefore, your main task is to create enough confidence in investors, so that they believe that if they give you the money you are requesting, you will deliver as promised.

Investors are usually canny people who have made other business deals and so they will look closely at the people who will be running the company and managing the filmmaking process. This is where a business plan is vitally important, along with a clear business model.

In this section we will look at the main methods for financing a film. Of course no two films are ever financed in the same way, and it is up to the producer to decide which is the best format for making the film a reality, and getting it distributed.

As far as the financiers and backers are concerned, this is the most important part of the plan. It is basically a finance and recoupment strategy. How will the finance be raised, how will the profits be distributed? The producer or studio executive does not have to be fully conversant with all the details; in fact it is highly unlikely that any individual could have a firm grasp of all the aspects of the finance plan, since it often involves tax accounting principles that the average accountant would struggle with. However, the producer needs a clear vision of what would be the most beneficial, and cost effective, way in which the film is likely to be financed, and the method for distributing the profits that will keep all the interested parties happy. Attempting to raise finance for a film is not for those easily put off or intimidated – just as, those investing in a film should not look for a safe investment. There are a thousand different ways to raise finance for a film, and none of them is considered easy. As they say, if it were easy then everybody would be doing it.

The Value Of A Film

Even when the film is finished, how much is it worth? The answer is that it is simply worth what somebody is willing to pay for it. You should never, when negotiating with a sales agent or a distributor, base the value of the film on what it cost to make. **Four Weddings And A Funeral** cost £2.2m to make, but has made many times that figure in world-wide sales. So, the value of a film is what you estimate the market will pay for it, and this will be based on the revenue it is likely to generate. That is why distributors and studios use revenue projections based on the past performance of similar films. But of course, this can never identify the new breakout, or crossover movie, that will have been made for relatively little and will garner massive box office takings. This unpredictability is what makes filmmaking so frustrating, and at the same time so fascinating.

Investors

Investors usually look at the Executive Summary first, and then, if they see what they like, they will turn to the financial section. If they find nothing wrong there, they will then read the rest of the plan. Remember, these are business people and are looking to make a deal that benefits them and possibly their organisation. They may be, to some extent, interested in the artistic merit of your film proposal, but they are more concerned about not seeing their investment disappear. Also, if they work for a production company, distributor, finance house or film studio, they want to keep their jobs, and picking the wrong films to invest in will soon cost them their jobs. So your job is to create enough confidence in those who can make your project happen, for them to say yes.

Finding The Best Deal For You

You need to think long and hard about what kind of overall package you really want. This is why you should spend between twelve and eighteen months fully focused on developing the project. It bears repeating that no film ever suffered from spending too much time in development. You need to decide how much artistic and creative control you want to maintain over the film.

Single Investor Or Studio

If artistic control is very important to you, and you are a new filmmaker or producer, you may not want to go to a single investor or a studio. These people usually want full control and you can understand why. If it is a studio they may reason, quite legitimately, that they have more experience than you and know how to market and promote the film once it is made. With this in mind, as we saw with distributors who invest in films, the studio, or single investor, may wish to have a big say in the film's content. Certainly, the studios will want to have the final say on how the film is edited, and once it has been screened before a test audience, they may wish to re-shoot certain sections of the film. So, be prepared; studios or single investors are likely to appoint their own producers who will have the final say on everything – including the ability to fire the director and what the final cut looks like.

Multiple Investors

On the other hand, having lots of investors may mean you can keep control by playing one off against the other, but it might also mean lots of intermediaries who all want fees and commissions for arranging the deals. Some investors may demand that their wife or husband plays the lead. See **Mulholland Drive**. Also, to protect their investments, some of the investors may demand that they are paid before anybody else. If more than one wants to be paid first, you have to do some skilful negotiation with all the parties. Most investors will want to be apprised of all the terms and conditions appertaining to the other investors. This is reasonable and prudent on their part since they want to make sure that they are being treated fairly and equitably in relation to the other investors. This can cause problems when GAP financing is being negotiated.

GAP Finance Or Finishing Funds

GAP finance is often sought at the end of filmmaking in order to finish the film, or complete the post-production phase. GAP finance is what it says: it fills a gap in the finances. However, companies who specialise in these finishing funds, or completion funds as they are sometimes known, almost invariably want to be last in and first out. That is, they only put their money in when everybody else has committed theirs, and then when any money is made they want to be paid first. Or, they want to be paid back within a set time-frame. Needless to say, this can cause problems with the initial investors since they may have provided the bulk of the money for the film, and lost interest on it while it was being used for making the film, and now they are being relegated to an inferior position when the money is going to be recouped. It has been know that some investors feel so strongly about the terms asked for by GAP providers, that they are willing to see the film not get finished rather than allow what they feel are inequitable arrangements to prevail.

Keep The Faith

But do not be disheartened; there are a lot of people out there who would like to invest in films. What they need is for you to provide them with a film project that has been well thought through, follows the rules and practices of good business management and has a potential market. The more you research and develop your skills and contacts, the more experienced you will become and so be ready to take advantage of the opportunities when they arise. Remember, luck is 90% preparation and 10% opportunity. So, if you are well prepared, because you have developed your ideas, script and business plan, when the opportunity arises you can take advantage of it. The market for films is constantly changing and in a state of flux; if this weren't so, then everybody would be making the right film at the right time. This clearly is not happening, not even in the US with the studio system. Executives in the studio system come and go all the time because they are only as good as their first big mistake, either backing a no-hoper or passing on the next big breakout movie. It's true that nobody knows anything, but being well prepared means you stand a much greater chance than other newcomers to seeing your film project come to life.

Some films are hawked around for years, such as **Rambo** and **Forrest Gump**, and then, when the time is right, the film gets made. So, have faith, but also be realistic and when one of your film projects is clearly no longer viable, put it into storage and concentrate on other projects.

Be Careful What You Promise Investors

In her book, **Filmmakers & Financing**, Louise Levison cautions filmmakers to be very circumspect about what they promise investors, what investors promise them and what financial schemes to use. If you say **"we will seek presales in order to offset some of the production costs"**, this is a statement that means you will attempt to get some money before shooting starts. It is not a declaration of what will actually happen. But if you say **"we will obtain presales, or a distribution agreement, in order to meet some of the filmmaking costs"**, then you are stating that this is what you will do. In that case, the investors will expect you to do just that; and, being business people, they may well hold you to account if you fail to obtain any pre-sales or a distribution agreement.

Also, when informing the investors as to what the film can expect to be sold for, be careful what sums you quote. There are tables that state what prices have been paid for independent US, UK and

European films, but, as said before, a film is worth what someone is willing to pay for it.

Sometimes investors, if they are not familiar with the film industry, assume that profit margins will be the same as other industries and so they may expect profits to be in the region of twice what the film cost to make, assuming a 100% mark-up to be the norm. Make sure that investors are made aware that there is no set profit margin for a film. That a film is only worth what a distributor is willing to pay for it. It has been known that investors have refused to accept a distribution agreement because they thought the price was too low. Again, if you can keep full control of the process right from the beginning, then you are free to do whatever deal you wish. Therefore, the aim should be to construct the financial package in a way that suits you best.

Be Careful What Investors Promise You

You will find there are a lot of people who are specialists in Bovine Excrement. Often, people don't mean to be, they just like the sound of their own voice and appearing to be a player. Film festivals are full of these people. Or it might be that they genuinely think they can help you, but when push comes to shove they find they have overreached themselves. If as many cheques were "in the post" as people say, then the postal service would grind to a halt. Remember, you don't have the money until the cash is in the production account. Also, unless it is your lawyer who has drawn up the agreement, you should check the small-print carefully. All investors want the best deal they can get, and this doesn't always tie in with what is best for you or the film.

Know What You Are Saying

Be careful that you do not use financial, or business, concepts or terms that you do not fully understand. Also, do not state that you will be using financing schemes, especially international ones, that are not well understood and used by the filmmaking community. If you do, and it is shown that either you don't understand the financial constructs you are using, or the schemes are not clearly viable, then you will look at best amateur and at worst a con-merchant.

Investors often invest in people more than projects, and they seek reassurance that the person whom they are investing in knows what they are doing. They don't like to take chances with their hard-earned money, and are much more likely to come on board if the methods you are using have a proven track record. That is why the marketing aspect is so important in proving there is an audience for the finished film, and there is a distribution strategy in place.

There are some people who say that they can find you the money for the film, but you will need to pay them a fee up-front. Do not do this. If they are good at their job they will be willing to accept a finder's fee, which will be a percentage of what they bring in. If it is a good project, that is a hot script with the right talent attached, then an experienced intermediary who has the right contacts will accept a finder's fee.

Giving Away Equity

When people invest in your film project, they will expect to take a portion of your film. It may be that the investors, between them, have all the equity in your film and you, the producer, receive only a fee. This is very common in independent productions, especially if the producer is not well established. You must learn to see things from the point of view of the investors who are putting in all the money. They are the ones taking the risks, and so they want the ownership. He who pays the piper...

Friends And Family

If you do decide to approach friends and family, be careful. You need to think about what the consequences would be if you lost all the money that your family and friends invested in your enterprise. Of course, if you don't like your friends and don't get on with your relatives, then OK. But if you would like to continue to look them in the eye, then you need to make sure that they fully understand the risks involved in investing in filmmaking. Remember, most films lose money and so, along with your film being a financial disaster, you lose your friends and relatives as well.

Film folklore has it that Ed Burns raised the money for **The Brothers McMullen** with credit cards. Also, Kevin Smith funded the $26,575 (£15,056) budget for **Clerks** with credit card advances, the sale of his comic book collection and a loan from his mum and dad. These films were successful, but that is incredibly rare. Be realistic and honest, especially with those close to you.

Angels

These are the people who invest in projects because they like the subject matter rather than the chances of the investment making money for them. They do this for all sorts of reasons. It may be they want to be associated with the glamour of the movie business; because they believe in the story and feel it needs to be told; they want to be associated with art. However, be careful about changing your film to suit private investors who may want to send a message to the world. Your first aim is to entertain. If you want to send a message, use email and a website.

The Financial Deal

The Split

As a model, you should aim for a 50/50 split between yourself as the filmmaker or producer and those investing in the project. This is the norm in the US, but not in the UK. In fact, the Relph Report cited this lack of funds going back to the producer as one of the reasons the UK film industry doesn't have a strong base. So, if you can, try to offer the equity investors 50% of the producer's share in the film. Do your best not to give away any more than 50%. After all, your aim is to build a company and create a capital base from which you can finance future films. If you are a first-time producer, this can be hard to achieve. However, you want to see the film made and so you may be willing to accept any deal that allows this to happen.

If you have a strong and well thought out business plan and model, and it is a hot script with the right talent, then you are in a strong negotiating position. If they are seasoned investors, they will know that they can make returns on their investments undreamed of outside the gambling casinos.

90/10

The distributor and the investors have to be paid first for their investment: that is, the actual costs of producing and distributing the film. It is usual in the US, and so try to get it written into your deal, that as the money is coming in, the distributor and the investors will get 90% and the producer 10%. Then, if you have negotiated well, when the costs have been met, the producer gets 50% of the net profit.

This is the format to aim for, but each deal is different and some distributors and investors will demand 100% of the incoming revenue until their initial outlays have been met. In fact, they may also demand interest on the money they have invested.

Low Budget Big Return

Sometimes, the lure for the investor is that they will make a big killing on a small investment. This can sometimes mean the potential of 500 to 1,000 percent return on an investment. Of course, such investments also carry a high risk and this must be explained to the investors. However, if you have done your homework and created a good business model, you can show potential investors that here is a good chance they will get a good return on their money, and they may possibly hit the jackpot.

Never promise a risk-free investment. No such thing exists, no matter how much your friends and family tell you your are a genius and the script is the best they have ever read. Remember, as in all viable businesses plans, it is what is on the bottom line that convinces investors.

Points

Lots of filmmakers, including myself, give away **points** in the film. Of course, this has to be agreed with the investors if it is to come out of the initial inflow of revenues. Points are a form of equity in that if a director or actor has one point in the gross take of the film, then for each hundred pounds that come in, they get one pound. Of course this kind of deal is usually only given to A list talent who have the box-office power to negotiate points from the gross take of the film. What is usual is that the points the producer offers to the talent or crew, come from the producer's net share.

If you have managed to negotiate a good deal that means you get 50% of the gross once the cost of the film has been met, these points can come out of the producer's 50%. This is a much more attractive proposition to talent and crew and if you can offer this then maybe you can attract box office power and so make the film more viable.

Non-Financial Considerations

Credits

Be careful who you promise credits to and keep a note of to whom you have offered, and exactly what you have offered. Remember, people are likely to invest in your film for all sorts of reasons, and often it is the kudos of being at parties and being able to say they produced such-and-such film. That means, they want the credit of Executive Producer. Executive Producers are usually the ones who put the money and resources in, so that the film can be made – producers are usually the ones with the ideas for the film who develop the script and find the talent and the investors. More of a creative role, but, remember, this can be taken away from them if there are major investors such as studios.

So, it is always wise to give away the executive producer's tag as a last resort; reserve this credit for those who will not part with their money without it.

Presales

Presales are agreements between the producer and distributors in various territories. The producer agrees to give distribution rights to the distributor in exchange for an up-front fee. These agreements are signed before the film is made, and can often be a major source of funding for the film. Also, obtaining pre-sale agreements gives confidence to other investors that the film will be distributed and is therefore likely to recoup the investment. Pictures at the lowest end of the production scale will be expected to recoup their costs mostly from their home territory. This especially applies to independent films.

Money from pre-sales can be not only the theatrical rights, but also the ancillary rights such as video, satellite and broadcast. When projecting the likely income from presales you can calculate it as a percentage of the total budget. Ballpark figures for the presales to the main territories are as follows:

As a % of total budget

- US – 40%

- UK – 10%

- Germany & Austria – 10%

- Japan – 10% to 12%

- Italy – 8%

- France – 6%

- Spain – 4%

- Australasia – 2% to 3%

Also, there are charts that give you the minimum and maximum revenues you can expect from different territories for a low budget UK or European film.

Finding The Right Figures

Each deal is different, and these figures are based on historical revenues. However, distributors are notoriously reluctant to publicise all the revenues from their films, so fully accurate figures are hard to come by. The pre-sale is a commitment from the distributor, or other form of buyer, from each territory to buy the film from you once it is completed. Once this deal is signed, you can take it to a bank which specialises in such deals, such as Barclays in Soho Square, and they can lend you money to make the film. However, the bank must believe that the distributors, or those who have signed the deal, will actually pay once the film is made. Then, as well as wanting you to return the money they have lent you to make the film, they charge interest on the amount they lend.

Selling Territories

The distributors who buy the rights to the individual film, keep all the revenues that the film generates within their territory. Of course an individual distributor may have the distribution rights to more than one territory. The distributor is usually given the territory rights for between 5 and 15 years, with seven being customary. But new filmmakers are often forced into giving more, such as 25 years. It depends on your powers of negotiation and how badly the distributor wants the film.

You may wish to vary the deal for different territories, so you may give the film for a particular length of time, or you may be able to put a revenue cap on the deal. Revenue capped deals are structured so that when, say, the film makes $300,000 (£170,454) in the Japanese market, the revenues to the Japanese distributor stop and revert to you. You may wish, at this point, to renegotiate a new agreement that gives you a percentage of the revenue.

US Rights

The main territory you are seeking to sell, is the US rights. If you can secure this in the form of a presale, then you will have no trouble raising the rest of the money to make the film. The distribution rights for the US, usually represent 40% of the total cost of making the film. Once you have pre-sold the US rights, raising the rest of the money is usually very easy because it means you have a distribution deal in the world's largest market and therefore the film stands a good chance of recouping

Advances From Ancillary Rights

Sometimes you may be able to get an advance from a cable TV company, or DVD/Video distributor, in a certain territory. If it is a low budget film, this could be a large amount of the money you need. However, be careful; this divides the rights within individual territories, which can be a handicap once the film is made. Most likely, a distributor will want all the rights to a territory. This may be because they calculate that they won't earn much from the theatrical rights and so are relying on the ancillary rights to make a profit. Most films, even the ones produced by the Hollywood majors, do not earn enough from box-office takings at the cinemas to cover the cost of making the film.

Disadvantages Of Pre-selling

One of the major disadvantages of pre-selling all the distribution rights to the film is that you may, if the film is a big hit, sacrifice future profits. If the film is a potential cross over film and was made for say £2.2m ($3.8m), and then, like **Four Weddings and A Funeral** or **The Full Monty**, goes on to generate over $200m (£113.6m) in world-wide sales, you lose all those potential earnings. The received wisdom is to sell all the territories you can, but keep the US and, if possible, your home rights such as the UK rights if it was made in the UK.

Another disadvantage is that not all pre-sale agreements are bankable. The bank has to believe that the distributor will honour the agreement, so, do a lot of research and talk to a specialist bank before you sign these agreements. It may also be the case that if you are not a well established producer the bank may not be confident that you will deliver the film according to the agreement and so will not commit money if they think you might be a risk.

So, there is a lot to think about. Each film project will be different and you will need to weigh up the pros and cons for each project.

Straight Sales

This occurs when you have completed the film and you take it to festivals or distributors and they buy the complete package from you for a fee. This is what happened to the **Blair Witch Project**. Sundance is a festival where many independent films are bought outright after they are completed. Of course it means you have to find all the money up-front to make the film in the first place, but if you can create a buzz about the film before it gets to the festival, you might be lucky enough to create a bidding war amongst distributors all wanting your film.

Co-production Deals

These deals are governed by the treaties between various countries. These deals are usually put together to take advantage of the various tax incentives and grants from participating countries. For instance, a Canadian film of which only 40% is created in the UK, is eligible for 100% tax relief on the cost of the film. Hence, lots of Canadian co-production deals take place in the UK. If the co-production deal is simply a money raising strategy, then this is not always good for the film.

Euro-Puddings

Be careful that you don't sacrifice vital elements in the film in order to make it fit the requirements of the co-production deal. Some films have been described as Euro-Puddings, because they have raised the money for the film by creating co-production deals with several countries. Each country will have its own reasons for participating and to satisfy these individual requirements can often mean trying to make the film be all things to all men, which often means the film lacks coherence and a single theme and vision. This then makes it almost impossible to market.

However, sometimes it can be the right thing for the film. A filmmaker I know wants to make a film about boy soldiers fighting in an African civil war. The producer is based in the UK and would have difficulty liaising with an African country for shooting purposes. But France has lots of deals with African countries and even has a special state financial incentive to help those wishing to film in Africa, so the filmmaker is exploring a UK – French co-production deal because this seems the best route for the film.

First decide what is right for the film and then look closely at the various requirements of each participating country. The best kind of co-production deals are those where each of the participants all want to make the same kind of film and have a clear idea what the finished film will look like. It may be that the producer and scriptwriter are British and the director and key crew are French and the film will be shot in France, Britain and Africa. If everybody is making the same film, with the same vision, then it is likely that co-production is the best way.

Negative Pickup

Negative Pickup is when the studio, or distributor, agrees to pay the cost of shooting the film, once it is completed. The studio or distributor is paying for the costs of producing the negative of the film that can then be used to market and distribute the film. Just like presales, it is an agreement that the producer can take to the bank and draw money down on. Again, this all rests on the bank's attitude towards the filmmaker and the studio. The bank has to believe that the producer will complete the film; that the distributor, or studio, will pay the costs once the negative has been delivered, which can be up to one year after the actual shooting of the film has been completed.

There are many attractions to a negative pickup deal. One is that the producer does not give away any of the company equity or lose artistic control. Another is that a negative pickup deal with a major studio or distributor means that you don't have to go round searching for a distributor.

The disadvantages can be that distributors, and sometimes majors, have financial troubles and cannot honour agreements. It has been known for distributors go out of business and so the bank then forecloses on the producer and takes control of the film. Another possible disadvantage is that you must deliver the film as promised; any change in the script, no matter how minor it may seem to you, can cause cancellation. Therefore, always keep in constant communication with the distributor or studio, and apprise them of any changes. At the same time it is a good idea to get their written agreement to the changes.

The other thing is that the finished film must meet the studio's or distributor's standards of quality. So, even if the film is shot exactly like it said it would be in the shooting script, and all the changes were signed and agreed, the distributor or studio can say the film's qualities, or values, are not up to their standards. This is rare and contestable. Recently a US major agreed a negative pickup deal with a small independent UK company and then, when the film was delivered to them, tried to say the film was not what they had initially agreed to. The filmmakers contested this and won. So, the big boys do not always have it all their own way.

The important thing is to show the documents to your bank or a lawyer and see if the agreement is equitable and reasonable. If possible, do this with all agreements, especially distribution deals, you are thinking of entering into.

Completion Guarantees

Another element of the financial package to be considered is the notion of a completion guarantee. These are basically akin to insurance policies. The guarantor's role is to provide an assurance that the film will be completed and delivered to the distributor.

Because the company providing the guarantee is the most vulnerable should things go wrong, the contract will stipulate that they have the power to take over the film at any time. This would only usually occur if for some reason the production company looked like it wasn't going to be able to complete the film as required.

The company offering the completion guarantee enters into a bond that the film will be made. However, the company will not give a bond until ALL of the funding is in place – this needs to be explained to all the investors, especially those not familiar with the financing protocol of the film industry.

The fee charged is based on the film's budget, but is flexible and very often depends on what is happening in the bond market. Given the risks involved, especially with new producers and directors, getting a completion bond for low budget film can be difficult, but not impossible. In the past few years the market for film completion bonds has been fraught with difficulty. A few years ago, two of the US's biggest bonding companies ran into trouble when high budget films failed. So it does happen. But all markets recover and at any one time there are opportunities – you must believe in yourself and your project and be prepared when the doors open.

A completion bond is something to aim to acquire, because it protects the producer and the investors financially, and makes you look professional. After all, what you are aiming to do is to build a career, and this will only happen when you make good contacts and create a reputation for sound financial management, good judgement of viable film projects and the ability to implement management strategies that will make the most of the resources available.

Accidents and bad weather do happen, as Terry Guilliam found out when filming **Don Quixote**. Do watch the film **The Road To**

La Mancha, which documents the disasters that befell the film. Watch it and learn!

Perhaps the best thing would be to tell investors that you are going to seek a completion bond.

Minimum Guarantee

These are monies the distributor gives to the sales agent in advance of the film being made. This commits the sales agent to delivering the film to the distributor. The distributor might find this attractive since once the film is made, it might have such a buzz that a bidding war starts and the distributor would have to pay a lot more for the film. The usual form is for the distributor to agree to hand over a certain amount of money once the film is completed and delivered to the distributor. The completed package the distributor will be looking for usually includes: The completed film; a trailer of the film; poster-ready artwork. The deal may also include a number of items that can be used for promoting the film to the press.

Overages

Once the film is in the cinemas, TV, video, DVD or any ancillary format and is earning money, if the amount accrued is more than the minimum amount guaranteed by the distributor to the sales agent, these are called **overages** and will be split between the sales agent and the distributor. Each deal is different.

Cross-Collateralisation

This is something to be avoided. It can take many different forms, but the basis of it is that your film becomes part of a slate of films held by the distributor or sales agent. The sales agent or distributor then offsets money earned in one territory for the film, against losses in another territory. Often, agents or distributors put losses from a completely different film against gains from your film, so that although your film makes money, you never get any because it is set against losses that had nothing to do with your film.

Development Funds

Development finance is always difficult and unless there are some key people, like stars or a well know director attached to your project, it is unlikely that any development money will be forthcoming. Various government schemes are available in the UK and Europe, and these are well worth checking out. But don't hold your breath and the amounts given are not big.

Financial Terms

When negotiating finance deals you must always look at the small print and make sure you understand what all the terms mean. There is no standard definition for all the terms such as Gross Profits, Net Profits, Adjusted Gross Profits. You may be wishing to get a gross deal and accept an "adjusted gross deal" only to find that in reality it is a "net profits deal". Do not be afraid to negotiate and of course, if you can, consult a lawyer. The following terms are pretty standard in the film industry, but take nothing for granted and check the definitions.

Box Office Receipts: This is the money collected by the exhibitor, cinema owner, from the public who go to see your film.

Film Rental: This is the agreed portion of the box office receipts paid to the distributor. In the US it is about 50% of the box office but in the UK and Europe it is often a smaller figure, sometimes as low as 25%.

Gross Receipts: This is the full amount the distributor or studio receives from all revenue streams – cinema, DVD sales and rentals etc.

Gross Participation: This is a good deal for the filmmaker or anybody else who gets this kind of deal. It is sometimes given to stars to get them to play the parts. This deal means that you are paid from the distributor's film rental receipts. It should be borne in mind that gross in this instance does not mean gross box office.

Gross After Break-Even: The filmmaker and the distributor may agree a breakeven point after which the filmmaker will participate in a share of the film rental.

Adjusted Gross Participation: This is participation in a share of the profits after certain deductions have been made. These deductions are usually apply to the costs of making the prints and promoting the film. The thing to be aware of is that if there are too many deductions allowed then the deal becomes a net profit one. This deal is also known as a **Rolling Gross Deal**.

Net Profit: Often seen in contracts as the producer's net profit. All too often this amounts to nothing. Given all the ongoing costs involved in distributing a film, very few films ever make a net profit. Also, distributors and studios pile on indirect costs such paying for part of the studio's running costs, or first class travel and accommodation to various festivals where they "promote your film".

Arbitration

It is always worthwhile including an arbitration clause in any agreement. This might not always be possible, especially if you are dealing with the major Hollywood studios who have "their way" of doing things. But if you can include an arbitration deal then this can save a lot of money if disagreements arise. Also, try to make the agreement legally binding on both parties and to include legal fees.

What To Include In Your Business Plan

Investors and studio executives are busy people and believe in clarity and brevity. Therefore, only, at the beginning of negotiations, give them essential financial information. There is no need to include all the options for finance, just those you are actively going to pursue. After that, give details, and show you understand them, of those financing strategies you are going to use. The film industry is a strange beast and so many successful business investors will have never come across some of the methods used for financing films.

Here are a few examples of how UK films have been financed

<u>Film A</u>

Budget

- £4.4m ($7.7m)

Talent

- First time director

- Well known UK cast

Pre-Deal

- Powerful UK distributor

- Viable box office cast

Financial Elements

- Public Equity   44%
  (Film Council. Regional Bodies)

- Tax equity   8%
  (EIS)

- Super Sale & Leaseback   0%
  (Including 10% equity. Last out)

- Tax Equity   22%
  (Section 48 fund. Commissioning Producer)

- Deferments   6%

Film B

Budget

- £4.2m ($7.3m)

Talent

- Well known director

- Well known UK cast

Pre-Deal

- International Sales Agent

- US distributor

Financial Elements

- Public Equity
  (Film Council) 40%

- Sale & Leaseback 10%

- UK Broadcast Pre-sale 11%

- UK Broadcast Equity 9%

- US Negative Pick-Up 30%

John Sweeney

<u>Film C</u>

Budget

- £18m ($31.68m)

Talent

- International director

- Well-known UK cast

Pre-Deal

- International Sales Agent

- US distributor

Financial Elements

• Public Equity	15%
• Tax Equity	35%
• US Negative Pick-Up	30%
• US Distribution & International Sales	20%

Film D

Budget

- £2.37m ($4.17m)

Pre-Deal

- Sales Agent

- Strong Story

- Co-production: UK – Scottish – Canada

Financial Elements

- Public Equity   19%

- Pre-sales   30%

- Sale & Leaseback   11%

- Bank Gap Finance   16%
  (To obtain GAP your project usually needs to have low equity and lots of presales)

- Co-production   24%
  German/Scotland

Film E

This is an example of many of the UK, co-finance, co-production deals that are put together. Many of these are between the UK and Canada. However, as we go to print, there are changes taking place concerning the tax break opportunities for co-production deals, so check the current legislation.

Financial Elements

- UK Tax Equity & Sale & Leaseback.   20%

- Foreign Investment   80%

Summing-up

There is no right or wrong way to finance a film. What should happen is that the financial package should reflect and enhance the aims and objectives of the company. This means that if the company aims to retain as much equity or gross participation points in the film as possible, then these are the kind of deals they should pursue. What is important is that the filmmaker does not give away all his or her rights in the film, just to get it made. Therefore, allotting sufficient time to planning and development is vital.

<u>**Financing Strategies Data File**</u>

Have you a clear idea of the market value for your film?

Have you a worked out the best financial deal for you?

Do you have a list of the territories you will be targeting as well as the estimated revenues from these territories?

Have you a clear strategy for awarding the valuable non-financial considerations such as main credits for the executive producers?

Do you have examples of financial packages recently used to make UK films?

A model of any kind, especially a film business model, should not be an end in itself, but rather a facilitator; there to structure the efforts, both creative and technical, of all those engaged in the enterprise of creating art through film. A good film business model should provide a basis on which to build and express the vision of what you want to create. The model will also allow you to understand how the filmmaking process works, and this gives you freedom to experiment and find the best format for your own, unique voice.

There is no shortage of money waiting to be invested in the making and distribution of films. What prevents filmmaking from being highly attractive to investors, given the potentially high returns on investment, is their perception of filmmakers as not appreciating the need for professional financial management. Having a comprehensive business model that is structured around the kind of films you want to make, will allow you to speak the same language as the investor or distributor and so greatly increase the chances of having your films made.

By being able to communicate effectively with financiers and distributors via a business model, does not mean creativity is restricted; rather, the model, by providing a framework, allows creativity to be released. As with music, the structure such as notes, bars, movements do not make the music, they facilitate it. So to, business models are to be used to facilitate the making of films, which must have an aesthetic life completely separate from the model.

I love watching films and genuinely believe they are destined to be the premier art form of the future. Therefore, as with all vital art forms throughout history, film must express the pain, joy, hopes and defeats of humanity as experienced by the citizenry of the world.

Too many potentially good or great films, that express these crucial issues of humanity, never get made. Hopefully, in some small way, this book will help to redress that situation and this will enrich us all.

Robert McKee, one of the finest minds addressing the way screenplays are structured and created, says that cinema is " the foremost media for creative expression in the world today..." and that it can produce "... works of beauty and meaning that help shape our vision of reality..."

Therefore, go forth and create the great films of the future.

Appendices

Appendix 1:

   –   **Delivery List**

Appendix 2:

   –   **Page Of A Screenplay In Industry Format**

Appendix 3:

   –   **Example of Below The Line Costings For a Low Budget Film**

Appendix 4:

   –   **Film Production Jobs**

Appendix 5:

   –   **Chain Of Title**

Appendix 1

Delivery List

1) Release Print

- 35mm. Combined Optical print
- 35mm. Interpositive
- 35mm. Internegative
- 35mm. Optical Sound negative

2) Magnetic Sound Master

3) Music and Effects Mix (M&E)

4) Textless Title Background

5) Trailer

6) DVD or CD of film with tracks 1 and 2 stereo sound and tracks 3 and 4 M&E

7) Amended screenplay of final cut and with all music cues.

8) Music cue sheet

9) Continuities – full action and dialogues continuity

10) Chain of title with all production and cast contracts

11) Distribution restrictions – if any

12) Certificate of origin

13) Certificate of nationality

14) Certificate of authorship

15) List of screen credits

16) Copy of Errors and Omissions policy

Press Kit

1) Story synopsis – about half a page long.

2) Cast list. Just the main ones. Include key crew, such as the Director of Photography, if they have gained positive reputations.

3) Director's biography – one page.

4) Producer's biography – one page.

5) Still Photos – black and white 8X10.

6) Stills of crew and cast whilst making the film – 30 to 100 colour transparencies.

7) Action shots of the director and principle cast while making the film.

8) Tip Sheet:

- **Genre**
- **Running time**
- **Medium the film was shot in – 35mm colour, black and white, digital**
- **Locations**

9) Trailer. Duplicated on ½ VHS tape.

10) DVD or Betacam of clips from the film and trailer

11) An invitation to the next screening of your film.

12) A brief description – one to three pages – of events and happenings that took place during the pre-production, production or post-production that you think would help publicise the film. Do not include negative stories or happenings, unless they help generate good publicity.

Electronic Press Kit

This is vitally important to the successful distribution and marketing of the film. If you have a full and comprehensive EPK then it is one more element that helps you sell the film to a distributor.

It is therefore vitally important that the EPK is planned during the pre-production stages, since many of the elements it contains will be created during the shoot. Once the shoot is finished it can prove costly or even be impossible to create a full EPK.

The elements to be included in the press kit

Usually a press kit will be shot on 35m and may be transferred to video or disc for broadcast. Therefore, it is important that the quality of the film is good. That is why if these publicity and marketing materials are created during the shoot they will be of the same quality as the film. Also, during the shoot you will have all the resources to hand including lights and sound equipment, the camera crew and the stars. Trying to get the stars back once the film is finished can be costly or impossible, especially if they are working on another film.

Interviews with

- The principal cast members

- The director

- The producer

- Others, including the crew, such as the DOP, who might have interesting things to say about the production

Footage

- Interesting behind the scenes footage, especially if they are humorous and the film is a comedy.

- Production footage showing how the film was made and any interesting insights into

- Difficulties overcome or locations that were special.

Audio

There should be four discrete tracks, each containing:

- Dialogue

- Voice over or narration

- Music

- Effects

The running time of the interviews with the stars etc between 10 and 20 minutes.

Page Of A Screenplay In Industry Format

INT. MORNING. MADDOX FOYER AS SEEN THROUGH A SURVEILLANCE CAMERA

The image on the surveillance camera shows the foyer is empty except for JEAN-PAUL and JANE. Throughout this scene, the screen is filled with the image coming through the surveillance camera, and JANE'S and JEAN-PAUL'S voices are heard through the surveillance camera. JEAN-PAUL beckons to JANE and takes her to a relief on the wall. The camera follows them.

> JEAN-PAUL
> Look at this.

> JANE
> It's just like your work.

> JEAN-PAUL
> Almost. But it's wrong. It's not a true
> replica.

> JANE looks.

> JEAN-PAUL
> Look at the blue.

> JANE looks and shrugs.

> JANE
> It's a beautiful blue.

John Sweeney

JEAN-PAUL

Exactly! It's too blue. For this to be a true replica of late renaissance Italian, you need to use the third wash.

JANE

Of course dear. How silly of me. Now, off you go to your exhibition, where true genius resides, and I'll see you there this evening.

JEAN-PAUL sighs.

JEAN-PAUL

Sometimes I feel all alone.

JANE

I wonder why.

As JANE and JEAN-PAUL leave the foyer the surveillance camera image gets smaller on screen as it becomes a monitor on Marcus's desk. MARCUS reaches forward and turns the screen off.

310

Example of Below The Line Costings For a Low Budget Film

Film Z

These cost parameters have been used to make two low budget features. Depending on available finance, this list can be expanded or reduced. The crew were divided into three bands; all the members within each band were paid the same money and all knew what each other was receiving.

I accept that it will meet with some criticism from those who think the "going rate" should be paid for all film projects. But this doesn't happen in the real world, either here or in the US.

The payments were supplemented by contractual deferred payments and points in the film. The deferred payments were negotiated on what the producers thought the individual was contributing to the film. For instance, if the film had a great deal of dance sequences and original music in it and the success or failure of the film depended on how well the dance and music elements were received, then the crew members responsible for these aspects might receive greater deferred payments than other members of the crew. If this happens it is important that the other crew members were aware of this, and accepted it is fair.

Crew Banding Status and Remuneration

For a ten week shoot – six days a week

Crew A

Job	Remuneration
Production Co-ord	£10k + 1 Gross point + Deferred payment
DOP:	£10k + 1 Gross point + Deferred payment
1st AD:	£10k + 1 Gross point + Deferred payment
Make-up:	£10k + 1 Gross point + Deferred payment
Wardrobe:	£10k + 1 Gross point + Deferred payment
Production Designer:	£10k + 1 Gross point + Deferred payment
Sound:	£10k + 1 Gross point + Deferred payment
Editor:	£10k + 1 Gross point + Deferred payment
Choreographer:	£10k + 1 Gross point + Deferred payment
Music:	£10k + 1 Gross point + Deferred payment

Total: £100k

Crew B

Job	Remuneration
Gaffer:	£5k + ½ Gross point + Deferred payment
Continuity:	£5k + ½ Gross point + Deferred payment
Focus puller:	£5k + ½ Gross point + Deferred payment
Locations Manager:	£5k + ½ Gross point + Deferred payment

Total: £20,000

Crew C

Job	Remuneration
Clapper Loader:	£2,500 + Deferred
Boom Op:	£2,500 + Deferred
2nd AD:	£2,500 + Deferred
Costume Assistant:	£2,500 + Deferred
Hair/Make-up Assistant:	£2,500 + Deferred
Office Manager:	£2,500 + Deferred
Set Design Ass:	£2,500 + Deferred

To receive, on a pro-rata basis, a share of 2% of net profits.

Total: £17,500

Runners

To receive expenses and a share of 2% of the producer's net profits. (If the budget allows, then the runners should be paid a wage; but realistically, even on big shoots, the job of a runner is seen as being occupied by those new to the film industry and who are seeking work experience).

Job

3rd AD

Costume Assistant 2

Hair/Make-up Assistant 2

Office Assistant

Set Design

Total: £2,500

Total Up Front Crew Costs: £140,000-00

Deferred payments

As previously discussed, it is a matter of trust if deferred payments are made. If the film is bought by a big international distributor, then the responsibility for meeting the deferred payments may be taken out of the hands of the producers or filmmakers who made the film. However, wherever possible the producer or filmmaker must try to ensure that any contractual obligations that are passed on to new owners of the film are met. If not, then the original producers should explain why.

Film Production Jobs

This is a list that has been used to make two low budget features. Depending on available finance, this list can be expanded or reduced.

Job Titles:

- *Producer*

- *Line Producer*

- *Director*

- *Director of Photography (DOP)*

- *Production manager*

- *1st assistant director*

- *Focus puller*

- *Clapper loader*

- *Grip*

- *Camera Assistant*

- *Script supervisor*

- *Costume designer*

- **Assist costume designer**

- **Editor**

- **Gaffer**

- **Spark**

- **Make-up / hair artist**

- **Make-up / hair assistant**

- **Director of music**

- **Production designer**

- **Art dept. assistant**

- **Sound Recordist**

- **Runners**

- **Driver**

- **Stills photographer**

- **Documentary filmmaker of the film**

Chain Of Title

A chain of title is a group of documents that prove ownership of all the elements that have gone into making the finished film. No distributor will accept a film unless there is clear proof that the producer or filmmaker owns all the rights and has not infringed, in making the film, anyone else's rights. A chain of title will usually include, as a minimum, the following:

- An agreement that the producer owns the script and all the rewrites, or has legally obtained it, or has employed the writer under a signed contract.

- Signed release agreements from all the actors and those who appear in the film

- Contracts of employment, including deferred payment agreements, for all the cast and crew.

- You will also need a license, unless it is in the public domain, if you have used someone else's music, artwork, film-footage, photograph, painting or anything that has copyright.

Glossary of Terms

As with all industries the film industry has generated its own jargon and ways of describing situations and terms of agreement. The following are the ones most relevant for the independent producer or filmmaker and I have attempted to describe each in the simplest and most straightforward of terms. Others, perhaps more experienced than I, will disagree with some of the definitions or even the terms themselves, but this is to be expected in an industry that is international and in a state of constant flux and development.

Above The Line Costs

The top sheet of the budget for a film, which summarises all the costs of making the film, is divided into various sections. The first of these sections summarises what are known as above the line costs and these usually comprise the creative elements such as the purchase of the story rights and screenplay, the salaries of the executive producer and producer, director and the principal cast. See also below the line costs.

Access Letter

A letter which states that a film laboratory agrees to honour orders placed by a distributor. This can be important if the laboratory is owed money by the company making the film.

Acquisitions

These are films that have been acquired by a distributor or studio for distribution, but which have been independently financed and produced.

Adjusted Gross Deal

This is an agreement between the film's distributor and the film's producer. The distributor usually meets all the costs of promoting and distributing the film, but with this kind of deal the distributor deducts the advertising costs from the gross receipts and then divides the balance with the producer. This balance is the "the adjusted gross". The producer needs to be aware that the distributor may cut back on the advertising and promotion budget if he thinks the adjusted gross receipts will not cover his expenses and this could harm the commercial success of the film since the marketing and promotion campaign is vital in getting the film seen by its target audience.

Advances

This is money paid when a distribution deal is agreed or the finished film is delivered ready for distribution. These advances of money are paid in anticipation of future profits.

All-Media Distribution Agreement

This is exactly what it says: an agreement whereby all the rights for distribution, including theatrical and ancillary, are exclusively assigned to an individual distributor.

Ancillary Rights

These are rights that pertain to all the aspects of a film that can be commercially exploited other than the film itself. These rights often include the sound track including the publishing rights, TV, merchandising, computer games and indeed anything that can be identified as emanating from the production or development of the film.

Angel (Private investor)

Usually an individual who invests in films, or theatre productions, for reasons other than just financial gain.

Answer Print

This is the first complete assembly of all the various aspects of the film on a negative print. It is made up of the film itself, which will have been graded for colour and texture, the sound and music track as well as optical effects. This print is then seen by the producer and or director for approval and then returned to the laboratory for copies to be made, ready for distribution.

Assignment By Way Of Security

This is when certain rights in the film, such as the copyright to the film or the soundtrack, are legally assigned to an investor in the film as security for his or her investment in the film.

Auteur

This is the name sometimes given to a director whose films have a unique style or look to them. Sometimes the name auteur can be used pejoratively to criticise a director's film or films for being too self indulgent without due regard to the script or acting talent or the commercially viability of the film and that the director cares only for his or her vision.

Back End

What you are promised as the final profit from the film. This will include box office and all ancillary revenues.

Basic Points

These are points that are expressed as one hundredth of one percent. They are often used to define interest rates and so 20 basic points is 0.20%

Below The Line Costs

The top sheet of the budget for a film, which summarises all the costs of making the film, is divided into various sections. The section that deals with the cost of making the film without the creative costs such as the main actors is defined as Below The Line Costs. Producers when putting the idea for the film forward will often state the Below The Line costs as a bench mark for what the film will cost.

British Board of Film Classification (B.B.F.C.)

This is the organisation that views the finished film before it is released for distribution. It will award the film a category which will determine which age group can view it in the cinemas. It is important for the producer to think about whom the viewing audience will be and what the distribution strategy will be. For instance, a horror film will not have a large cinema release if it is categorised as being suitable for 18 year olds, but films for18 year olds do very well as videos. So if the film does not have built in box office appeal, then focusing on the video sales might be the best option.

Cash Flow

As its name implies it is the amount of cash that flows into the production budget once the film starts to be shot. Money for the development of the film is often difficult to obtain and so it is often only when the film is actually being shot that any money invested in the film becomes available.

Chain Of Title

This is very important for the producer since it details the legal transfers and assignments of rights that allow the producer to use copyright material. Without this Chain Of Title the producer will not be able to sell the film for distribution. (See appendix 5)

Collecting Society

A body that has the right to collect monies, on behalf of its members, for the use of copyright material. Often used in the music industry and hence used by producers to collect royalties on soundtracks.

Collection Agreement

An agreement usually made by the executive producer of the film, the one who raises the money, for the collection of monies owed for the exploitation of the film. The agent who collects is usually charged with distributing the money as set out in the finance plan.

Completion Guarantee

An agreement whereby an organisation, usually financial, guarantees that the film will be completed and delivered by a given date to its principal distributors in accordance with the relevant distribution agreements.

Film financiers, and anyone else who has invested in the film such as a distributor, like to have a completion guarantee in place since it protects them if anything goes wrong and guarantees that the film will be made and delivered as specified in the original agreement. The organisation underwriting the completion guarantee has the power to get involved with the filmmaking process at any time, and even replace the director or producers, in order to ensure that the film is completed. However, if a certain level of funding has already been advanced then the completion guarantor does not have to complete the film but does have to repay the financiers the amounts they have invested. This cut off point is known as the strike price. The completion guarantor may, even though the strike price has been achieved, choose to complete the film and deliver it to the distributor since it may be the best option of not losing all the money they have guaranteed.

Completion Guarantor

As the name implies, it is an organisation that provides the completion guarantees for film projects.

The Completion Guarantor does not get involved in the artistic format of the film.

Contingency

The sum of money built into the film budget to provide for unforeseen expenses. It can vary from 5% to 20%. If filming in remote and hazardess locations, or where the shoot depends on the weather, then it is best to make as large a contingency fund as possible.

Co-operative Advertising

Usually refers to an agreement between the distributor and exhibitors, or distributor and producer, to share the costs of advertising the film.

Co-production Deal

This is a deal where the cost of producing the film is shared between one or more production entities. This can be between companies or entities in the same country or in different countries. Often this kind of deal happens between persons or entities in different countries in order to take advantage of the various tax breaks and other financial incentives offered by various governments.

Co-production Treaty

Co-production treaties allow producers from different countries to co-operate in the making of a film. It is seen as a cost effective way to make films since it allows the producers to use subsidies from both countries.

Costs Off The Top Deal

This kind of agreement favours the producer since the distributor's expenses are paid from the gross takings and then the remaining money is then divided between the producer and the distributor on an agreed basis. Given that the distributor's fees are usually about 35% of the gross receipts and his expenses are also deducted from the gross take, then this deal means the distributor gets less than he normally would. This kind of deal is only done with films that are certain to be box office hits such as **Star Wars**.

Cross Collateralisation

This form of agreement favours the distributor or agent to the detriment of the producer and should if possible be avoided at all times. This agreement means that money earned from one film can be used to off-set losses on another film. So if one producer's film makes a lot of money, he or she may never see it because the distributor or sales agent uses these funds to promote another film that might not make any money. Investors in your film will not be happy to find they have been saddled with this kind of deal.

John Sweeney

Debenture

This is usually a legal agreement to pay a set sum of money in return for an investment in the film. The problem with this kind of agreement is that even if the film does not make any profits you must still pay the agreed sum for borrowing the money. However, the reverse is true and if the film makes lots of money then the producer keeps all the extra profit and repays only the fixed amount.

Deferment

This is where the agreed fees, be they for the writer, actors or anyone else connected with the film, are deferred until the film is distributed or sold and revenue is accrued. It is widely used in the independent filmmaking sector where a small amount of money is paid to the actors or others along with an agreed deferred fee.

Development Deal

This is a deal whereby funding is given to a producer or filmmaker during the pre-production stages of a film project. This money is usually very hard to come by in the UK and Europe, although it is considered vital to the proper development of the script. There are many forms of development funding and they can be given to writers and directors as well as producers. It should also be noted that even if you are in receipt of a development deal, it doesn't mean the film will be made. It is estimated that each major Hollywood studio has up to 5,000 projects in active development at any one time, of which about 200 will be given the green-light (the decision to go into production) but only 12 will eventually be made.

326

Distribution Agreement

This is any form of agreement whereby the rights to distribute a film are granted. All of these deals will vary depending on the rights being granted, such as theatrical rights or video rights, and in what territories.

Distributor

A person or organisation that ensures that the finished film is shown in cinemas or other forms of exploitation. The distributor also pays for the marketing and promotion of the film which can be a considerable expense.

Domestic Rights

Even if the film in not made in North America the domestic market is the US and Canada. The rights for the rest of the world are called foreign.

Electronic Press Kit

This comprises all the key promotional and publicity materials that will help sell and market the film. The contents of the EPK should be planned during the pre-production stages, since many of its elements will need to be created during the shoot. (See appendix 1 for a full list)

Equity

The trade union for British actors.

John Sweeney

Errors and Omissions (E&O) Insurance

This kind of insurance is very important unless all the rights to the copyright material are in the hands of the producer. This is often the case with independent filmmakers when the film is written and directed by the same person. But if the producer has acquired rights from a third party then it is wise to get this kind of insurance since it protects the film from litigation arising from infringements of copyrights, unauthorised use of any kind of name be they trademarks, well known characters or brands. It also protects against claims for slander or defamation.

It is a good idea for the producer to get their name onto the E&O policy so that if there are any claims they are protected.

Escrow Account.

It is often the case, to protect all the investors, that the producer will be asked to set up an escrow account. Money paid into this account cannot be drawn upon until all the money, the film budget total, has been paid in. If the budget is £12 million and one investor puts in £2m but the producer is unable to raise the rest, then if some of that £2m has been spent development an other costs, the original investor will never be able to get his/her money back because the film will not be made.

The Film Council (UK)

This is the UK body that distributes public funds for film development and production. There are three sections: The Development Fund which does what is says and gives money for script development; the New Cinema Fund which gives money for innovative ideas especially when using new technology; the Premier Fund which can give large amounts of money for film projects. As with all public bodies the rules for distributing the funds change so see their website for up to date details.

Final Cut

This is the last edited version of the film before it goes on general release. Most directors do not have the final say on what the film will look like; this right will usually lie with the producers. However, some major directors have this right and guard it jealously.

Fine Cut

A term often applied to he final edited cut of the film.

First Look Deal

This is when a studio or distributor pays a regular amount of money to a writer or producer, or assists in some other way, in return for having the first look at any new projects they create. The studio or distributor may decide to offer further funds for a full development of the project or turn it down and then the originator of the project can take it elsewhere. This sometimes known as turnaround and certain constraints are usually applied, such as the original funder of the development process retaining certain financial rights if the film ever is made and released.

First Trial Print

This is another term for the Answer Print. (See above)

Floating Rate

When money is borrowed or advanced for the making of a film and the interest charged on the loan is not fixed, but floats up or down according to the base rate. Producers would be well advised to avoid this kind of agreement since although extra money could be forthcoming if the base rate falls, it can also mean that if the base rate rises then money assigned for making, editing or promoting the film has to be used to pay the extra charges. With a fixed interest rate a producer has more control over his or her cash-flow.

Foreign Rights

These are all the non-domestic rights to exploit the film. I.e. all those outside North America.

Four Walling

If a producer feels confident enough in his or her film and feels that it can be effectively promoted to the target audience, then he or she rents all the seats in a cinema, usually for less than the normal price, and then puts on his or her film and keeps all the box-office money.

Free M & E Track

Sound tracks that are left blank so that foreign language versions of the film can be made.

Free TV

Television stations that broadcast their programmes for free, or for the price of a TV licence, as with the BBC in the UK.

Fringe Benefits or Packages

These may be financial or other benefits offered to the cast or crew over and above their normal wage. These vary greatly from pension payments to an ongoing financial interest in the film or TV programme. If an actor or member of the crew has a long ongoing relationship with the production company then these benefits may include paying tax and national insurance payments for pension and social security rights on behalf of the actor or crew member.

Gap Financing

As its name implies, this kind of finance is used to fill the gap between the amount of money that has been raised for the production of the film and what is actually needed. The problem with this kind of finance is that the company offering the loan usually want to be "last in and first out". This means that the money they lend will be the final amount needed, so they are sure all the money to make the film has been raised, and first out in that as soon as any money is made from the exploitation of the film they are paid first. If as a producer or filmmaker you enter this kind of agreement, make sure that all your investors are aware of the fact, since somebody putting up the majority of the finance may not be happy for somebody else to be paid first, especially if the film does not make enough to repay the investors.

Gearing

Sometimes referred to as leverage, gearing refers to the ratio between what a company owns in terms of equity, that which can be converted to cash, and what the company owes. If the company is worth $1 million in cash terms and owes $10 million, then it has a 1 to 10 gearing ratio. Needless to say the higher the gearing ratio the more difficult it is for companies to borrow extra money or sell shares in the company. However, the peculiar circumstances pertaining to the film industry often means investors are willing to commit finance to a film project when the company making the film is technically bankrupt or has a gearing ratio that passes the 100 mark.

Gross Points Participation

This is something that can only really be demanded by major box-office artists. The Gross Income is the money generated from the box office receipts. If an artist has gross points, say 10, then they receive 10% of the income from cinema ticket sales. Most producers and other participants do not receive any monies from the gross income. Often the only income the producer receives is the fee he or she is paid up-front for producing the film. However, the producer along with those with deferred payment contracts (see Deferred Payments above) will have clauses in their contract to receives monies from the "producer's net profits". It is crucial that the producer looks carefully at the clauses governing these agreements since net-profits in the film industry are considered to be as rare as the sightings of the genuine Father Christmas.

Grossing-up Clause

This is a clause that is sometimes included in a loan agreement. It provides that in the event of the person or company who has borrowed the money having to pay taxes on the money to be repaid, then the borrowing company will make up the shortfall and pay the loan company in full. That means that the borrowing company will pay the loaning company the equivalent amount of the tax so that the loaning company receives all their money in full, so they "Gross-up".

Hedging

This is when the producer attempts to protect his or her cashflow against movements and fluctuations in interests rates and/or currency exchange rates. This is very important if the producer is filming in more than one country and has set aside sums of money for each foreign location. One way producers can protect themselves is to ensure that all the contracts for each foreign location stipulate that all payments will be made in the local currency. A producer can then buy the separate amounts of currency needed for each location. If an individual country's currency is not being traded internationally, such as currently the Russian Rouble, then when filming in Russia you may be able to make all payments in US dollars. It is a sad fact that many films are not completed because they run out of money, therefore planning by the producer for all eventualities is vital.

Holdback

This happens when some form of exploitation of the film is withheld for a set time period. It used to be that video and DVD exploitation happened three or six months after the theatrical release of the film. Or, that the film was released in the US and then shown in Europe some months later. However, because of the advent of all forms of piracy most films are now released for most avenues of exploitation within a short time frame. The obvious exception to this is TV. For films to be shown on TV and on what kind of channel will depend on the theatrical success of the film.

Housekeeping Deal

This is when a studio has a financial deal to pay for all the overheads and running costs of a production company. This deal may be in the form of a "first look deal", or it may be that all the production company's output is owned and controlled by the studio. This kind of deal is not confined to the film industry and can be found in the business relationship of many suppliers to the big supermarkets.

Increased Costs Clause

This kind of clause is usually inserted into agreements by banks in order to protect themselves against changes to statutory requirements that result in the bank's profit on loans being reduced. It basically means that the producer, or whoever loans the money from the bank, must compensate the bank if any changes in the regulations that govern financial agreements result in the bank not making as much profit on the loan as it intended. The producer would be well advised to avoid this one-sided deal, since, in my humble opinion, banks are in a much better position to absorb unforeseen loses than the average film producer.

In-House Product

As the name suggests, it is a film project developed and produced in-house by a producer and or distributor.

Internal Rate of Return or IRR

All investors in a film project, including the distributor, are mainly interested in how safe and sound their investments are. One method of appraising the likely rate of return on an investment is to use a technique known as discounted cash flow yield. This method attempts to ascertain the likely income and expenditure of a project and so project a cash-flow scenario that will show when the project is likely to be in profit, if at all. From this can be deduced the rate of return on the amount invested. The problem with cashflows is that they are "guestimates", that is a cross between an estimate and a guess. This kind of prediction is difficult with cashflows for companies that have predictable products and markets; it is much more difficult in an industry where "nobody knows anything" and a film's success and therefore profitability can depend on such imponderables as the weather or what is happening on the opening weekend of the film's release.

Inter-party Agreement

This form of agreement is very important. Often the filmmaker or producer will enter into a variety of different agreements between various parties who have a vested interest in the film project or projects. Because of this the filmmaker or producer must ensure that all parties to a specific agreement or film project are equally aware of all the ramifications of the various agreements. If some investors have special agreements about profit participation then this must be common knowledge amongst all the investors. Needless to say, withholding this kind of information from one or more of the investors could amount to fraud, even if the information was not disclosed through ignorance or by mistake.

Therefore, in order to ensure that all is open and above board an agreement needs to be drawn up that regulates the relationship between all the participating parties. This is especially important as regards the participation of each of the parties in any profits and the methods and sequence of any payments made. The filmmaker or producer should attempt to build a reputation for sound financial and business management and this means being open an honest about all agreements, especially financial ones, between all those who have a vested interest in the film project.

Interpositive

This is a positive print of the film made from the original negative of the final version of the film. From this positive, sometimes known as a master positive, a duplicate negative is made. It is then possible to make many prints of the film, from this duplicate, for screening in cinemas without damaging the original negative. The original negative is seen and considered a valuable commodity that needs to be protected and secured.

Lead Bank

Often, on big budget films, there will be more than one bank or organisation investing in the film. This often requires that a bank or financial organisation is appointed by the producer to explain to existing and potential investors the terms on which the producer is seeking investment. This can be important since this kind of syndicated loan can be very complex and it is in the interests of the producer to have on board, and leading the negotiations, a bank or organisation who is familiar with the normal requirements, legal and otherwise, of this kind of investment. Of course the bank or organisation leading the negotiations will charge a fee for their services.

Loss Payee Endorsement

Sometimes the person or organisation providing the Completion Guarantee decides to take out insurance themselves in case the film runs into trouble and they are called upon to honour their financial commitment under the terms of the agreement. By taking out this insurance they are in effect insuring themselves against the possibility of not being able to meet their commitments. The film's financiers sometimes ask for this kind of reinsurance to be taken out since if the organisation who has agreed to give the completion guarantee gets into trouble and cannot meet its commitments, then the financiers can look to the insurance company to make payments under the terms of the reinsurance policy. Therefore the film's financiers will want to have written confirmation from the reinsurer that the terms and conditions of the reinsurance policy meet their requirements.

Margin Above Base Rate

This the amount of money the producer has to pay over and above the base rate. So, if the bank base rate is 5% and the loan company charges the producer 5% above base rate the producer is paying 10% interest on all monies borrowed. Finance organisations apply a larger margin if they think the project is risky. Gap financiers often charge rates way above the base rate. These can be crippling for the producer and so should only be entered into as a last resort.

Minimum Guarantee

This is a guaranteed amount the distributor will pay to the producer for the right to distribute the film. This may be for one or more territories. This money can be paid as soon as the film is delivered to the distributor or it may be that the money will be due after a certain period. Either way this kind of guarantee can help the producer raise money for the financing the production of the film. Minimum Guarantee agreements can be combined with pre-sale agreements when the full distribution and exploitation rights for individual territories are sold before the film is shot. Again, this kind of agreement is very useful but difficult for the independent producer to acquire unless they have a track record of producing commercially viable films or their current film has box office talent attached.

Motion Picture Association of America (MPAA)

This organisation does a similar job in the US as the BBFC does in the UK in that it gives a film a rating as to which age group can view it.

National Television System Code (NTSC)

This is the colour television broadcast system used in the USA and Japan. It uses 525 lines as opposed to the European PAL system which uses 625 lines.

Negative Pick-up Deal

The negative is the print from which all other copies of the film will be made for showing in cinemas. This deal provides that as soon as the negative is handed over to the distributor he or she must pay the agreed sum to the producer. This kind of deal must be entered into with caution and the fine print scrutinised and agreed by all parties. It is in the interests of the producer to try to secure as much money as possible "up front", that is before the film is distributed, because the "back-end" of the deal, final profits, may produce no money. Because this is common knowledge in the industry the exhibitor will try to offer no more than what the film cost to make, while the producer will try to secure the production cost and as much of the anticipated profits as he can.

You can further protect your position as producer by keeping possession of the original negative, which remains in the lab for safekeeping, and give the distributor a "lab access letter". If the distributor reneges on any promises then you can stop him having access to the original negative. Try also to keep the originals of the key art work such as for the poster and stills for the EPK.

Non-Disclosure Agreement

This is an agreement that can stand on its own or be part of a larger contract. It basically ensures that any information given by one part to another must not be disclosed to a third party. This form of agreement is useful when filmmakers or producers feel they have a unique idea for a film, either in the form of a pitch, treatment or script, and want to protect it and stop it from being stolen. The only problem is that you cannot copyright ideas, so if you only have an idea or short treatment, then unless you really trust the person to whom you are pitching the idea, the best thing is to develop the idea into a script and have it registered.

Optical Sound Negative

The master copy of the magnetic sound mix is rerecorded optically. This optical sound negative is then synchronised and printed with the final cut of the film to make the negative for the making of prints for distribution.

Option

This is the right to use copyright material, usually for the making of a film. Most often it is a book or article that has been published.

Overages

As its name implies, it is the amount of money over and above what the distributor agreed to pay the producer. This money is only due after the distributor has recouped the payments, usually minimum guarantees, he or she has already paid out to the producer.

P&A (Promotion and Advertising) Spend Commitment

The amount a distributor spends on promoting and advertising the film can have a profound effect on the success of the film. Therefore, the producer may seek a legally binding agreement with a distributor as to how much the minimum P&A will be, before he or she agrees to give the distribution rights away.

Packaging

This usually refers to the development process whereby a producer will put a package together and sell it on. This package may consist of a screenplay along with a director or box office actor. There are some producers in Hollywood who make a good living by just packaging projects and selling them on.

Pay or Play

This type of deal can be very risky for a producer no matter how experienced. This is because this kind of agreement stipulates that the producer will pay the director or actor the agreed sum for their services even if the film is not made and the actor's or director's services are never used – hence you pay or they play, one or the other.

Phase Alternative Line (PAL)

This is the colour television broadcast system used in the UK and many parts of Europe. TV programmes are transmitted using 625 lines.

Pledge Holder Agreement

This agreement allows the film's financiers to protect their interests by preventing the processing laboratory from parting with the original negative of the film without their express permission.

Points

This usually means shares in terms of percentage points in the net profits of a film as opposed to gross points which are a share of the box office receipts.

Prequel

This kind of film tells a story about what happened before the events in a previously released film. Star Wars has used this form of filmmaking. Most filmmakers look to make sequels but prequels have become popular in recent years.

Pre-sale

If pre-sales can be obtained then they are very useful to the producer. Pre-sales are most often the rights to distribute or exploit the film in various territories or through various ancillary activities such as video or TV and are sold before the film goes into production. These sales are important in that they can help finance the production of the film and also ensure that it is distributed once the film is made.

Priority Agreement

As the financial aspects of the film are put together it is sometimes necessary to agree on the rights and priorities each of the investors, or others with an interest in the film, has in relation to each other. These rights and priorities will be set out in the Inter-party Agreement (See above).

Producers' Alliance for Cinema and Television (PACT)

This is a UK trade association founded and run by film and television producers.

Production Finance & Distribution (PFD) Agreement

This kind of agreement is usually only obtained from major Hollywood studios and major production companies with links to major distributors. It does make the whole process much easier since the deal means that the finance for the film as well as production costs are met along with a distribution deal.

Put Picture

This is a film that will be put on the screen without having to go through the normal processes of development such as having the script approved.

Recoupment Order

Again this is a document that needs careful consideration since it sets out the order in which each investor will receive any monies accruing from the financial and commercial exploitation of the film. It may be that this kind of document involves distribution agreements and so will affect how monies are paid from revenues from the various territories.

Remake

Often thought of as the refuge of the uninspired since it basically means remaking a film that has already been made and has gained some form of kudos. Recent remakes have included the UK hits **Alfie** and **Get Carter,** which were not well received critically or commercially.

Residual

This is an agreement to pay monies directly associated with the commercial exploitation of the film in specific territories or in ancillary forms and markets. These monies may be due to the actors or directors or others associated with the film. If, say an actor has box office appeal in Japan, he or she might have a specific agreement to receive a higher percentage of the film's revenue emanating from Japan than other territories such as the UK.

Roll Over Relief

This is associated with tax due to be paid from capital gains or corporation tax. This payment can be deferred or "rolled over" and invested in more assets or qualifying projects. If the individual or company does not reinvest qualifying projects, then the tax becomes due.

Sales Agent

The role of the sales agent has diminished somewhat in recent years as the competition in the international film market place has increased. The sales agent would normally act for a director or producer and try to sell their films to the distributors. They would often have detailed knowledge about specific markets and film festivals and acquire films and then sell them on. Now it is much more difficult to find original material that can be sold on for a profit. The drop in the price paid for films by national broadcasting television companies has meant that the sales agents' profit margins have been dramatically reduced. However, it is still worthwhile for a filmmaker or producer to attempt to acquire a sales agent to act on their behalf since these agents have many contacts within the industry.

The Screen Actors Guild (SAG)

The American equivalent of the actors' association Equity in the UK. SAG, like equity, sets minimum rates of pay for its members.

Secondary Rights

This is sometimes the name given to the rights pertaining to non-theatrical exploitation of the film such as DVD and TV. However, they may also be referred to as ancillary rights (See above).

Slate

This is the total amount of films a production company will be in the process of developing. These films can be at various stages of development, from a short treatment to a completed film ready for distribution. Once the film has been released and acquired, or remains with the production company, it is said to be part of a library. A company's library of films is a valuable asset.

Source Material

This is the original material on which the script for the film is based or derived from. It could be a true-life story from a newspaper, a book or article in a magazine. The producer needs to make sure that they have secured the copyright for this material or that the writer of the screenplay has the right to use this source material.

Step Deal

This is a deal whereby a studio or distributor will agree to provide funds to a producer or writer or director for the development of a script. The studio or distributor will want to see that each stage, or step, of the process has been completed before handing over more funds. The studio or distributor can decide to halt the process at any stage or step in the process. If this happens, then the work on the script that has been completed often forms the basis for a turnaround deal (see below).

Stop-date

If a performer or director or any other key person associated with the making of the film has other commitments, then they might include a stop-date in their contract which stipulates the date beyond which they are not contractually obliged to work. This can be very difficult and expensive if the film runs over time and the director or actor has another contract to work on a new film. If it's the actor who has the stop-date then it can be catastrophic since the whole film would have to be re-shot. The producer either needs to be very confident about his or her scheduling or avoid this kind of clause.

Strike Price

This involves the person or company who has provided the completion guarantee. The strike price is determined by the amount of money already invested in the production of the film. This figure will have previously been agreed between the producer and the investors and the company providing the completion guarantee. When this strike price has been reached the completion guarantor does not have to complete the film but does have to repay the financiers the amounts they have invested. This is why the producer needs to apprise the investors of the strike price and agree it with them. On reaching the strike price, it is up to the completion guarantor to decide whether or not to complete the film and deliver it to the distributor, or pay the investors the sums so far invested in the film. It may be in the best interests of the completion guarantor to finish the film and release it and so hope not to lose all the money they have guaranteed. (See also Completion Guarantee above)

Syndicated Loan

As its name implies, a sum of money from a number of sources that are interrelated, usually by an agreement to lend to one project such as a single film or slate of films from one production company or producer.

Theatrical Rights

These stipulate the right to show the film in cinemas for viewing by the general public.

Turnaround

If a studio or production company has been developing a film project, usually to the point of a finished first draft of the script, and then decides not to make the film they can place the project in "turnaround". This means that the producer or writer who is involved with the development of the project can take the idea to other studios or production companies. However, the original studio or production company often keeps a stake in the project since they have spent money developing it. This stake varies considerably, but usually involves a share in the gross profits if the film goes on to be made by another studio and is a commercial success.

John Sweeney

Under-spend

This is unusual in the film industry, but it refers to the amount of money that was not spent on making the film and yet was in the budget to be spent.

Further reading concerning the sources of ideas contained in this book

Starting and Running a Company

Colin Barrow **The Complete Small Business Guide** Capstone Publishing 2002

Lloyds TSB Small Business Guide London Press Vitesse 2002

D. McMullan **Be Your Own Boss** Kogan Page 1997

Rosthorn, Haldane, Blackwell, Wholey **The Small Business Action Kit** Kogan Page 1995

D. William **Running Your Own Business** Nicholas Brealey 1995

The Film Industry

Jake Eberts and Terry Ilott **My Indecision Is Final *The rise and fall of Goldcrest Films**. Faber and Faber 1990

Robert Evans **The Kid Stays In The Picture** – 1994 Faber & Faber

William Goldman **Which Lie Did I Tell *More Adventures In The Screen Trade*** - Bloomsbury Publishing Plc. 2000

Gregory Goodell **Independent Feature Film Production** St. Martin's Griffin 1998

John Sweeney

Sidney Lumet **Making Movies** – Bloomsbury 1996

James Park **British Cinema – The Lights That Failed** B.T. Batsford Ltd, London 1990

Building a Sustainable UK Film Industry - Keynote speech by Sir Alan Parker as Chairman of the Film Council November 2002

Producing The Goods? UK Film Production Since 1991 British Film Institute National Library - 2003

The Relph Report, *The British Film Industry* - UK Film Council 2002

Alexander Walker **Icons In the Fire** *The decline and fall of almost everybody in the British film industry. 1984-2000.* Orion books ltd   2004

Harris Watts **On Camera** *How to produce film and video* – BBC Books BBC Enterprises Ltd. 1992

Co-production – Media European

<u>Script Writing And Development</u>

G.P. Baker **Dramatic Technique** Da Capo Press 1976

Lajos Egri **The Art of Dramatic Writing** Simon & Schuster

Michael Hague **Writing Screenplays That Sell** Elm Tree Books 1989
Robert McKee **Story** Methuen 1999

Georges Polti **The Thirty Six Dramatic Situations** The Writer Inc. 1993

Jeffrey Sweet **The Dramatist's Toolkit** Heineman 1993

Christopher Vogler **The Writer's Journey** Pan Books 1998

Management

J. Stacy Adams Essay: Inequity In Social Exchange **Advances in Experimental Social Psychology** (Ed.) L. Berkowitz Vol 2 New York Academic Press

Buchanan & Huczynski **Organisational Behaviour** Prentice Hall 1997

De Bono –**Lateral Thinking : Creativity Step by Step** Harper Paperbacks; Reissue edition (October 29, 1973)

Joseph DeVito **The Interpersonal Communications Book** Harper and Row 1989

D.Evans **People Communications and Organisations** Pitman 1990

J.R. Hackman and J.L. Suttle (eds) **Improving Life At Work** Goodyear 1976

J.R. Hackman and G.R.Oldham **Work Redesign** Addison- Wesley 1980

Handy **Understanding Organisations** Penguin 1985
Robert Heller **The Complete Guide To Modern Management** Mercury Books 1991

Tom Lloyd **The Nice Company** Bloombury 1990

Maslow, Abraham H**, Motivation and Personality**, 2nd. ed., New York, Harper & Row 1955

Tom Peters and Robert Waterman Warner Books Reissue edition 1988 **In Search of Excellence**

L.W. Porter and E.E. Lawler **Managerial Attitudes and Performance** Homewood Ill. Irwin 1968

J. Rawlinson **Creative Thinking & Brainstorming** Gower 1989

Scanlon & Keys **Management & Organisational Behaviour** Wiley 1983

V.H. Vroom **Work and Motivation** New York – John Wiley 1964

M. A. Wahba & L. G. Bridwell **Maslow reconsidered: A review of research on the need hierarchy theory.** Organizational Behavior and Human Performance, 15, 212-240. (1976).

Marketing

Michael Baker **The Marketing Book** Butterworth Heinmann 1992

D. Bird **Commonsense Direct Marketing** Kogan Page 1993

A. Fairbey **How to Produce Successful Advertising** Kogan Page 1995

Robin Fairlie **Database Marketing & Direct Mail** Kogan Page 1993

Ferrell, Lucas and Luck _**Strategic Marketing Management** South Western Publishing 1994

Lancaster and Massingham **The Essentials of Marketing** McGraw Hill 1993

Terence Ship **Integrated marketing Communications** The Dryden Press 1997

P. Smith **Marketing Communications** Kogan Page 1995

D. Yadin **Creating Effective Marketing Communications** Kogan Page 1993

Finance

Caroline Hancock and Nic Wistreich **Get Your Film Financed** 2004 Shooting People www.shootingpeople.org

William Johnson **Baffled By Balance Sheets** Kogan Page 1988

Louise Levison **Filmmakers & Financing *Business Plans for Independents*** Focal Press 2001

Index